NON SANS DROICT.

THE TRAGEDY OF
King Richard the third.

Containing,
His treacherous Plots against his brother Clarence:
the pittiefull murther of his iunocent nephewes:
his tyrannicall vsurpation : with the whole course
of his detested life, and most deserued death.

As it hath beene lately Acted by the
Right honourable the Lord Chamber-
laine his seruants.

AT LONDON
Printed by Valentine Sims, for Andrew Wise,
dwelling in Paules Chuch-yard, at the
Signe of the Angell.
1597.

The First Quarto (1597) of *Richard III*, the earliest printed version of
the play

William Shakespeare

The Tragedy of
Richard the Third

With New and Updated
Critical Essays
and a Revised Bibliography

Edited by Mark Eccles

The Signet Classics Shakespeare
General Editor: Sylvan Barnet

SIGNET CLASSICS

SIGNET CLASSICS
Published by New American Library, a division of
Penguin Group (USA) Inc., 375 Hudson Street,
New York, New York 10014, USA
Penguin Group (Canada), 90 Eglinton Avenue East, Suite 700, Toronto,
Ontario M4P 2Y3, Canada (a division of Pearson Penguin Canada Inc.)
Penguin Books Ltd., 80 Strand, London WC2R 0RL, England
Penguin Ireland, 25 St. Stephen's Green, Dublin 2,
Ireland (a division of Penguin Books Ltd.)
Penguin Group (Australia), 250 Camberwell Road, Camberwell, Victoria 3124,
Australia (a division of Pearson Australia Group Pty. Ltd.)
Penguin Books India Pvt. Ltd., 11 Community Centre, Panchsheel Park,
New Delhi - 110 017, India
Penguin Group (NZ), 67 Apollo Drive, Rosedale, North Shore 0632,
New Zealand (a division of Pearson New Zealand Ltd.)
Penguin Books (South Africa) (Pty.) Ltd., 24 Sturdee Avenue,
Rosebank, Johannesburg 2196, South Africa

Penguin Books Ltd., Registered Offices:
80 Strand, London WC2R 0RL, England

Published by Signet Classics, an imprint of New American Library, a division
of Penguin Group (USA) Inc. The Signet Classics edition of *Richard III* was
first published in 1964, and an updated edition was published in 1988.

First Signet Classics Printing (Second Revised Edition), July 1998
30 29 28 27

Contents

Shakespeare: An Overview

Biographical Sketch

Between the record of his baptism in Stratford on 26 April 1564 and the record of his burial in Stratford on 25 April 1616, some forty official documents name Shakespeare, and many others name his parents, his children, and his grandchildren. Further, there are at least fifty literary references to him in the works of his contemporaries. More facts are known about William Shakespeare than about any other playwright of the period except Ben Jonson. The facts should, however, be distinguished from the legends. The latter, inevitably more engaging and better known, tell us that the Stratford boy killed a calf in high style, poached deer and rabbits, and was forced to flee to London, where he held horses outside a playhouse. These traditions are only traditions; they may be true, but no evidence supports them, and it is well to stick to the facts.

Mary Arden, the dramatist's mother, was the daughter of a substantial landowner; about 1557 she married John Shakespeare, a tanner, glove-maker, and trader in wool, grain, and other farm commodities. In 1557 John Shakespeare was a member of the council (the governing body of Stratford), in 1558 a constable of the borough, in 1561 one of the two town chamberlains, in 1565 an alderman (entitling him to the appellation of "Mr."), in 1568 high bailiff—the town's highest political office, equivalent to mayor. After 1577, for an unknown reason he drops out of local politics. What *is* known is that he had to mortgage his wife's property, and that he was involved in serious litigation.

The birthday of William Shakespeare, the third child and the eldest son of this locally prominent man, is unrecorded, but the Stratford parish register records that the infant was baptized on 26 April 1564. (It is quite possible that he was born on 23 April, but this date has probably been assigned by tradition because it is the date on which, fifty-two years later, he died, and perhaps because it is the feast day of St. George, patron saint of England.) The attendance records of the Stratford grammar school of the period are not extant, but it is reasonable to assume that the son of a prominent local official attended the free school—it had been established for the purpose of educating males precisely of his class—and received substantial training in Latin. The masters of the school from Shakespeare's seventh to fifteenth years held Oxford degrees; the Elizabethan curriculum excluded mathematics and the natural sciences but taught a good deal of Latin rhetoric, logic, and literature, including plays by Plautus, Terence, and Seneca.

On 27 November 1582 a marriage license was issued for the marriage of Shakespeare and Anne Hathaway, eight years his senior. The couple had a daughter, Susanna, in May 1583. Perhaps the marriage was necessary, but perhaps the couple had earlier engaged, in the presence of witnesses, in a formal "troth plight" which would render their children legitimate even if no further ceremony were performed. In February 1585, Anne Hathaway bore Shakespeare twins, Hamnet and Judith.

That Shakespeare was born is excellent; that he married and had children is pleasant; but that we know nothing about his departure from Stratford to London or about the beginning of his theatrical career is lamentable and must be admitted. We would gladly sacrifice details about his children's baptism for details about his earliest days in the theater. Perhaps the poaching episode is true (but it is first reported almost a century after Shakespeare's death), or perhaps he left Stratford to be a schoolmaster, as another tradition holds; perhaps he was moved (like Petruchio in *The Taming of the Shrew*) by

> Such wind as scatters young men through the world,
> To seek their fortunes farther than at home
> Where small experience grows.   (1.2.49–51)

In 1592, thanks to the cantankerousness of Robert Greene, we have our first reference, a snarling one, to Shakespeare as an actor and playwright. Greene, a graduate of St. John's College, Cambridge, had become a playwright and a pamphleteer in London, and in one of his pamphlets he warns three university-educated playwrights against an actor who has presumed to turn playwright:

> There is an upstart crow, beautified with our feathers, that with his *tiger's heart wrapped in a player's hide* supposes he is as well able to bombast out a blank verse as the best of you, and being an absolute Johannes-factotum [i.e., jack-of-all-trades] is in his own conceit the only Shake-scene in a country.

The reference to the player, as well as the allusion to Aesop's crow (who strutted in borrowed plumage, as an actor struts in fine words not his own), makes it clear that by this date Shakespeare had both acted and written. That Shakespeare is meant is indicated not only by *Shake-scene* but also by the parody of a line from one of Shakespeare's plays, *3 Henry VI*: "O, tiger's heart wrapped in a woman's hide" (1.4.137). If in 1592 Shakespeare was prominent enough to be attacked by an envious dramatist, he probably had served an apprenticeship in the theater for at least a few years.

In any case, although there are no extant references to Shakespeare between the record of the baptism of his twins in 1585 and Greene's hostile comment about "Shake-scene" in 1592, it is evident that during some of these "dark years" or "lost years" Shakespeare had acted and written. There are a number of subsequent references to him as an actor. Documents indicate that in 1598 he is a "principal comedian," in 1603 a "principal tragedian," in 1608 he is one of the "men players." (We do not have, however, any solid information about which roles he may have played; later traditions say he played Adam in *As You Like It* and the ghost in *Hamlet*, but nothing supports the assertions. Probably his role as dramatist came to supersede his role as actor.) The profession of actor was not for a gentleman, and it occasionally drew the scorn of university men like Greene who resented writing speeches for persons less educated than themselves, but it was respectable enough; players, if prosperous, were in effect members of the bourgeoisie, and there is nothing to suggest that Stratford considered William Shakespeare less than a solid citizen. When, in 1596, the Shakespeares were granted a coat of arms—i.e., the right to be considered gentlemen—the grant was made to Shakespeare's father, but probably William Shakespeare had arranged the matter on his own behalf. In subsequent transactions he is occasionally styled a gentleman.

Although in 1593 and 1594 Shakespeare published two narrative poems dedicated to the Earl of Southampton, *Venus and Adonis* and *The Rape of Lucrece*, and may well have written most or all of his sonnets in the middle nineties, Shakespeare's literary activity seems to have been almost entirely devoted to the theater. (It may be significant that the two narrative poems were written in years when the plague closed the theaters for several months.) In 1594 he was a charter member of a theatrical company called the Chamberlain's Men, which in 1603 became the royal company, the King's Men, making Shakespeare the king's playwright. Until he retired to Stratford (about 1611, apparently), he was with this remarkably stable company. From 1599 the company acted primarily at the Globe theater, in which Shakespeare held a one-tenth interest. Other Elizabethan dramatists are known to have acted, but no other is known also to have been entitled to a share of the profits.

Shakespeare's first eight published plays did not have his name on them, but this is not remarkable; the most popular play of the period, Thomas Kyd's *The Spanish Tragedy*, went through many editions without naming Kyd, and Kyd's authorship is known only because a book on the profession of acting happens to quote (and attribute to Kyd) some lines on the interest of Roman emperors in the drama. What is remarkable is that after 1598 Shakespeare's name commonly appears on printed plays—some of which are not his. Presumably his name was a drawing card, and publishers used it to attract potential buyers. Another indication of his popularity comes from Francis Meres, author of *Palladis Tamia: Wit's Treasury* (1598). In this anthology of snippets accompanied by an essay on literature, many playwrights are mentioned, but Shakespeare's name occurs more often than any other, and Shakespeare is the only playwright whose plays are listed.

From his acting, his play writing, and his share in a playhouse, Shakespeare seems to have made considerable money. He put it to work, making substantial investments in Stratford real estate. As early as 1597 he bought New Place, the second-largest house in Stratford. His family moved in soon afterward, and the house remained in the family until a granddaughter died in 1670. When Shakespeare made his will in 1616, less than a month before he died, he sought to leave his property intact to his descendants. Of small bequests to relatives and to friends (including three actors, Richard Burbage, John Heminges, and Henry Condell), that to his wife of the second-best bed has provoked the most comment. It has sometimes been taken as a sign of an unhappy marriage (other supposed signs are the apparently hasty marriage, his wife's seniority of eight years, and his residence in London without his family). Perhaps the second-best bed was the bed the couple had slept in, the best bed being reserved for visitors. In any case, had Shakespeare not excepted it, the bed would have gone (with the rest of his household possessions) to his daughter and her husband.

On 25 April 1616 Shakespeare was buried within the chancel of the church at Stratford. An unattractive monument to his memory, placed on a wall near the grave, says that he died on 23 April. Over the grave itself are the lines, perhaps by Shakespeare, that (more than his literary fame) have kept his bones undisturbed in the crowded burial ground where old bones were often dislodged to make way for new:

> Good friend, for Jesus' sake forbear
> To dig the dust enclosed here.
> Blessed be the man that spares these stones
> And cursed be he that moves my bones.

A Note on the Anti-Stratfordians, Especially Baconians and Oxfordians

Not until 1769—more than a hundred and fifty years after Shakespeare's death—is there any record of anyone expressing doubt about Shakespeare's authorship of the plays and poems. In 1769, however, Herbert Lawrence nominated Francis Bacon (1561–1626) in *The Life and Adventures of Common Sense*. Since then, at least two dozen other nominees have been offered, including Christopher Marlowe, Sir Walter Raleigh, Queen Elizabeth I, and Edward de Vere, 17th earl of Oxford. The impulse behind all anti-Stratfordian movements is the scarcely concealed snobbish opinion that "the man from Stratford" simply could not have written the plays because he was a country fellow without a university education and without access to high society. Anyone, the argument goes, who used so many legal terms, medical terms, nautical terms, and so forth, and who showed some familiarity with classical writing, must have attended a university, and anyone who knew so much about courtly elegance and courtly deceit must himself have moved among courtiers. The plays do indeed reveal an author whose interests were exceptionally broad, but specialists in any given field—law, medicine, arms and armor, and so on—soon find that the plays do not reveal deep knowledge in specialized matters; indeed, the playwright often gets technical details wrong.

The claim on behalf of Bacon, forgotten almost as soon as it was put forth in 1769, was independently reasserted by Joseph C. Hart in 1848. In 1856 it was reaffirmed by W. H. Smith in a book, and also by Delia Bacon in an article; in 1857 Delia Bacon published a book, arguing that Francis Bacon had directed a group of intellectuals who wrote the plays.

Francis Bacon's claim has largely faded, perhaps because it was advanced with such evident craziness by Ignatius Donnelly, who in *The Great Cryptogram* (1888) claimed to break a code in the plays that proved Bacon had written not only the plays attributed to Shakespeare but also other Renaissance works, for instance the plays of Christopher Marlowe and the essays of Montaigne.

Consider the last two lines of the Epilogue in *The Tempest*:

As you from crimes would pardoned be,
Let your indulgence set me free.

What was Shakespeare—sorry, Francis Bacon, Baron Verulam—*really* saying in these two lines? According to Baconians, the lines are an anagram reading, "Tempest of Francis Bacon, Lord Verulam; do ye ne'er divulge me, ye words." Ingenious, and it is a pity that in the quotation the letter *a* appears only twice in the cryptogram, whereas in the deciphered message it appears three times. Oh, no problem; just alter "Verulam" to "Verul'm" and it works out very nicely.

Most people understand that with sufficient ingenuity one can torture any text and find in it what one wishes. For instance: Did Shakespeare have a hand in the King James Version of the Bible? It was nearing completion in 1610, when Shakespeare was forty-six years old. If you look at the 46th Psalm and count forward for forty-six words, you will find the word *shake*. Now if you go to the end of the psalm and count backward forty-six words, you will find the word *spear*. Clear evidence, according to some, that Shakespeare slyly left his mark in the book.

Bacon's candidacy has largely been replaced in the twentieth century by the candidacy of Edward de Vere (1550–1604), 17th earl of Oxford. The basic ideas behind the Oxford theory, advanced at greatest length by Dorothy and Charlton Ogburn in *This Star of England* (1952, rev. 1955), a book of 1297 pages, and by Charlton Ogburn in *The Mysterious William Shakespeare* (1984), a book of 892 pages, are these: (1) The man from Stratford could not possibly have had the mental equipment and the experience to have written the plays—only a courtier could have written them; (2) Oxford had the requisite background (social position, education, years at Queen Elizabeth's court); (3) Oxford did not wish his authorship to be known for two basic reasons: writing for the public theater was a vulgar pursuit, and the plays show so much courtly and royal disreputable behavior that they would have compromised Oxford's position at court. Oxfordians offer countless details to support the claim. For example, Hamlet's phrase "that ever I was born to set it right" (1.5.89) barely conceals "E. Ver, I was born to set it right," an unambiguous announcement of de Vere's authorship, according to *This Star of England* (p. 654). A second example: Consider Ben

Jonson's poem entitled "To the Memory of My Beloved Master William Shakespeare," prefixed to the first collected edition of Shakespeare's plays in 1623. According to Oxfordians, when Jonson in this poem speaks of the author of the plays as the "swan of Avon," he is alluding not to William Shakespeare, who was born and died in Stratford-on-Avon and who throughout his adult life owned property there; rather, he is alluding to Oxford, who, the Ogburns say, used "William Shakespeare" as his pen name, and whose manor at Bilton was on the Avon River. Oxfordians do not offer any evidence that Oxford took a pen name, and they do not mention that Oxford had sold the manor in 1581, forty-two years before Jonson wrote his poem. Surely a reference to the Shakespeare who was born in Stratford, who had returned to Stratford, and who had died there only seven years before Jonson wrote the poem is more plausible. And exactly why Jonson, who elsewhere also spoke of Shakespeare as a playwright, and why Heminges and Condell, who had acted with Shakespeare for about twenty years, should speak of Shakespeare as the author in their dedication in the 1623 volume of collected plays is never adequately explained by Oxfordians. Either Jonson, Heminges and Condell, and numerous others were in on the conspiracy, or they were all duped—equally unlikely alternatives. Another difficulty in the Oxford theory is that Oxford died in 1604, and some of the plays are clearly indebted to works and events later than 1604. Among the Oxfordian responses are: At his death Oxford left some plays, and in later years these were touched up by hacks, who added the material that points to later dates. *The Tempest*, almost universally regarded as one of Shakespeare's greatest plays and pretty clearly dated to 1611, does indeed date from a period after the death of Oxford, but it is a crude piece of work that should not be included in the canon of works by Oxford.

The anti-Stratfordians, in addition to assuming that the author must have been a man of rank and a university man, usually assume two conspiracies: (1) a conspiracy in Elizabethan and Jacobean times, in which a surprisingly large number of persons connected with the theater knew that the actor Shakespeare did not write the plays attributed to him but for some reason or other pretended that he did; (2) a conspiracy of today's Stratfordians, the professors who teach Shakespeare in the colleges and universities, who are said to have a vested interest in preserving Shakespeare as the author of the plays they teach. In fact, (1) it is inconceivable that the secret of Shakespeare's non-authorship could have been preserved by all of the people who supposedly were in on the conspiracy, and (2) academic fame awaits any scholar today who can disprove Shakespeare's authorship.

The Stratfordian case is convincing not only because hundreds or even thousands of anti-Stratford arguments—of the sort that say "ever I was born" has the secret double meaning "E. Ver, I was born"—add up to nothing at all but also because irrefutable evidence connects the man from Stratford with the London theater and with the authorship of particular plays. The anti-Stratfordians do not seem to understand that it is not enough to dismiss the Stratford case by saying that a fellow from the provinces simply couldn't have written the plays. Nor do they understand that it is not enough to dismiss all of the evidence connecting Shakespeare with the plays by asserting that it is perjured.

The Shakespeare Canon

We return to William Shakespeare. Thirty-seven plays as well as some nondramatic poems are generally held to constitute the Shakespeare canon, the body of authentic works. The exact dates of composition of most of the works are highly uncertain, but evidence of a starting point and/or of a final limiting point often provides a framework for informed guessing. For example, *Richard II* cannot be earlier than 1595, the publication date of some material to which it is indebted; *The Merchant of Venice* cannot be later than 1598, the year Francis Meres mentioned it. Sometimes arguments for a date hang on an alleged topical allusion, such as the lines about the unseasonable weather in *A Midsummer Night's Dream*, 2.1.81–117, but such an allusion, if indeed it is an allusion to an event in the real world, can be variously interpreted, and in any case there is always the possibility that a topical allusion was inserted years later, to bring the play up to date. (The issue of alterations in a text between the time that Shakespeare drafted it and the time that it was printed—alterations due to censorship or playhouse practice or Shakespeare's own second thoughts—will be discussed in "The Play Text as a Collaboration" later in this overview.) Dates are often attributed on the basis of style, and although conjectures about style usually rest on other conjectures (such as Shakespeare's development as a playwright, or the appropriateness of lines to character), sooner or later one must rely on one's literary sense. There is no documentary proof, for example, that *Othello* is not as early as *Romeo and Juliet*, but one feels that *Othello* is a later, more mature work, and because the first record of its performance is 1604, one is glad enough to set its composition at that date and not push it back into Shakespeare's early years. (*Romeo and Juliet* was first published in 1597, but evidence suggests that it was written a little earlier.) The following chronology, then, is indebted not only to facts but also to informed guesswork and sensitivity. The dates, necessarily imprecise for some works, indicate something like a scholarly consensus concerning the time of original composition. Some plays show evidence of later revision.

Plays. The first collected edition of Shakespeare, published in 1623, included thirty-six plays. These are all accepted as Shakespeare's, though for one of them, *Henry VIII*, he is thought to have had a collaborator. A thirty-seventh play, *Pericles*, published in 1609 and attributed to Shakespeare on the title page, is also widely accepted as being partly by Shakespeare even though it is not included in the 1623 volume. Still another play not in the 1623 volume, *The Two Noble Kinsmen*, was first published in 1634, with a title page attributing it to John Fletcher and Shakespeare. Probably most students of the subject now believe that Shakespeare did indeed have a hand in it. Of the remaining plays attributed at one time or another to Shakespeare, only one, *Edward III*, anonymously published in 1596, is now regarded by some scholars as a serious candidate. The prevailing opinion, however, is that this rather simple-minded play is not Shakespeare's; at most he may have revised some passages, chiefly scenes with the Countess of

Salisbury. We include *The Two Noble Kinsmen* but do not include *Edward III* in the following list.

1588–94	*The Comedy of Errors*
1588–94	*Love's Labor's Lost*
1589–91	*2 Henry VI*
1590–91	*3 Henry VI*
1589–92	*1 Henry VI*
1592–93	*Richard III*
1589–94	*Titus Andronicus*
1593–94	*The Taming of the Shrew*
1592–94	*The Two Gentlemen of Verona*
1594–96	*Romeo and Juliet*
1595	*Richard II*
1595–96	*A Midsummer Night's Dream*
1596–97	*King John*
1594–96	*The Merchant of Venice*
1596–97	*1 Henry IV*
1597	*The Merry Wives of Windsor*
1597–98	*2 Henry IV*
1598–99	*Much Ado About Nothing*
1598–99	*Henry V*
1599	*Julius Caesar*
1599–1600	*As You Like It*
1599–1600	*Twelfth Night*
1600–1601	*Hamlet*
1601–1602	*Troilus and Cressida*
1602–1604	*All's Well That Ends Well*
1603–1604	*Othello*
1604	*Measure for Measure*
1605–1606	*King Lear*
1605–1606	*Macbeth*
1606–1607	*Antony and Cleopatra*
1605–1608	*Timon of Athens*
1607–1608	*Coriolanus*
1607–1608	*Pericles*
1609–10	*Cymbeline*
1610–11	*The Winter's Tale*
1611	*The Tempest*

| 1612–13 | *Henry VIII* |
| 1613 | *The Two Noble Kinsmen* |

Poems. In 1989 Donald W. Foster published a book in which he argued that "A Funeral Elegy for Master William Peter," published in 1612, ascribed only to the initials W.S., *may* be by Shakespeare. Foster later published an article in a scholarly journal, *PMLA* 111 (1996), in which he asserted the claim more positively. The evidence begins with the initials, and includes the fact that the publisher and the printer of the elegy had published Shakespeare's *Sonnets* in 1609. But such facts add up to rather little, especially because no one has found any connection between Shakespeare and William Peter (an Oxford graduate about whom little is known, who was murdered at the age of twenty-nine). The argument is based chiefly on statistical examinations of word patterns, which are said to correlate with Shakespeare's known work. Despite such correlations, however, many readers feel that the poem does not sound like Shakespeare. True, Shakespeare has a great range of styles, but his work is consistently imaginative and interesting. Many readers find neither of these qualities in "A Funeral Elegy."

1592–93	*Venus and Adonis*
1593–94	*The Rape of Lucrece*
1593–1600	*Sonnets*
1600–1601	*The Phoenix and the Turtle*

Shakespeare's English

1. Spelling and Pronunciation. From the philologist's point of view, Shakespeare's English is modern English. It requires footnotes, but the inexperienced reader can comprehend substantial passages with very little help, whereas for the same reader Chaucer's Middle English is a foreign language. By the beginning of the fifteenth century the chief grammatical changes in English had taken place, and the final unaccented *-e* of Middle English had been lost (though it survives even today in spelling, as in *name*); during the fifteenth century the dialect of London, the commercial and political center, gradually displaced the provincial dialects, at least in writing; by the end of the century, printing had helped to regularize and stabilize the language, especially spelling. Elizabethan spelling may seem erratic to us (there were dozens of spellings of *Shakespeare*, and a simple word like *been* was also spelled *beene* and *bin*), but it had much in common with our spelling. Elizabethan spelling was conservative in that for the most part it reflected an older pronunciation (Middle English) rather than the sound of the language as it was then spoken, just as our spelling continues to reflect medieval pronunciation—most obviously in the now silent but formerly pronounced letters in a word such as *knight*. Elizabethan pronunciation, though not identical with ours, was much closer to ours than to that of the Middle Ages. Incidentally, though no one can be certain about what Elizabethan English sounded like, specialists tend to believe it was rather like the speech of a modern stage Irishman (*time* apparently was pronounced *toime*, *old* pronounced *awld*, *day* pronounced *die*, and *join* pronounced *jine*) and not at all like the Oxford speech that most of us think it was.

An awareness of the difference between our pronunciation and Shakespeare's is crucial in three areas—in accent, or number of syllables (many metrically regular lines may look irregular to us); in rhymes (which may not look like rhymes); and in puns (which may not look like puns). Examples will be useful. Some words that were at least on occasion stressed differently from today are *aspèct*, *còmplete*, *fòrlorn*, *revènue*, and *sepùlcher*. Words that sometimes had an additional syllable are *emp[e]ress*, *Hen[e]ry*, *mon[e]th*, and *villain* (three syllables, *vil-lay-in*). An additional syllable is often found in possessives, like *moon*'s (pronounced *moones*) and in words ending in *-tion* or *-sion*. Words that had one less syllable than they now have are *needle* (pronounced *neel*) and *violet* (pronounced *vilet*). Among rhymes now lost are *one* with *loan*, *love* with *prove*, *beast* with *jest*, *eat* with *great*. (In reading, trust your sense of metrics and your ear, more than your eye.) An example of a pun that has become obliterated by a change in pronunciation is Falstaff's reply to Prince Hal's "Come, tell us your reason" in *1 Henry IV*: "Give you a reason on compulsion? If reasons were as plentiful as blackberries, I would give no man a reason upon compulsion, I" (2.4.237–40). The *ea* in *reason* was pronounced rather like a long *a*, like the *ai* in *raisin*, hence the comparison with blackberries.

Puns are not merely attempts to be funny; like metaphors they often involve bringing into a meaningful relationship areas of experience normally seen as remote. In *2 Henry IV*, when Feeble is conscripted, he stoically says, "I care not. A man can die but once. We owe God a death" (3.2.242–43), punning on *debt*, which was the way *death* was pronounced. Here an enormously significant fact of life is put into simple commercial imagery, suggesting its commonplace quality. Shakespeare used the same pun earlier in *1 Henry IV*, when Prince Hal says to Falstaff, "Why, thou owest God a death," and Falstaff replies, " 'Tis not due yet: I would be loath to pay him before his day. What need I be so forward with him that calls not on me?" (5.1.126–29).

Sometimes the puns reveal a delightful playfulness; sometimes they reveal aggressiveness, as when, replying to Claudius's "But now, my cousin Hamlet, and my son," Hamlet says, "A little more than kin, and less than kind!" (1.2.64–65). These are Hamlet's first words in the play, and we already hear him warring verbally against Claudius. Hamlet's "less than kind" probably means (1) Hamlet is not of Claudius's family or nature, *kind* having the sense it still has in our word *mankind*; (2) Hamlet is not kindly (affectionately) disposed toward Claudius; (3) Claudius is not naturally (but rather unnaturally, in a legal sense incestuously) Hamlet's father. The puns evidently were not put in as sops to the groundlings; they are an important way of communicating a complex meaning.

2. *Vocabulary.* A conspicuous difficulty in reading Shakespeare is rooted in the fact that some of his words are no longer in common use—for example, words concerned with armor, astrology, clothing, coinage, hawking, horsemanship, law, medicine, sailing, and war. Shakespeare had a large vocabulary—something near thirty thousand words—but it was not so much a vocabulary of big words as a vocabulary drawn from a wide range of life, and it is partly

his ability to call upon a great body of concrete language that gives his plays the sense of being in close contact with life. When the right word did not already exist, he made it up. Among words thought to be his coinages are *accommodation, all-knowing, amazement, bare-faced, countless, dexterously, dislocate, dwindle, fancy-free, frugal, indistinguishable, lackluster, laughable, overawe, premeditated, sea change, star-crossed*. Among those that have not survived are the verb *convive*, meaning to feast together, and *smilet*, a little smile.

Less overtly troublesome than the technical words but more treacherous are the words that seem readily intelligible to us but whose Elizabethan meanings differ from their modern ones. When Horatio describes the Ghost as an "erring spirit," he is saying not that the ghost has sinned or made an error but that it is wandering. Here is a short list of some of the most common words in Shakespeare's plays that often (but not always) have a meaning other than their most usual modern meaning:

'a	he
abuse	deceive
accident	occurrence
advertise	inform
an, and	if
annoy	harm
appeal	accuse
artificial	skillful
brave	fine, splendid
censure	opinion
cheer	(1) face (2) frame of mind
chorus	a single person who comments on the events
closet	small private room
competitor	partner
conceit	idea, imagination
cousin	kinsman
cunning	skillful
disaster	evil astrological influence
doom	judgment
entertain	receive into service

envy	malice
event	outcome
excrement	outgrowth (of hair)
fact	evil deed
fancy	(1) love (2) imagination
fell	cruel
fellow	(1) companion (2) low person (often an insulting term if addressed to someone of approximately equal rank)
fond	foolish
free	(1) innocent (2) generous
glass	mirror
hap, haply	chance, by chance
head	army
humor	(1) mood (2) bodily fluid thought to control one's psychology
imp	child
intelligence	news
kind	natural, acting according to nature
let	hinder
lewd	base
mere(ly)	utter(ly)
modern	commonplace
natural	a fool, an idiot
naughty	(1) wicked (2) worthless
next	nearest
nice	(1) trivial (2) fussy
noise	music
policy	(1) prudence (2) stratagem
presently	immediately
prevent	anticipate
proper	handsome
prove	test
quick	alive
sad	serious
saw	proverb
secure	without care, incautious
silly	innocent

sensible	capable of being perceived by the senses
shrewd	sharp
so	provided that
starve	die
still	always
success	that which follows
tall	brave
tell	count
tonight	last night
wanton	playful, careless
watch	keep awake
will	lust
wink	close both eyes
wit	mind, intelligence

All glosses, of course, are mere approximations; sometimes one of Shakespeare's words may hover between an older meaning and a modern one, and as we have seen, his words often have multiple meanings.

3. Grammar. A few matters of grammar may be surveyed, though it should be noted at the outset that Shakespeare sometimes made up his own grammar. As E.A. Abbott says in *A Shakespearian Grammar,* "Almost any part of speech can be used as any other part of speech": a noun as a verb ("he childed as I fathered"); a verb as a noun ("She hath made compare"); or an adverb as an adjective ("a seldom pleasure"). There are hundreds, perhaps thousands, of such instances in the plays, many of which at first glance would not seem at all irregular and would trouble only a pedant. Here are a few broad matters.

Nouns: The Elizabethans thought the *-s* genitive ending for nouns (as in *man's*) derived from *his*; thus the line " 'gainst the count his galleys I did some service," for "the count's galleys."

Adjectives: By Shakespeare's time adjectives had lost the endings that once indicated gender, number, and case. About the only difference between Shakespeare's adjectives and ours is the use of the now redundant *more* or *most* with the comparative ("some more fitter place") or superlative

("This was the most unkindest cut of all"). Like double comparatives and double superlatives, double negatives were acceptable; Mercutio "will not budge for no man's pleasure."

Pronouns: The greatest change was in pronouns. In Middle English *thou, thy,* and *thee* were used among familiars and in speaking to children and inferiors; *ye, your,* and *you* were used in speaking to superiors (servants to masters, nobles to the king) or to equals with whom the speaker was not familiar. Increasingly the "polite" forms were used in all direct address, regardless of rank, and the accusative *you* displaced the nominative *ye.* Shakespeare sometimes uses *ye* instead of *you,* but even in Shakespeare's day *ye* was archaic, and it occurs mostly in rhetorical appeals.

Thou, thy, and *thee* were not completely displaced, however, and Shakespeare occasionally makes significant use of them, sometimes to connote familiarity or intimacy and sometimes to connote contempt. In *Twelfth Night* Sir Toby advises Sir Andrew to insult Cesario by addressing him as *thou:* "If thou thou'st him some thrice, it shall not be amiss" (3.2.46–47). In *Othello* when Brabantio is addressing an unidentified voice in the dark he says, "What are you?" (1.1.91), but when the voice identifies itself as the foolish suitor Roderigo, Brabantio uses the contemptuous form, saying, "I have charged thee not to haunt about my doors" (93). He uses this form for a while, but later in the scene, when he comes to regard Roderigo as an ally, he shifts back to the polite *you,* beginning in line 163, "What said she to you?" and on to the end of the scene. For reasons not yet satisfactorily explained, Elizabethans used *thou* in addresses to God—"O God, thy arm was here," the king says in *Henry V* (4.8.108)—and to supernatural characters such as ghosts and witches. A subtle variation occurs in *Hamlet.* When Hamlet first talks with the Ghost in 1.5, he uses *thou,* but when he sees the Ghost in his mother's room, in 3.4, he uses *you,* presumably because he is now convinced that the Ghost is not a counterfeit but is his father.

Perhaps the most unusual use of pronouns, from our point of view, is the neuter singular. In place of our *its, his* was often used, as in "How far that little candle throws *his* beams." But the use of a masculine pronoun for a neuter noun came to seem unnatural, and so *it* was used for the possessive as well as the nominative: "The hedge-sparrow fed the cuckoo so long / That it had it head bit off by it young." In the late sixteenth century the possessive form *its* developed, apparently by analogy with the *-s* ending used to indicate a genitive noun, as in *book*'s, but *its* was not yet common usage in Shakespeare's day. He seems to have used *its* only ten times, mostly in his later plays. Other usages, such as "you have seen Cassio and she together" or the substitution of *who* for *whom*, cause little problem even when noticed.

Verbs, Adverbs, and Prepositions: Verbs cause almost no difficulty: The third person singular present form commonly ends in *-s*, as in modern English (e.g., "He blesses"), but sometimes in *-eth* (Portia explains to Shylock that mercy "blesseth him that gives and him that takes"). Broadly speaking, the *-eth* ending was old-fashioned or dignified or "literary" rather than colloquial, except for the words *doth*, *hath*, and *saith*. The *-eth* ending (regularly used in the King James Bible, 1611) is very rare in Shakespeare's dramatic prose, though not surprisingly it occurs twice in the rather formal prose summary of the narrative poem *Lucrece*. Sometimes a plural subject, especially if it has collective force, takes a verb ending in *-s*, as in "My old bones aches." Some of our strong or irregular preterites (such as *broke*) have a different form in Shakespeare (*brake*); some verbs that now have a weak or regular preterite (such as *helped*) in Shakespeare have a strong or irregular preterite (*holp*). Some adverbs that today end in *-ly* were not inflected: "grievous sick," "wondrous strange." Finally, prepositions often are not the ones we expect: "We are such stuff as dreams are made on," "I have a king here to my flatterer."

Again, none of the differences (except meanings that have substantially changed or been lost) will cause much difficulty. But it must be confessed that for some elliptical passages there is no widespread agreement on meaning. Wise editors resist saying more than they know, and when they are uncertain they add a question mark to their gloss.

Shakespeare's Theater

In Shakespeare's infancy, Elizabethan actors performed wherever they could—in great halls, at court, in the courtyards of inns. These venues implied not only different audiences but also different playing conditions. The innyards must have made rather unsatisfactory theaters: on some days they were unavailable because carters bringing goods to London used them as depots; when available, they had to be rented from the innkeeper. In 1567, presumably to avoid such difficulties, and also to avoid regulation by the Common Council of London, which was not well disposed toward theatricals, one John Brayne, brother-in-law of the carpenter turned actor James Burbage, built the Red Lion in an eastern suburb of London. We know nothing about its shape or its capacity; we can say only that it may have been the first building in Europe constructed for the purpose of giving plays since the end of antiquity, a thousand years earlier. Even after the building of the Red Lion theatrical activity continued in London in makeshift circumstances, in marketplaces and inns, and always uneasily. In 1574 the Common Council required that plays and playing places in London be licensed because

> sundry great disorders and inconveniences have been found to ensue to this city by the inordinate haunting of great multitudes of people, specially youth, to plays, interludes, and shows, namely occasion of frays and quarrels, evil practices of incontinency in great inns having chambers and secret places adjoining to their open stages and galleries.

The Common Council ordered that innkeepers who wished licenses to hold performance put up a bond and make contributions to the poor.

The requirement that plays and innyard theaters be licensed, along with the other drawbacks of playing at inns and presumably along with the success of the Red Lion, led James Burbage to rent a plot of land northeast of the city walls, on property outside the jurisdiction of the city. Here he built England's second playhouse, called simply the Theatre. About all that is known of its construction is that it was wood. It soon had imitators, the most famous being the Globe (1599), essentially an amphitheater built across the Thames (again outside the city's jurisdiction), constructed with timbers of the Theatre, which had been dismantled when Burbage's lease ran out.

Admission to the theater was one penny, which allowed spectators to stand at the sides and front of the stage that jutted into the yard. An additional penny bought a seat in a covered part of the theater, and a third penny bought a more comfortable seat and a better location. It is notoriously difficult to translate prices into today's money, since some things that are inexpensive today would have been expensive in the past and vice versa—a pipeful of tobacco (imported, of course) cost a lot of money, about three pennies, and an orange (also imported) cost two or three times what a chicken cost—but perhaps we can get some idea of the low cost of the penny admission when we realize that a penny could also buy a pot of ale. An unskilled laborer made about five or sixpence a day, an artisan about twelve pence a day, and the hired actors (as opposed to the sharers in the company, such as Shakespeare) made about ten pence a performance. A printed play cost five or sixpence. Of course a visit to the theater (like a visit to a baseball game today) usually cost more than the admission since the spectator probably would also buy food and drink. Still, the low entrance fee meant that the theater was available to all except the very poorest people, rather as movies and most athletic events are today. Evidence indicates that the audience ranged from apprentices who somehow managed to scrape together the minimum entrance fee and to escape from their masters for a few hours, to prosperous members of the middle class and aristocrats who paid the additional fee for admission to the galleries. The exact proportion of men to women cannot be determined, but women of all classes certainly were present. Theaters were open every afternoon but Sundays for much of the year, except in times of plague, when they were closed because of fear of infection. By the way, no evidence suggests the presence of toilet facilities. Presumably the patrons relieved themselves by making a quick trip to the fields surrounding the playhouses.

There are four important sources of information about the

structure of Elizabethan public playhouses—drawings, a contract, recent excavations, and stage directions in the plays. Of drawings, only the so-called de Witt drawing (c. 1596) of the Swan—really his friend Aernout van Buchell's copy of Johannes de Witt's drawing—is of much significance. The drawing, the only extant representation of the interior of an Elizabethan theater, shows an amphitheater of three tiers, with a stage jutting from a wall into the yard or

Johannes de Witt, a Continental visitor to London, made a drawing of the Swan theater in about the year 1596. The original drawing is lost; this is Aernout van Buchell's copy of it.

center of the building. The tiers are roofed, and part of the stage is covered by a roof that projects from the rear and is supported at its front on two posts, but the groundlings, who paid a penny to stand in front of the stage or at its sides, were exposed to the sky. (Performances in such a playhouse were held only in the daytime; artificial illumination was not used.) At the rear of the stage are two massive doors; above the stage is a gallery.

The second major source of information, the contract for the Fortune (built in 1600), specifies that although the Globe (built in 1599) is to be the model, the Fortune is to be square, eighty feet outside and fifty-five inside. The stage is to be forty-three feet broad, and is to extend into the middle of the yard, i.e., it is twenty-seven and a half feet deep.

The third source of information, the 1989 excavations of the Rose (built in 1587), indicate that the Rose was fourteen-sided, about seventy-two feet in diameter with an inner yard almost fifty feet in diameter. The stage at the Rose was about sixteen feet deep, thirty-seven feet wide at the rear, and twenty-seven feet wide downstage. The relatively small dimensions and the tapering stage, in contrast to the rectangular stage in the Swan drawing, surprised theater historians and have made them more cautious in generalizing about the Elizabethan theater. Excavations at the Globe have not yielded much information, though some historians believe that the fragmentary evidence suggests a larger theater, perhaps one hundred feet in diameter.

From the fourth chief source, stage directions in the plays, one learns that entrance to the stage was by the doors at the rear (*"Enter one citizen at one door, and another at the other"*). A curtain hanging across the doorway—or a curtain hanging between the two doorways—could provide a place where a character could conceal himself, as Polonius does, when he wishes to overhear the conversation between Hamlet and Gertrude. Similarly, withdrawing a curtain from the doorway could "discover" (reveal) a character or two. Such discovery scenes are very rare in Elizabethan drama, but a good example occurs in *The Tempest* (5.1.171), where a stage direction tells us, *"Here Prospero discovers Ferdinand and Miranda playing at chess."* There was also some sort of playing space "aloft" or "above" to represent, for instance, the top of a city's walls or a room above the street. Doubtless each theater had its own peculiarities, but perhaps we can talk about a "typical" Elizabethan theater if we realize that no theater need exactly fit the description, just as no mother is the average mother with 2.7 children.

This hypothetical theater is wooden, round, or polygonal (in *Henry V* Shakespeare calls it a "wooden *O*") capable of holding some eight hundred spectators who stood in the yard around the projecting elevated stage—these spectators were the "groundlings"—and some fifteen hundred additional spectators who sat in the three roofed galleries. The stage, protected by a "shadow" or "heavens" or roof, is entered from two doors; behind the doors is the "tiring house" (attiring house, i.e., dressing room), and above the stage is some sort of gallery that may sometimes hold spectators but can be used (for example) as the bedroom from which Romeo—according to a stage direction in one text—"goeth down." Some evidence suggests that a throne can be lowered onto the platform stage, perhaps from the "shadow"; certainly characters can descend from the stage through a trap or traps into the cellar or "hell." Sometimes this space beneath the stage accommodates a sound-effects man or musician (in *Antony and Cleopatra* "*music of the hautboys* [oboes] *is under the stage*") or an actor (in *Hamlet* the "*Ghost cries under the stage*"). Most characters simply walk on and off through the doors, but because there is no curtain in front of the platform, corpses will have to be carried off (Hamlet obligingly clears the stage of Polonius's corpse, when he says, "I'll lug the guts into the neighbor room"). Other characters may have fallen at the rear, where a curtain on a doorway could be drawn to conceal them.

Such may have been the "public theater," so called because its inexpensive admission made it available to a wide range of the populace. Another kind of theater has been called the "private theater" because its much greater admission charge (sixpence versus the penny for general admission at the public theater) limited its audience to the wealthy or the prodigal. The private theater was basically a large room, entirely roofed and therefore artificially illuminated, with a stage at one end. The theaters thus were distinct in two ways: One was essentially an amphitheater that catered to the general public; the other was a hall that catered to the wealthy. In 1576 a hall theater was established in Blackfriars, a Dominican priory in London that had been suppressed in 1538 and confiscated by the Crown and thus was not under the city's jurisdiction. All the actors in this Blackfriars theater were boys about eight to thirteen years old (in the public theaters similar boys played female parts; a boy Lady Macbeth played to a man Macbeth). Near the end of this section on Shakespeare's theater we will talk at some length about possible implications in this convention of using boys to play female roles, but for the moment we should say that it doubtless accounts for the relative lack of female roles in Elizabethan drama. Thus, in *A Midsummer Night's Dream*, out of twenty-one named roles, only four are female; in *Hamlet*, out of twenty-four, only two (Gertrude and Ophelia) are female. Many of Shakespeare's characters have fathers but no mothers—for instance, King Lear's daughters. We need not bring in Freud to explain the disparity; a dramatic company had only a few boys in it.

To return to the private theaters, in some of which all of the performers were children—the "eyrie of . . . little eyases" (nest of unfledged hawks—2.2.347–48) which Rosencrantz mentions when he and Guildenstern talk with Hamlet. The theater in Blackfriars had a precarious existence, and ceased operations in 1584. In 1596 James Burbage, who had already made theatrical history by building the Theatre, began to construct a second Blackfriars theater. He died in 1597, and for several years this second Blackfriars theater was used by a troupe of boys, but in 1608 two of Burbage's sons and five other actors (including Shakespeare) became joint operators of the theater, using it in the winter when the open-air Globe was unsuitable. Perhaps such a smaller theater, roofed, artificially illuminated, and with a tradition of a wealthy audience, exerted an influence in Shakespeare's late plays.

Performances in the private theaters may well have had intermissions during which music was played, but in the public theaters the action was probably uninterrupted, flowing from scene to scene almost without a break. Actors would enter, speak, exit, and others would immediately enter and establish (if necessary) the new locale by a few properties and by words and gestures. To indicate that the scene took place at night, a player or two would carry a torch. Here are some samples of Shakespeare establishing the scene:

> This is Illyria, lady.   (*Twelfth Night,* 1.2.2)

> Well, this is the Forest of Arden.   (*As You Like It,* 2.4.14)

> This castle has a pleasant seat; the air
> Nimbly and sweetly recommends itself
> Unto our gentle senses.   (*Macbeth,* 1.6.1–3)

> The west yet glimmers with some streaks of day.
>   (*Macbeth,* 3.3.5)

Sometimes a speech will go far beyond evoking the minimal setting of place and time, and will, so to speak, evoke the social world in which the characters move. For instance, early in the first scene of *The Merchant of Venice* Salerio suggests an explanation for Antonio's melancholy. (In the following passage, *pageants* are decorated wagons, floats, and *cursy* is the verb "to curtsy," or "to bow.")

> Your mind is tossing on the ocean,
> There where your argosies with portly sail—
> Like signiors and rich burghers on the flood,
> Or as it were the pageants of the sea—
> Do overpeer the petty traffickers
> That cursy to them, do them reverence,   .
> As they fly by them with their woven wings.   (1.1.8–14)

Late in the nineteenth century, when Henry Irving produced the play with elaborate illusionistic sets, the first scene showed a ship moored in the harbor, with fruit vendors and dock laborers, in an effort to evoke the bustling and exotic life of Venice. But Shakespeare's words give us this exotic, rich world of commerce in his highly descriptive language when Salerio speaks of "argosies with portly sail" that fly with "woven wings"; equally important, through Salerio Shakespeare conveys a sense of the orderly, hierarchical society in which the lesser ships, "the petty traffickers," curtsy and thereby "do . . . reverence" to their superiors, the merchant prince's ships, which are "Like signiors and rich burghers."

On the other hand, it is a mistake to think that except for verbal pictures the Elizabethan stage was bare. Although Shakespeare's Chorus in *Henry V* calls the stage an "unworthy scaffold" (Prologue 1.10) and urges the spectators to "eke out our performance with your mind" (Prologue 3.35), there was considerable spectacle. The last act of *Macbeth*, for instance, has five stage directions calling for *"drum and colors,"* and another sort of appeal to the eye is indicated by the stage direction *"Enter Macduff, with Macbeth's head."* Some scenery and properties may have been substantial; doubtless a throne was used, but the pillars supporting the roof would have served for the trees on which Orlando pins his poems in *As You Like It*.

Having talked about the public theater—"this wooden *O*"—at some length, we should mention again that Shakespeare's plays were performed also in other locales. Alvin Kernan, in *Shakespeare, the King's Playwright: Theater in the Stuart Court 1603–1613* (1995) points out that "several of [Shakespeare's] plays contain brief theatrical performances, set always in a court or some noble house. When Shakespeare portrayed a theater, he did not, except for the choruses in *Henry V*, imagine a public theater" (p. 195). (Examples include episodes in *The Taming of the Shrew*, *A Midsummer Night's Dream*, *Hamlet*, and *The Tempest*.)

A Note on the Use of Boy Actors in Female Roles

Until fairly recently, scholars were content to mention that the convention existed; they sometimes also mentioned that it continued the medieval practice of using males in female roles, and that other theaters, notably in ancient Greece and in China and Japan, also used males in female roles. (In classical Noh drama in Japan, males still play the female roles.) Prudery may have been at the root of the academic failure to talk much about the use of boy actors, or maybe there really is not much more to say than that it was a convention of a male-centered culture (Stephen Greenblatt's view, in *Shakespearean Negotiations* [1988]). Further, the very nature of a convention is that it is not thought about: Hamlet is a Dane and Julius Caesar is a Roman, but in Shakespeare's plays they speak English, and we in the audience never give this odd fact a thought. Similarly, a character may speak in the presence of others and we understand, again without thinking about it, that he or she is not heard by the figures on the stage (the aside); a character alone on the stage may speak (the soliloquy), and we do not take the character to be unhinged; in a realistic (box) set, the fourth wall, which allows us to see what is going on, is miraculously missing. The no-nonsense view, then, is that the boy actor was an accepted convention, accepted unthinkingly—just as today we know that Kenneth Branagh is not Hamlet, Al Pacino is not Richard III, and Denzel Washington is not the Prince of Aragon. In this view, the audience takes the performer for the role, and that is that; such is the argument we now make for race-free casting, in which African-Americans and Asians can play roles of persons who lived in medieval Denmark and ancient Rome. But gender perhaps is different, at least today. It is a matter of abundant academic study: The Elizabethan theater is now sometimes called a transvestite theater, and we hear much about cross-dressing.

Shakespeare himself in a very few passages calls attention to the use of boys in female roles. At the end of *As You Like It* the boy who played Rosalind addresses the audience, and says, "O men, . . . if I were a woman, I would kiss as many of you as had beards that pleased me." But this is in the Epilogue; the plot is over, and the actor is stepping out of the play and into the audience's everyday world. A second reference to the practice of boys playing female roles occurs in *Antony and Cleopatra*, when Cleopatra imagines that she and Antony will be the subject of crude plays, her role being performed by a boy:

> The quick comedians
> Extemporally will stage us, and present
> Our Alexandrian revels: Antony
> Shall be brought drunken forth, and I shall see
> Some squeaking Cleopatra boy my greatness.   (5.2.216–20)

In a few other passages, Shakespeare is more indirect. For instance, in *Twelfth Night* Viola, played of course by a boy, disguises herself as a young man and seeks service in the house of a lord. She enlists the help of a Captain, and (by way of explaining away her voice and her beardlessness) says,

> I'll serve this duke
> Thou shalt present me as an eunuch to him.   (1.2.55–56)

In *Hamlet*, when the players arrive in 2.2, Hamlet jokes with the boy who plays a female role. The boy has grown since Hamlet last saw him: "By'r Lady, your ladyship is nearer to heaven than when I saw you last by the altitude of a chopine" (a lady's thick-soled shoe). He goes on: "Pray God your voice . . . be not cracked" (434–38).

Exactly how sexual, how erotic, this material was and is, is now much disputed. Again, the use of boys may have been unnoticed, or rather not thought about—an unexamined convention—by most or all spectators most of the time, perhaps *all* of the time, except when Shakespeare calls the convention to the attention of the audience, as in the passages just quoted. Still, an occasional bit seems to invite erotic thoughts. The clearest example is the name that Rosalind takes in *As You Like It*, Ganymede—the beautiful youth whom Zeus abducted. Did boys dressed to play female roles carry homoerotic appeal for straight men (Lisa Jardine's view, in *Still Harping on Daughters* [1983]), or for gay men, or for some or all women in the audience? Further, when the boy actor played a woman who (for the purposes of the plot) disguised herself as a male, as Rosalind, Viola, and Portia do—so we get a boy playing a woman playing a man—what sort of appeal was generated, and for what sort of spectator?

Some scholars have argued that the convention empowered women by letting female characters display a freedom unavailable in Renaissance patriarchal society; the convention, it is said, undermined rigid gender distinctions. In this view, the convention (along with plots in which female characters for a while disguised themselves as young men) allowed Shakespeare to say what some modern gender

critics say: Gender is a constructed role rather than a bio-
logical given, something we make, rather than a fixed binary
opposition of male and female (see Juliet Dusinberre, in
Shakespeare and the Nature of Women [1975]). On the other
hand, some scholars have maintained that the male disguise
assumed by some female characters serves only to reaffirm
traditional social distinctions since female characters who
don male garb (notably Portia in *The Merchant of Venice*
and Rosalind in *As You Like It*) return to their female garb
and at least implicitly (these critics say) reaffirm the status
quo. (For this last view, see Clara Claiborne Park, in an
essay in *The Woman's Part*, ed. Carolyn Ruth Swift Lenz et
al. [1980].) Perhaps no one answer is right for all plays; in
As You Like It cross-dressing empowers Rosalind, but in
Twelfth Night cross-dressing comically traps Viola.

Shakespeare's Dramatic Language: Costumes, Gestures and Silences; Prose and Poetry

Because Shakespeare was a dramatist, not merely a poet,
he worked not only with language but also with costume,
sound effects, gestures, and even silences. We have already
discussed some kinds of spectacle in the preceding section,
and now we will begin with other aspects of visual language;
a theater, after all, is literally a "place for seeing." Consider
the opening stage direction in *The Tempest*, the first play in
the first published collection of Shakespeare's plays: *"A
tempestuous noise of thunder and Lightning heard: Enter a
Ship-master, and a Boteswain."*

Costumes: What did that shipmaster and that boatswain
wear? Doubtless they wore something that identified them
as men of the sea. Not much is known about the costumes
that Elizabethan actors wore, but at least three points are
clear: (1) many of the costumes were splendid versions of
contemporary Elizabethan dress; (2) some attempts were
made to approximate the dress of certain occupations and of
antique or exotic characters such as Romans, Turks, and
Jews; (3) some costumes indicated that the wearer was

supernatural. Evidence for elaborate Elizabethan clothing can be found in the plays themselves and in contemporary comments about the "sumptuous" players who wore the discarded clothing of noblemen, as well as in account books that itemize such things as "a scarlet cloak with two broad gold laces, with gold buttons down the sides."

The attempts at approximation of the dress of certain occupations and nationalities also can be documented from the plays themselves, and it derives additional confirmation from a drawing of the first scene of Shakespeare's *Titus Andronicus*—the only extant Elizabethan picture of an identifiable episode in a play. (See pp. xxxviii–xxxix.) The drawing, probably done in 1594 or 1595, shows Queen Tamora pleading for mercy. She wears a somewhat medieval-looking robe and a crown; Titus wears a toga and a wreath, but two soldiers behind him wear costumes fairly close to Elizabethan dress. We do not know, however, if the drawing represents an actual stage production in the public theater, or perhaps a private production, or maybe only a reader's visualization of an episode. Further, there is some conflicting evidence: In *Julius Caesar* a reference is made to Caesar's doublet (a close-fitting jacket), which, if taken literally, suggests that even the protagonist did not wear Roman clothing; and certainly the lesser characters, who are said to wear hats, did not wear Roman garb.

It should be mentioned, too, that even ordinary clothing can be symbolic: Hamlet's "inky cloak," for example, sets him apart from the brightly dressed members of Claudius's court and symbolizes his mourning; the fresh clothes that are put on King Lear partly symbolize his return to sanity. Consider, too, the removal of disguises near the end of some plays. For instance, Rosalind in *As You Like It* and Portia and Nerissa in *The Merchant of Venice* remove their male attire, thus again becoming fully themselves.

Gestures and Silences: Gestures are an important part of a dramatist's language. King Lear kneels before his daughter Cordelia for a benediction (4.7.57–59), an act of humility that contrasts with his earlier speeches banishing her and that contrasts also with a comparable gesture, his ironic

kneeling before Regan (2.4.153–55). Northumberland's failure to kneel before King Richard II (3.3.71–72) speaks volumes. As for silences, consider a moment in *Coriolanus*: Before the protagonist yields to his mother's entreaties (5.3.182), there is this stage direction: *"Holds her by the hand, silent."* Another example of "speech in dumbness" occurs in *Macbeth*, when Macduff learns that his wife and children have been murdered. He is silent at first, as Malcolm's speech indicates: "What, man! Ne'er pull your hat upon your brows. Give sorrow words" (4.3.208–09). (For a discussion of such moments, see Philip C. McGuire's *Speechless Dialect: Shakespeare's Open Silences* [1985].)

Of course when we think of Shakespeare's work, we think primarily of his language, both the poetry and the prose.

Prose: Although two of his plays (*Richard II* and *King John*) have no prose at all, about half the others have at least one quarter of the dialogue in prose, and some have notably more: *1 Henry IV* and *2 Henry IV*, about half; *As You Like It*

and *Twelfth Night*, a little more than half; *Much Ado About Nothing*, more than three quarters; and *The Merry Wives of Windsor*, a little more than five sixths. We should remember that despite Molière's joke about M. Jourdain, who was amazed to learn that he spoke prose, most of us do not speak prose. Rather, we normally utter repetitive, shapeless, and often ungrammatical torrents; prose is something very different—a sort of literary imitation of speech at its most coherent.

Today we may think of prose as "natural" for drama; or even if we think that poetry is appropriate for high tragedy we may still think that prose is the right medium for comedy. Greek, Roman, and early English comedies, however, were written in verse. In fact, prose was not generally considered a literary medium in England until the late fifteenth century; Chaucer tells even his bawdy stories in verse. By the end of the 1580s, however, prose had established itself on the English comic stage. In tragedy, Marlowe made some use of prose, not simply in the speeches of clownish servants but even in the speech of a tragic hero, Doctor Faustus. Still, before Shakespeare, prose normally was used in the theater only for special circumstances: (1) letters and proclamations, to set them off from the poetic dialogue; (2) mad characters, to indicate that normal thinking has become disordered; and (3) low comedy, or speeches uttered by clowns even when they are not being comic. Shakespeare made use of these conventions, but he also went far beyond them. Sometimes he begins a scene in prose and then shifts into verse as the emotion is heightened; or conversely, he may shift from verse to prose when a speaker is lowering the emotional level, as when Brutus speaks in the Forum.

Shakespeare's prose usually is not prosaic. Hamlet's prose includes not only small talk with Rosencrantz and Guildenstern but also princely reflections on "What a piece of work is a man" (2.2.312). In conversation with Ophelia, he shifts from light talk in verse to a passionate prose denunciation of women (3.1.103), though the shift to prose here is perhaps also intended to suggest the possibility of madness. (Consult Brian Vickers, *The Artistry of Shakespeare's Prose* [1968].)

Poetry: Drama in rhyme in England goes back to the Middle Ages, but by Shakespeare's day rhyme no longer dominated poetic drama; a finer medium, blank verse (strictly speaking, unrhymed lines of ten syllables, with the stress on every second syllable) had been adopted. But before looking at unrhymed poetry, a few things should be said about the chief uses of rhyme in Shakespeare's plays. (1) A couplet (a pair of rhyming lines) is sometimes used to convey emotional heightening at the end of a blank verse speech; (2) characters sometimes speak a couplet as they leave the stage, suggesting closure; (3) except in the latest plays, scenes fairly often conclude with a couplet, and sometimes, as in *Richard II*, 2.1.145–46, the entrance of a new character within a scene is preceded by a couplet, which wraps up the earlier portion of that scene; (4) speeches of two characters occasionally are linked by rhyme, most notably in *Romeo and Juliet*, 1.5.95–108, where the lovers speak a sonnet between them; elsewhere a taunting reply occasionally rhymes with the previous speaker's last line; (5) speeches with sententious or gnomic remarks are sometimes in rhyme, as in the duke's speech in *Othello* (1.3.199–206); (6) speeches of sardonic mockery are sometimes in rhyme—for example, Iago's speech on women in *Othello* (2.1.146–58)—and they sometimes conclude with an emphatic couplet, as in Bolingbroke's speech on comforting words in *Richard II* (1.3.301–2); (7) some characters are associated with rhyme, such as the fairies in *A Midsummer Night's Dream*; (8) in the early plays, especially *The Comedy of Errors* and *The Taming of the Shrew*, comic scenes that in later plays would be in prose are in jingling rhymes; (9) prologues, choruses, plays-within-the-play, inscriptions, vows, epilogues, and so on are often in rhyme, and the songs in the plays are rhymed.

Neither prose nor rhyme immediately comes to mind when we first think of Shakespeare's medium: It is blank verse, unrhymed iambic pentameter. (In a mechanically exact line there are five iambic feet. An iambic foot consists of two syllables, the second accented, as in *away*; five feet make a pentameter line. Thus, a strict line of iambic pentameter contains ten syllables, the even syllables being stressed more heavily than the odd syllables. Fortunately, Shakespeare usually varies the line somewhat.) The first speech in *A Midsummer Night's Dream*, spoken by Duke Theseus to his betrothed, is an example of blank verse:

> Now, fair Hippolyta, our nuptial hour
> Draws on apace. Four happy days bring in
> Another moon; but, O, methinks, how slow
> This old moon wanes! She lingers my desires,
> Like to a stepdame, or a dowager,
> Long withering out a young man's revenue.   (1.1.1–6)

As this passage shows, Shakespeare's blank verse is not mechanically unvarying. Though the predominant foot is the iamb (as in *apace* or *desires*), there are numerous variations. In the first line the stress can be placed on "fair," as the regular metrical pattern suggests, but it is likely that "Now" gets almost as much emphasis; probably in the second line "Draws" is more heavily emphasized than "on," giving us a trochee (a stressed syllable followed by an unstressed one); and in the fourth line each word in the phrase "This old moon wanes" is probably stressed fairly heavily, conveying by two spondees (two feet, each of two stresses) the oppressive tedium that Theseus feels.

In Shakespeare's early plays much of the blank verse is end-stopped (that is, it has a heavy pause at the end of each line), but he later developed the ability to write iambic pentameter verse paragraphs (rather than lines) that give the illusion of speech. His chief techniques are (1) enjambing, i.e., running the thought beyond the single line, as in the first three lines of the speech just quoted; (2) occasionally replacing an iamb with another foot; (3) varying the position of the chief pause (the caesura) within a line; (4) adding an occasional unstressed syllable at the end of a line, traditionally called a feminine ending; (5) and beginning or ending a speech with a half line.

Shakespeare's mature blank verse has much of the rhythmic flexibility of his prose; both the language, though richly figurative and sometimes dense, and the syntax seem natural. It is also often highly appropriate to a particular character. Consider, for instance, this speech from *Hamlet*, in which Claudius, King of Denmark ("the Dane"), speaks to Laertes:

> And now, Laertes, what's the news with you?
> You told us of some suit. What is't, Laertes?
> You cannot speak of reason to the Dane
> And lose your voice. What wouldst thou beg, Laertes,
> That shall not be my offer, not thy asking?   (1.2.42–46)

Notice the short sentences and the repetition of the name "Laertes," to whom the speech is addressed. Notice, too, the shift from the royal "us" in the second line to the more intimate "my" in the last line, and from "you" in the first three lines to the more intimate "thou" and "thy" in the last two lines. Claudius knows how to ingratiate himself with Laertes.

For a second example of the flexibility of Shakespeare's blank verse, consider a passage from *Macbeth*. Distressed by the doctor's inability to cure Lady Macbeth and by the imminent battle, Macbeth addresses some of his remarks to the doctor and others to the servant who is arming him. The entire speech, with its pauses, interruptions, and irresolution (in "Pull't off, I say," Macbeth orders the servant to remove the armor that the servant has been putting on him), catches Macbeth's disintegration. (In the first line, *physic* means "medicine," and in the fourth and fifth lines, *cast the water* means "analyze the urine.")

> Throw physic to the dogs, I'll none of it.
> Come, put mine armor on. Give me my staff.
> Seyton, send out.—Doctor, the thanes fly from me.—
> Come, sir, dispatch. If thou couldst, doctor, cast
> The water of my land, find her disease
> And purge it to a sound and pristine health,
> I would applaud thee to the very echo,
> That should applaud again.—Pull't off, I say.—
> What rhubarb, senna, or what purgative drug,
> Would scour these English hence? Hear'st thou of them?

(5.3.47–56)

Blank verse, then, can be much more than unrhymed iambic pentameter, and even within a single play Shakespeare's blank verse often consists of several styles, depending on the speaker and on the speaker's emotion at the moment.

The Play Text as a Collaboration

Shakespeare's fellow dramatist Ben Jonson reported that the actors said of Shakespeare, "In his writing, whatsoever he penned, he never blotted out line," i.e., never crossed out material and revised his work while composing. None of Shakespeare's plays survives in manuscript (with the possible exception of a scene in *Sir Thomas More*), so we cannot fully evaluate the comment, but in a few instances the published work clearly shows that he revised his manuscript. Consider the following passage (shown here in facsimile) from the best early text of *Romeo and Juliet*, the Second Quarto (1599):

> *Ro.* Would I were sleepe and peace so sweet to rest
> The grey eyde morne smiles on the frowning night,
> Checkring the Easterne Clouds with streaks of light,
> And darknesse fleckted like a drunkard reeles,
> From forth daies pathway, made by *Tytans* wheeles.
> Hence will I to my ghostly Friers close cell,
> His helpe to craue, and my deare hap to tell.
>
> *Exit.*
>
> *Enter Frier alone with a basket.*   (night,
> *Fri.* The grey-eyed morne smiles on the frowning
> Checking the Easterne clowdes with streaks of light:
> And fleckeld darknesse like a drunkard reeles,
> From forth daies path, and *Titans* burning wheeles:
> Now ere the sun aduance his burning eie,

Romeo rather elaborately tells us that the sun at dawn is dispelling the night (morning is smiling, the eastern clouds are checked with light, and the sun's chariot—Titan's wheels—advances), and he will seek out his spiritual father, the Friar. He exits and, oddly, the Friar enters and says pretty much the same thing about the sun. Both speakers say that "the gray-eyed morn smiles on the frowning night," but there are small differences, perhaps having more to do with the business of printing the book than with the author's composition: For Romeo's "checkring," "fleckted," and "pathway," we get the Friar's "checking," "fleckeld," and "path." (Notice, by the way, the inconsistency in Elizabethan spelling: Romeo's "clouds" become the Friar's "clowdes.")

Both versions must have been in the printer's copy, and it seems safe to assume that both were in Shakespeare's manuscript. He must have written one version—let's say he first wrote Romeo's closing lines for this scene—and then he decided, no, it's better to give this lyrical passage to the Friar, as the opening of a new scene, but he neglected to delete the first version. Editors must make a choice, and they may feel that the reasonable thing to do is to print the text as Shakespeare intended it. But how can we know what he intended? Almost all modern editors delete the lines from

Romeo's speech, and retain the Friar's lines. They don't do this because they know Shakespeare's intention, however. They give the lines to the Friar because the first published version (1597) of *Romeo and Juliet* gives only the Friar's version, and this text (though in many ways inferior to the 1599 text) is thought to derive from the memory of some actors, that is, it is thought to represent a performance, not just a script. Maybe during the course of rehearsals Shakespeare—an actor as well as an author—unilaterally decided that the Friar should speak the lines; if so (remember that we don't know this to be a fact) his final intention was to give the speech to the Friar. Maybe, however, the actors talked it over and settled on the Friar, with or without Shakespeare's approval. On the other hand, despite the 1597 version, one might argue (if only weakly) on behalf of giving the lines to Romeo rather than to the Friar, thus: (1) Romeo's comment on the coming of the daylight emphasizes his separation from Juliet, and (2) the figurative language seems more appropriate to Romeo than to the Friar. Having said this, in the Signet edition we have decided in this instance to draw on the evidence provided by earlier text and to give the lines to the Friar, on the grounds that since Q1 reflects a production, in the theater (at least on one occasion) the lines were spoken by the Friar.

A playwright sold a script to a theatrical company. The script thus belonged to the company, not the author, and author and company alike must have regarded this script not as a literary work but as the basis for a play that the actors would create on the stage. We speak of Shakespeare as the author of the plays, but readers should bear in mind that the texts they read, even when derived from a single text, such as the First Folio (1623), are inevitably the collaborative work not simply of Shakespeare with his company—doubtless during rehearsals the actors would suggest alterations—but also with other forces of the age. One force was governmental censorship. In 1606 parliament passed "an Act to restrain abuses of players," prohibiting the utterance of oaths and the name of God. So where the earliest text of *Othello* gives us "By heaven" (3.3.106), the first Folio gives "Alas," presumably reflecting the compliance of stage practice with the law. Similarly, the 1623 version of *King Lear* omits the oath "Fut" (probably from "By God's foot") at 1.2.142, again presumably reflecting the line as it was spoken on the stage. Editors who seek to give the reader the play that Shakespeare initially conceived—the "authentic" play conceived by the solitary Shakespeare— probably will restore the missing oaths and references to God. Other editors, who see the play as a collaborative work, a construction made not only by Shakespeare but also by actors and compositors and even government censors, may claim that what counts is the play as it was actually performed. Such editors regard the censored text as legitimate, since it is the play that was (presumably) finally put on. A performed text, they argue, has more historical reality than a text produced by an editor who has sought to get at what Shakespeare initially wrote. In this view, the text of a play is rather like the script of a film; the script is not the film, and the play text is not the performed play. Even if we want to talk about the play that Shakespeare "intended," we will find ourselves talking about a script that he handed over to a company with the intention that it be implemented by actors. The "intended" play is the one that the actors—we might almost say "society"—would help to construct.

Further, it is now widely held that a play is also the work of readers and spectators, who do not simply receive meaning, but who create it when they respond to the play. This idea is fully in accord with contemporary post-structuralist critical thinking, notably Roland Barthes's "The Death of the Author," in *Image-Music-Text* (1977) and Michel Foucault's "What Is an Author?," in *The Foucault Reader* (1984). The gist of the idea is that an author is not an isolated genius; rather, authors are subject to the politics and other social structures of their age. A dramatist especially is a worker in a collaborative project, working most obviously with actors—parts may be written for particular actors—but working also with the audience. Consider the words of Samuel Johnson, written to be spoken by the actor David Garrick at the opening of a theater in 1747:

> The stage but echoes back the public voice;
> The drama's laws, the drama's patrons give,
> For we that live to please, must please to live.

The audience—the public taste as understood by the playwright—helps to determine what the play is. Moreover, even members of the public who are not part of the playwright's immediate audience may exert an influence through censorship. We have already glanced at governmental censorship, but there are also other kinds. Take one of Shakespeare's most beloved characters, Falstaff, who appears in three of Shakespeare's plays, the two parts of *Henry IV* and *The Merry Wives of Windsor*. He appears with this name in the earliest printed version of the first of these plays, *1 Henry IV*, but we know that Shakespeare originally called him (after an historical figure) Sir John Oldcastle. Oldcastle appears in Shakespeare's source (partly reprinted in the Signet edition of *1 Henry IV*), and a trace of the name survives in Shakespeare's play, 1.2.43–44, where Prince Hal punningly addresses Falstaff as "my old lad of the castle." But for some reason—perhaps because the family of the historical Oldcastle complained—Shakespeare had to change the name. In short, the play as we have it was (at least in this detail) subject to some sort of censorship. If we think that a text should present what we take to be the author's intention, we probably will want to replace *Falstaff* with *Oldcastle*. But if we recognize that a play is a collaboration, we may welcome the change, even if it was forced on Shakespeare. Somehow *Falstaff*, with its hint of *false-staff*, i.e., inadequate prop, seems just right for this fat knight who, to our delight, entertains the young prince with untruths. We can go as far as saying that, at least so far as a play is concerned, an insistence on the author's original intention (even if we could know it) can sometimes impoverish the text.

The tiny example of Falstaff's name illustrates the point that the text we read is inevitably only a version—something in effect produced by the collaboration of the playwright with his actors, audiences, compositors, and editors—of a fluid text that Shakespeare once wrote, just as the *Hamlet* that we see on the screen starring Kenneth Branagh is not the *Hamlet* that Shakespeare saw in an open-air playhouse starring Richard Burbage. *Hamlet* itself, as we shall note in a moment, also exists in several versions. It is not surprising that there is now much talk about the *instability* of Shakespeare's texts.

Because he was not only a playwright but was also an actor and a shareholder in a theatrical company, Shakespeare probably was much involved with the translation of the play from a manuscript to a stage production. He may or may not have done some rewriting during rehearsals, and he may or may not have been happy with cuts that were made. Some plays, notably *Hamlet* and *King Lear*, are so long that it is most unlikely that the texts we read were acted in their entirety. Further, for both of these plays we have more than one early text that demands consideration. In *Hamlet*, the Second Quarto (1604) includes some two hundred lines not found in the Folio (1623). Among the passages missing from the Folio are two of Hamlet's reflective speeches, the "dram of evil" speech (1.4.13–38) and "How all occasions do inform against me" (4.4.32–66). Since the Folio has more numerous and often fuller stage directions, it certainly looks as though in the Folio we get a theatrical version of the play, a text whose cuts were probably made—this is only a hunch, of course—not because Shakespeare was changing his conception of Hamlet but because the playhouse demanded a modified play. (The problem is complicated, since the Folio not only cuts some of the Quarto but adds some material. Various explanations have been offered.)

Or take an example from *King Lear*. In the First and Second Quarto (1608, 1619), the final speech of the play is given to Albany, Lear's surviving son-in-law, but in the First Folio version (1623), the speech is given to Edgar. The Quarto version is in accord with tradition—usually the highest-ranking character in a tragedy speaks the final words. Why does the Folio give the speech to Edgar? One possible answer is this: The Folio version omits some of Albany's speeches in earlier scenes, so perhaps it was decided (by Shakespeare? by the players?) not to give the final lines to so pale a character. In fact, the discrepancies are so many between the two texts, that some scholars argue we do not simply have texts showing different theatrical productions. Rather, these scholars say, Shakespeare substantially revised the play, and we really have two versions of *King Lear* (and of *Othello* also, say some)—two different plays—not simply two texts, each of which is in some ways imperfect.

In this view, the 1608 version of *Lear* may derive from Shakespeare's manuscript, and the 1623 version may derive from his later revision. The Quartos have almost three hundred lines not in the Folio, and the Folio has about a hundred lines not in the Quartos. It used to be held that all the texts were imperfect in various ways and from various causes— some passages in the Quartos were thought to have been set from a manuscript that was not entirely legible, other passages were thought to have been set by a compositor who was new to setting plays, and still other passages were thought to have been provided by an actor who misremembered some of the lines. This traditional view held that an editor must draw on the Quartos and the Folio in order to get Shakespeare's "real" play. The new argument holds (although not without considerable strain) that we have two authentic plays, Shakespeare's early version (in the Quarto) and Shakespeare's—or his theatrical company's—revised version (in the Folio). Not only theatrical demands but also Shakespeare's own artistic sense, it is argued, called for extensive revisions. Even the titles vary: Q1 is called *True Chronicle Historie of the life and death of King Lear and his three Daughters*, whereas the Folio text is called *The Tragedie of King Lear*. To combine the two texts in order to produce what the editor thinks is the play that Shakespeare intended to write is, according to this view, to produce a text that is false to the history of the play. If the new view is correct, and we do have texts of two distinct versions of *Lear* rather than two imperfect versions of one play, it supports in a textual way the poststructuralist view that we cannot possibly have an unmediated vision of (in this case) a play by Shakespeare; we can only recognize a plurality of visions.

Editing Texts

Though eighteen of his plays were published during his lifetime, Shakespeare seems never to have supervised their publication. There is nothing unusual here; when a playwright sold a play to a theatrical company he surrendered his ownership to it. Normally a company would not publish the play, because to publish it meant to allow competitors to acquire the piece. Some plays did get published: Apparently hard-up actors sometimes pieced together a play for a publisher; sometimes a company in need of money sold a play; and sometimes a company allowed publication of a play that no longer drew audiences. That Shakespeare did not concern himself with publication is not remarkable; of his contemporaries, only Ben Jonson carefully supervised the publication of his own plays.

In 1623, seven years after Shakespeare's death, John Heminges and Henry Condell (two senior members of Shakespeare's company, who had worked with him for about twenty years) collected his plays—published and unpublished—into a large volume, of a kind called a folio. (A folio is a volume consisting of large sheets that have been folded once, each sheet thus making two leaves, or four pages. The size of the page of course depends on the size of the sheet—a folio can range in height from twelve to sixteen inches, and in width from eight to eleven; the pages in the 1623 edition of Shakespeare, commonly called the First Folio, are approximately thirteen inches tall and eight inches wide.) The eighteen plays published during Shakespeare's lifetime had been issued one play per volume in small formats called quartos. (Each sheet in a quarto has been folded twice, making four leaves, or eight pages, each page being about nine inches tall and seven inches wide, roughly the size of a large paperback.)

Heminges and Condell suggest in an address "To the great variety of readers" that the republished plays are presented in better form than in the quartos:

> Before you were abused with diverse stolen and surreptitious copies, maimed and deformed by the frauds and stealths of injurious impostors that exposed them; even those, are now offered to your view cured and perfect of their limbs, and all the rest absolute in their numbers, as he [i.e., Shakespeare] conceived them.

There is a good deal of truth to this statement, but some of the quarto versions are better than others; some are in fact preferable to the Folio text.

Whoever was assigned to prepare the texts for publication

in the first Folio seems to have taken the job seriously and yet not to have performed it with uniform care. The sources of the texts seem to have been, in general, good unpublished copies or the best published copies. The first play in the collection, *The Tempest*, is divided into acts and scenes, has unusually full stage directions and descriptions of spectacle, and concludes with a list of the characters, but the editor was not able (or willing) to present all of the succeeding texts so fully dressed. Later texts occasionally show signs of carelessness: in one scene of *Much Ado About Nothing* the names of actors, instead of characters, appear as speech prefixes, as they had in the Quarto, which the Folio reprints; proofreading throughout the Folio is spotty and apparently was done without reference to the printer's copy; the pagination of *Hamlet* jumps from 156 to 257. Further, the proofreading was done while the presses continued to print, so that each play in each volume contains a mix of corrected and uncorrected pages.

Modern editors of Shakespeare must first select their copy; no problem if the play exists only in the Folio, but a considerable problem if the relationship between a Quarto and the Folio—or an early Quarto and a later one—is unclear. In the case of *Romeo and Juliet*, the First Quarto (Q1), published in 1597, is vastly inferior to the Second (Q2), published in 1599. The basis of Q1 apparently is a version put together from memory by some actors. Not surprisingly, it garbles many passages and is much shorter than Q2. On the other hand, occasionally Q1 makes better sense than Q2. For instance, near the end of the play, when the parents have assembled and learned of the deaths of Romeo and Juliet, in Q2 the Prince says (5.3.208–9),

Come, *Montague;* for thou art early vp
To see thy sonne and heire, now earling downe.

The last three words of this speech surely do not make sense, and many editors turn to Q1, which instead of "now earling downe" has "more early downe." Some modern editors take only "early" from Q1, and print "now early down"; others take "more early," and print "more early down." Further, Q1 (though, again, quite clearly a garbled and abbreviated text) includes some stage directions that are not found in Q2, and today many editors who base their text on Q2 are glad to add these stage directions, because the directions help to give us a sense of what the play looked like on Shakespeare's stage. Thus, in 4.3.58, after Juliet drinks the potion, Q1 gives us this stage direction, not in Q2: *"She falls upon her bed within the curtains."*

In short, an editor's decisions do not end with the choice of a single copy text. First of all, editors must reckon with Elizabethan spelling. If they are not producing a facsimile, they probably modernize the spelling, but ought they to preserve the old forms of words that apparently were pronounced quite unlike their modern forms—*lanthorn, alablaster*? If they preserve these forms are they really preserving Shakespeare's forms or perhaps those of a compositor in the printing house? What is one to do when one finds *lanthorn* and *lantern* in adjacent lines? (The editors of this series in general, but not invariably, assume that words should be spelled in their modern form, unless, for instance, a rhyme is involved.) Elizabethan punctuation, too, presents problems. For example, in the First Folio, the only text for the play, Macbeth rejects his wife's idea that he can wash the blood from his hand (2.2.60–62):

> No: this my Hand will rather
> The multitudinous Seas incarnardine,
> Making the Greene one, Red.

Obviously an editor will remove the superfluous capitals, and will probably alter the spelling to "incarnadine," but what about the comma before "Red"? If we retain the comma, Macbeth is calling the sea "the green one." If we drop the comma, Macbeth is saying that his bloody hand will make the sea ("the Green") *uniformly* red.

An editor will sometimes have to change more than spelling and punctuation. Macbeth says to his wife (1.7.46–47):

> I dare do all that may become a man,
> Who dares no more, is none.

For two centuries editors have agreed that the second line is unsatisfactory, and have emended "no" to "do": "Who dares do more is none." But when in the same play (4.2.21–22) Ross says that fearful persons

> Floate vpon a wilde and violent Sea
> Each way, and moue,

need we emend the passage? On the assumption that the compositor misread the manuscript, some editors emend "each way, and move" to "and move each way"; others emend "move" to "none" (i.e., "Each way and none"). Other editors, however, let the passage stand as in the original. The editors of the Signet Classic Shakespeare have restrained themselves from making abundant emendations. In their minds they hear Samuel Johnson on the dangers of emendation: "I have adopted the Roman sentiment, that it is more honorable to save a citizen than to kill an enemy." Some departures (in addition to spelling, punctuation, and lineation) from the copy text have of course been made, but the original readings are listed in a note following the play, so that readers can evaluate the changes for themselves.

Following tradition, the editors of the Signet Classic Shakespeare have prefaced each play with a list of characters, and throughout the play have regularized the names of the speakers. Thus, in our text of _Romeo and Juliet_, all speeches by Juliet's mother are prefixed "Lady Capulet," although the 1599 Quarto of the play, which provides our copy text, uses at various points seven speech tags for this one character: _Capu. Wi._ (i.e., Capulet's wife), _Ca. Wi._, _Wi._, _Wife_, _Old La._ (i.e., Old Lady), _La._, and _Mo._ (i.e., Mother). Similarly, in _All's Well That Ends Well_, the character whom we regularly call "Countess" is in the Folio (the copy text) variously identified as _Mother, Countess, Old Countess, Lady,_ and _Old Lady_. Admittedly there is some loss in regularizing, since the various prefixes may give us a hint of the way Shakespeare (or a scribe who copied Shakespeare's manuscript) was thinking of the character in a particular scene—for instance, as a mother, or as an old lady. But too much can be made of these differing prefixes, since the social relationships implied are *not* always relevant to the given scene.

We have also added line numbers and in many cases act and scene divisions as well as indications of locale at the beginning of scenes. The Folio divided most of the plays into acts and some into scenes. Early eighteenth-century editors increased the divisions. These divisions, which provide a convenient way of referring to passages in the plays, have been retained, but when not in the text chosen as the basis for the Signet Classic text they are enclosed within square brackets, [ ], to indicate that they are editorial additions. Similarly, though no play of Shakespeare's was equipped with indications of the locale at the heads of scene divisions, locales have here been added in square brackets for the convenience of readers, who lack the information that costumes, properties, gestures, and scenery afford to spectators. Spectators can tell at a glance they are in the throne room, but without an editorial indication the reader may be puzzled for a while. It should be mentioned, incidentally, that there are a few authentic stage directions—perhaps Shakespeare's, perhaps a prompter's—that suggest locales, such as *"Enter Brutus in his orchard,"* and *"They go up into the Senate house."* It is hoped that the bracketed additions in the Signet text will provide readers with the sort of help provided by these two authentic directions, but it is equally hoped that the reader will remember that the stage was not loaded with scenery.

Shakespeare on the Stage

Each volume in the Signet Classic Shakespeare includes a brief stage (and sometimes film) history of the play. When we read about earlier productions, we are likely to find them eccentric, obviously wrongheaded—for instance, Nahum Tate's version of *King Lear*, with a happy ending, which held the stage for about a century and a half, from the late seventeenth century until the end of the first quarter of the nineteenth. We see engravings of David Garrick, the greatest actor of the eighteenth century, in eighteenth-century garb as King Lear, and we smile, thinking how absurd the production must have been. If we are more thoughtful, we say, with the English novelist L. P. Hartley, "The past is a foreign country: they do things differently there." But if the eighteenth-century staging is a foreign country, what of the plays of the late sixteenth and seventeenth centuries? A foreign language, a foreign theater, a foreign audience.

Probably all viewers of Shakespeare's plays, beginning with Shakespeare himself, at times have been unhappy with the plays on the stage. Consider three comments about production that we find in the plays themselves, which suggest Shakespeare's concerns. The Chorus in *Henry V* complains that the heroic story cannot possibly be adequately staged:

> But pardon, gentles all,
> The flat unraisèd spirits that hath dared
> On this unworthy scaffold to bring forth
> So great an object. Can this cockpit hold
> The vasty fields of France? Or may we cram
> Within this wooden *O* the very casques
> That did affright the air at Agincourt?
>
> . . . .
>
> Piece out our imperfections with your thoughts.
>
> (Prologue 1.8–14,23)

Second, here are a few sentences (which may or may not represent Shakespeare's own views) from Hamlet's longish lecture to the players:

> Speak the speech, I pray you, as I pronounced it to you, trippingly on the tongue. But if you mouth it, as many of our players do, I had as lief the town crier spoke my lines. . . . O, it offends me to the soul to hear a robustious periwig-pated fellow tear a passion to tatters, to very rags, to split the ears of the groundlings. . . . And let those that play your clowns speak no more than is set down for them, for there be of them that will themselves laugh, to set on some quantity of barren spectators to laugh too, though in the meantime some necessary question of the play be then to be considered. That's villainous and shows a most pitiful ambition in the fool that uses it. (3.2.1–47)

Finally, we can quote again from the passage cited earlier in this introduction, concerning the boy actors who played the female roles. Cleopatra imagines with horror a theatrical version of her activities with Antony:

> The quick comedians
> Extemporally will stage us, and present
> Our Alexandrian revels: Antony
> Shall be brought drunken forth, and I shall see
> Some squeaking Cleopatra boy my greatness
> I' th' posture of a whore.   (5.2.216–21)

It is impossible to know how much weight to put on such passages—perhaps Shakespeare was just being modest about his theater's abilities—but it is easy enough to think that he was unhappy with some aspects of Elizabethan production. Probably no production can fully satisfy a playwright, and for that matter, few productions can fully satisfy *us;* we regret this or that cut, this or that way of costuming the play, this or that bit of business.

One's first thought may be this: Why don't they just do "authentic" Shakespeare, "straight" Shakespeare, the play as Shakespeare wrote it? But as we read the plays—words written to be performed—it sometimes becomes clear that we do not know *how* to perform them. For instance, in *Antony and Cleopatra* Antony, the Roman general who has succumbed to Cleopatra and to Egyptian ways, says, "The nobleness of life / Is to do thus" (1.1.36–37). But what is "thus"? Does Antony at this point embrace Cleopatra? Does he embrace and kiss her? (There are, by the way, very few scenes of kissing on Shakespeare's stage, possibly because boys played the female roles.) Or does he make a sweeping gesture, indicating the Egyptian way of life?

This is not an isolated example; the plays are filled with lines that call for gestures, but we are not sure what the gestures should be. *Interpretation* is inevitable. Consider a passage in *Hamlet*. In 3.1, Polonius persuades his daughter, Ophelia, to talk to Hamlet while Polonius and Claudius eavesdrop. The two men conceal themselves, and Hamlet encounters Ophelia. At 3.1.131 Hamlet suddenly says to her, "Where's your father?" Why does Hamlet, apparently out of nowhere—they have not been talking about Polonius—ask this question? Is this an example of the "antic disposition" (fantastic behavior) that Hamlet earlier (1.5.172) had told Horatio and others—including us—he would display? That is, is the question about the whereabouts of her father a seemingly irrational one, like his earlier question (3.1.103) to Ophelia, "Ha, ha! Are you honest?" Or, on the other hand, has Hamlet (as in many productions) suddenly glimpsed Polonius's foot protruding from beneath a drapery at the rear? That is, does Hamlet ask the question because he has suddenly seen something suspicious and now is testing Ophelia? (By the way, in productions that do give Hamlet a physical cue, it is almost always Polonius rather than Claudius who provides the clue. This itself is an act of interpretation on the part of the director.) Or (a third possibility) does Hamlet get a clue from Ophelia, who inadvertently betrays the spies by nervously glancing at their place of hiding? This is the interpretation used in the BBC television version, where Ophelia glances in fear toward the hiding place just after Hamlet says "Why wouldst thou be a breeder of sinners?" (121–22). Hamlet, realizing that he is being observed, glances here and there *before* he asks "Where's your father?" The question thus is a climax to what he has been doing while speaking the preceding lines. Or (a fourth interpretation) does Hamlet suddenly, without the aid of any clue whatsoever, intuitively (insightfully, mysteriously, wonderfully) sense that someone is spying? Directors must decide, of course—and so must readers.

Recall, too, the preceding discussion of the texts of the plays, which argued that the texts—though they seem to be before us in permanent black on white—are unstable. The Signet text of *Hamlet*, which draws on the Second Quarto (1604) and the First Folio (1623) is considerably longer than any version staged in Shakespeare's time. Our version, even if spoken very briskly and played without any intermission, would take close to four hours, far beyond "the two hours' traffic of our stage" mentioned in the Prologue to *Romeo and Juliet*. (There are a few contemporary references to the duration of a play, but none mentions more than three hours.) Of Shakespeare's plays, only *The Comedy of Errors*, *Macbeth*, and *The Tempest* can be done in less than three hours without cutting. And even if we take a play that exists only in a short text, *Macbeth*, we cannot claim that we are experiencing the very play that Shakespeare conceived, partly because some of the Witches' songs almost surely are non-Shakespearean additions, and partly because we are not willing to watch the play performed without an intermission and with boys in the female roles.

Further, as the earlier discussion of costumes mentioned, the plays apparently were given chiefly in contemporary, that is, in Elizabethan dress. If today we give them in the costumes that Shakespeare probably saw, the plays seem not contemporary but curiously dated. Yet if we use our own dress, we find lines of dialogue that are at odds with what we see; we may feel that the language, so clearly not our own, is inappropriate coming out of people in today's dress. A common solution, incidentally, has been to set the plays in the nineteenth century, on the grounds that this attractively distances the plays (gives them a degree of foreignness, allowing for interesting costumes) and yet doesn't put them into a museum world of Elizabethan England.

Inevitably our productions are adaptations, *our* adaptations, and inevitably they will look dated, not in a century but in twenty years, or perhaps even in a decade. Still, we cannot escape from our own conceptions. As the director Peter Brook has said, in *The Empty Space* (1968):

> It is not only the hair-styles, costumes and make-ups that look dated. All the different elements of staging—the shorthands of behavior that stand for emotions; gestures, gesticulations and tones of voice—are all fluctuating on an invisible stock exchange all the time. . . . A living theatre that thinks it can stand aloof from anything as trivial as fashion will wilt. (p. 16)

As Brook indicates, it is through today's hairstyles, costumes, makeup, gestures, gesticulations, tones of voice—this includes our *conception* of earlier hairstyles, costumes, and so forth if we stage the play in a period other than our own—that we inevitably stage the plays.

It is a truism that every age invents its own Shakespeare, just as, for instance, every age has invented its own classical world. Our view of ancient Greece, a slave-holding society in which even free Athenian women were severely circum-scribed, does not much resemble the Victorians' view of ancient Greece as a glorious democracy, just as, perhaps, our view of Victorianism itself does not much resemble theirs. We cannot claim that the Shakespeare on our stage is the true Shakespeare, but in our stage productions we find a Shakespeare that speaks to us, a Shakespeare that our ances-tors doubtless did not know but one that seems to us to be the true Shakespeare—at least for a while.

Our age is remarkable for the wide variety of kinds of staging that it uses for Shakespeare, but one development deserves special mention. This is the now common practice of race-blind or color-blind or nontraditional casting, which allows persons who are not white to play in Shakespeare. Previously blacks performing in Shakespeare were limited to a mere three roles, Othello, Aaron (in *Titus Andronicus*), and the Prince of Morocco (in *The Merchant of Venice*), and there were no roles at all for Asians. Indeed, African-Americans rarely could play even one of these three roles, since they were not welcome in white companies. Ira Aldridge (c.1806–1867), a black actor of undoubted talent, was forced to make his living by performing Shakespeare in England and in Europe, where he could play not only Othello but also—in whiteface—other tragic roles such as King Lear. Paul Robeson (1898–1976) made theatrical his-tory when he played Othello in London in 1930, and there was some talk about bringing the production to the United States, but there was more talk about whether American audiences would tolerate the sight of a black man—a real black man, not a white man in blackface—kissing and then killing a white woman. The idea was tried out in summer stock in 1942, the reviews were enthusiastic, and in the fol-lowing year Robeson opened on Broadway in a production that ran an astounding 296 performances. An occasional all-black company sometimes performed Shakespeare's plays, but otherwise blacks (and other minority members) were in effect shut out from performing Shakespeare. Only since about 1970 has it been common for nonwhites to play major roles along with whites. Thus, in a 1996–97 production of *Antony and Cleopatra*, a white Cleopatra, Vanessa Red-grave, played opposite a black Antony, David Harewood.

Multiracial casting is now especially common at the New York Shakespeare Festival, founded in 1954 by Joseph Papp, and in England, where even siblings such as Claudio and Isabella in *Measure for Measure* or Lear's three daughters may be of different races. Probably most viewers today soon stop worrying about the lack of realism, and move beyond the color of the performers' skin to the quality of the performance.

Nontraditional casting is not only a matter of color or race; it includes sex. In the past, occasionally a distinguished woman of the theater has taken on a male role—Sarah Bernhardt (1844–1923) as Hamlet is perhaps the most famous example—but such performances were widely regarded as eccentric. Although today there have been some performances involving cross-dressing (a drag *As You Like It* staged by the National Theatre in England in 1966 and in the United States in 1974 has achieved considerable fame in the annals of stage history), what is more interesting is the casting of women in roles that traditionally are male but that need not be. Thus, a 1993–94 English production of *Henry V* used a woman—*not* cross-dressed—in the role of the governor of Harfleur. According to Peter Holland, who reviewed the production in *Shakespeare Survey* 48 (1995), "having a female Governor of Harfleur feminized the city and provided a direct response to the horrendous threat of rape and murder that Henry had offered, his language and her body in direct connection and opposition" (p. 210). Ten years from now the device may not play so effectively, but today it speaks to us. Shakespeare, born in the Elizabethan Age, has been dead nearly four hundred years, yet he is, as Ben Jonson said, "not of an age but for all time." We must understand, however, that he is "for all time" precisely because each age finds in his abundance something for itself and something of itself.

And here we come back to two issues discussed earlier in this introduction—the instability of the text and, curiously, the Bacon/Oxford heresy concerning the authorship of the plays. *Of course* Shakespeare wrote the plays, and we should daily fall on our knees to thank him for them—and yet there is something to the idea that he is not their only author. Every editor, every director and actor, and every reader to some degree shapes them, too, for when we edit, direct, act, or read, we inevitably become Shakespeare's collaborator and re-create the plays. The plays, one might say, are so cunningly contrived that they guide our responses, tell us how we ought to feel, and make a mark on us, but (for better or for worse) we also make a mark on them.

—SYLVAN BARNET
Tufts University

Introduction

Richard III is above all a play for the stage. It was Shakespeare's first great success, a sudden leap up from his three plays on the reign of Henry VI. Richard Burbage made his reputation by playing Richard III; so did David Garrick when he conquered London in the eighteenth century. *Richard III* was the first Shakespeare play acted professionally in America, in 1750; it was a favorite of Lincoln, who knew by heart "Now is the winter of our discontent"; and the Shakespeare Festival of Canada opened with a brilliant production. Sir Laurence Olivier brought Richard to life again on the stage and on the screen.

When Shakespeare wrote this play, about 1592 or 1593, his audiences were eager for plays on English history. Such plays were like mirrors in which they could see what had happened to England in past crises and what might happen to themselves in the near future after the death of Queen Elizabeth. Would their next ruler be one who could unite his people, like Henry V or Henry VII, or one who would bring on civil war, like Henry VI or Richard III? The most popular plays on English history had dramatized wars and struggles for power: *The Famous Victories of Henry V*, *The Troublesome Reign of King John*, and the one great historical tragedy before Shakespeare's, Marlowe's *The Troublesome Reign and Lamentable Death of Edward II, King of England, with the Tragical Fall of Proud Mortimer*. Shakespeare emphasized as leading ideas of his English history plays the danger of division and the necessity of union: "United we stand, divided we fall."

Richard III is a tragedy of crimes punished by divine justice. Both branches of the royal Plantagenets, Lancaster and York, had committed cruel murders. Queen Margaret, the "she-wolf of France," had beheaded Richard, Duke of York; in revenge York's sons murdered her son, Prince Edward, and her husband, Henry VI. The murderers of Clarence tell him that he deserves God's vengeance for stabbing Prince Edward and for breaking his oath to God to fight for King Henry. Richard III must pay with his life for causing the deaths of his brother, his nephews, his wife, and his best friends. The demands for vengeance made by Queen Margaret are fulfilled; for, as Holinshed expressed the traditional religious view of history, "such is God's justice, to leave no unrepentant wickedness unpunished." God used Richard as a scourge to punish the sins of others; the "high All-Seer" then raised up Richmond to cancel Richard, "One that hath ever been God's enemy."

Yet it is one of Shakespeare's paradoxes that God's enemy is so much more fascinating than the puppet Richmond, who speaks with no voice of his own. Richard is alive; he is himself alone; he is what part of ourselves would like to be, free from the censor conscience. He can win women; he can win power; he can enjoy using his power to destroy, to do whatever he wants to do. We know he will not get away with it in the end; but meanwhile, what fun he is having! His gay soliloquies make us share his enjoyment:

> Was ever woman in this humor wooed?
> Was ever woman in this humor won?
> I'll have her, but I will not keep her long.
>
> (1.2.227–29)

Richard is the actor making up his part as he goes along, and making sure that it is the leading part.

How did Shakespeare create an acting role which has held so many audiences spellbound? For one thing, he made Richard a devil masked as a man: able to put on in turn the masks of the loyal brother, the impassioned lover, the kindly uncle, the self-sacrificing king. The masks are both tragic and comic; they hide death, and they mock at human folly. We pity Richard's victims, but we feel superior to them; we, of course, would never be taken in. For another thing, Richard is the underdog who fights his way to the top, one man against the world, with everything against him. The climb to power is a treacherous one, dangerous to Richard, deadly to anyone who blocks his path; he climbs over their bodies till he stands, though not for long, where he had determined to stand. This triumph of will is exciting theater; at the same time it is sharply ironic—so many years to rise, to fall in one day.

Richard dominates the play; he appears in fourteen out of twenty-five scenes, and his shadow hangs over the rest. It is the longest of Shakespeare's history plays, and longer than any other of Shakespeare's except *Hamlet*. Richard himself speaks nearly a third of the lines, and five of his ten soliloquies come in the first three scenes, so that we see him at once take the center of the stage. His opening speech is masterly. Winter is now summer, the killing is over, it is time to live and love, but not for Richard; his keenest pleasures are to come, and the first will be to destroy his brother. Shakespeare had shown Richard's will to power in *Henry VI, Part 3*, 1.2:

> How sweet a thing it is to wear a crown,
> Within whose circuit is Elysium,
> And all that poets feign of bliss and joy.   (29–31)

In 3.2 of the same play Richard had planned his strategy for winning the crown:

> Why, I can smile, and murder whiles I smile,
> And cry "Content" to that which grieves my heart,
> And wet my cheeks with artificial tears,
> And frame my face to all occasions. . . .
> I can add colors to the chameleon,
> Change shapes with Proteus for advantages,
> And set the murderous Machiavel to school.
> Can I do this, and cannot get a crown?   (182–85, 191–94)

And in 5.6, after stabbing King Henry in the Tower, he had promised that Clarence would be next:

> I have no brother, I am like no brother;
> And this word "love," which graybeards call divine,

> Be resident in men like one another
> And not in me: I am myself alone.   (80–83)

In the first scene of *Richard III* he is in high spirits as he speaks with and without the mask: "your imprisonment shall not be long" (114) to Clarence, and then, to himself, "I do love thee so / That I will shortly send thy soul to heaven" (118–19). Richard Crookback has a crooked but original sense of humor.

Why did Shakespeare invent the famous scene of Richard's wooing of Lady Anne? The soliloquy which ends the scene provides, I think, the key to Shakespeare's purpose. Richard took up the challenge of a task that seemed impossible; if he could succeed against such odds, for him nothing would be impossible:

> What! I that killed her husband and his father
> To take her in her heart's extremest hate . . .
> And yet to win her, all the world to nothing!
>   (1.2.230–31, 237)

He chose a time which presented the greatest obstacles, so that he could overcome them: a time when she was calling for vengeance upon him as the murderer of King Henry and of her husband. He provoked her to attack him with words and then gave her a chance to act, to kill him with his own sword. His will proved stronger than hers. Her change is sudden, but Shakespeare means it to be. Theatrically, he achieves the shock of surprise; dramatically, he convinces us that Richard will find hardly any difficulty too great for him to master.

Shakespeare created most of the first act from his own imagination; and such history as he used he rearranged for dramatic effect. He read in Holinshed that Richard, in 1471, murdered Henry VI, whose body was brought to St. Paul's and then buried at Chertsey; Shakespeare imagined the scene between Richard and Anne. In 1478 Edward IV had Clarence condemned to death by parliament and drowned in wine at the Tower; Shakespeare made Richard plot his brother's death, and he invented the whole vivid scene of Clarence's dream and murder. Queen Margaret had left

England to live in France; Shakespeare brought her into the third scene to prophesy retribution for the house of York and especially for Richard. Margaret, Clarence, Edward IV, and Hastings were omitted from the acting version by Colley Cibber which held the stage from 1700 to 1877, a travesty of the play which contained more Cibber than Shakespeare. All are essential to Shakespeare's drama. Margaret, for example, invokes the justice of God to punish the crimes of her enemies. Recalling the bloody past, she calls for the future to pay blood for blood. As York's dread curse had prevailed with heaven to make her suffer the loss of her husband, her son, and her kingdom, so she prays that her rival Elizabeth may "Die neither mother, wife, nor England's Queen" (1.3.208). Richard deserves to suffer the worst plagues of all: the worm of conscience, suspicion and betrayal, and the terror of tormenting dreams. Shakespeare makes Margaret no ghost crying for revenge, but a bitter, passionate woman. Yet he gives her a major function in the play: to thunder with the power of a prophetess, sent to warn that no sinner can escape his doom.

The first doom fell upon Clarence. Nothing in his life became him like the dream of his death, for while he slept, his conscience was awake. If he escaped the Tower, he feared he would find himself in hell, facing the father-in-law he had betrayed and the King's son he had stabbed to death. His repentance was genuine, but it came too late to save his life; when he warned his murderers of God's vengeance, they reminded him that he himself was a murderer. Shakespeare packs the scene with tragic irony: Clarence supposing that Richard caused his death in the dream by chance, not by design, and assuring the murderers that Richard would reward them for saving his life. The reluctant Second Murderer might still have saved him by listening to the dregs of conscience; he tried, perhaps, to warn him by crying "Look behind you, my lord!" and immediately afterward he wished he could wash his hands of the murder. Shakespeare ends the first act with Richard one step closer to the crown.

After Act 1 Shakespeare dramatizes the history of only two years, from the death of Edward IV in 1483 to the battle of Bosworth Field in 1485. Again and again he heightens the dramatic effect of events already full of drama. He brings

Richard to the deathbed of Edward in 2.1 to play-act the lover of peace and then to explode the news of Clarence's death and blame "the guilty kindred of the Queen," when he alone is guilty. No sooner does Richard mount the throne in 4.2 than Shakespeare shows him trying to incite Buckingham to murder the Princes, with the result that he drives his strongest supporter into rebellion. Above all, in 5.3 Shakespeare changes Richard's dream of "images like terrible devils," as Holinshed calls them, into a vision of the souls of all whom he has murdered, crying out "Despair and die!" Here Shakespeare makes Richard look into himself with fear and horror and see how he has cut himself off from mankind:

> I shall despair. There is no creature loves me;
> And if I die, no soul will pity me.   (201–2)

Though no one pities Richard, Shakespeare builds up recurring scenes of pity for those who suffer during this reign of terror. In 2.2 he shows three generations—mother, wife, and children—left desolate by the loss of Edward and of Clarence. In 4.1 the old Duchess of York longs for peace in the grave; Anne, who has had no rest with Richard, wishes that her crown were red-hot steel; and Queen Elizabeth, thinking only of her children, seeks pity for them from the stones of the Tower. The murderers of the two boys tell their deaths' sad story (4.3); and the next scene rises to a chorus of grief in the laments of their mother, of their grandmother, and of Queen Margaret. Each of these scenes intensifies emotion by a threefold pattern, as though the sorrow were too great to be expressed by only one person, and even Tyrrel shares the remorse of Dighton and Forrest. The killing of the Princes is a massacre of the innocents, and their mother is like Rachel weeping for her children.

Shakespeare secures a more complex response in scenes which present characters of mixed good and evil, persons who suffer for their sins and yet who call forth pity for their suffering. Hastings and Buckingham, together with Clarence and the shadowy Rivers, Grey, and Vaughan, are neither ruthless tyrants nor innocent children. Hastings is shown hoping for revenge upon his enemies, the Queen's kinsmen (1.1), hiding his hate under a vow of love for Rivers and Dorset (2.1), and then rejoicing at the execution of Rivers and the rest (3.2). When he is condemned to die the same day (3.4), he repents his too triumphant joy that his enemies were butchered and admits that Margaret's curse, for standing by when her son was murdered, has lighted on his head. On the other hand, he dies for loyalty to the true king, for refusing to help Richard usurp the throne. Shakespeare brings out the drama of his sudden fall when he least expects it, and the irony of his overconfident belief that Richard loves him well and that the boar will use him kindly. His last words, "They smile at me who shortly shall be dead" (105), foretell a parallel fall for Buckingham, who mocked at Hastings and yet still trusts Richard. Blinded by infatuation, Buckingham has already disregarded Margaret's warning to beware of Richard (1.3). He digs a pit for himself when he prays in 2.1 that if ever he harms Queen Elizabeth or her family God may punish him with hate where he expects most love, and yet becomes Richard's right-hand man to plot against her and her sons. Hesitating only at murder, he gains a crown for Richard and death for himself, and in 5.1 he acknowledges the justice of his death. As with Hastings, he is both sinning and sinned against, and his tragic recognition of his errors leads in the end to pity for his fall.

The blank verse in *Richard III* marches to a strong, emphatic rhythm. The pause at the end of the line, or sometimes of two lines (as in 1.1.1–4, 10–13), lets the actor dwell on the meaning with clarity and force. Shakespeare, who constructs his sonnets with three quatrains and a couplet, likes to build dramatic monologues also in groups of four lines. Richard's first speech is composed in quatrains, expanded twice to five lines and once to six. The second scene begins and ends with monologues which contain many quatrains, as well as groups of three or five lines. The dialogues show more variety, but Shakespeare makes striking use of stichomythia, which sets single line against single line, in Richard's duels of words with Anne in 1.2, York in 3.1, and Queen Elizabeth in 4.4. The verse of

Richard III is far from subtle, but its careful design contributes to its power.

Shakespeare heightens the dramatic effect of speech by an extraordinary range of rhetoric. The opening scene is rich in antitheses, between war and peace, the lover and the villain, true Edward and treacherous Richard and simple, plain Clarence. Anne expresses the intensity of her grief by figures of repetition and parallelism: "Set down, set down," "bloodless . . . blood," "O cursèd . . . Cursèd," "If ever he have child . . . If ever he have wife." Queen Margaret gives force to her prophetic curse in 1.3.187 ff. by pouring forth questions and exclamations, by reiterating key words like "curse," "heaven," and "death," and by emphasizing parallel constructions: "Edward thy son, that now is Prince of Wales, / For Edward our son, that was Prince of Wales" (198–99) or "Thyself a queen, for me that was a queen" (201). All these and more appear in 4.4: paradoxical antithesis in "Dead life, blind sight, poor mortal living ghost" (26), repeated questions like "Where is thy husband now? Where be thy brothers?" (92) and emphatic parallels, as in lines 20–21, 40–46, and 98–104. The conscious eloquence of the orations in 5.3 contrasts with the more intense rhetoric which expresses fear and despair in Richard's soliloquy. *Richard III* shows Shakespeare rejoicing in his mastery over language, though he has not yet learned the art of concealing his art.

The play is not merely a melodrama, although it tends towards melodrama in its exaggeration of Richard's villainy. It is the tragedy of a man, of a family, and of a nation. The tragedy is ironic in that Richard, by destroying others, brings destruction upon himself. Right does not triumph without probability, as in melodrama, but as a probable result of human actions. Richard rises steadily until he orders the murder of his nephews (4.2); from that moment he turns friends into enemies, till "He hath no friends but what are friends for fear" (5.2.20). But he does not have the inner conflict of Macbeth, who inspires pity as well as fear. Retributive justice strikes down not only Richard but the whole family of Plantagenet. The sons of York pay for the murder of Henry VI and his son by their own deaths and the murder of Edward's sons. Finally, Shakespeare shows how the people of England suffered from tyranny and civil war, when "The brother blindly shed the brother's blood" (5.5.24). He ends the play with a heartfelt prayer that his country, united, may now live in peace.

—MARK ECCLES
University of Wisconsin

Enter Richard Duke of Glocester, solus.

Now is the winter of our discontent,
Made glorious summer by this sonne of Yorke:
And all the cloudes that lowrd vpon our house,
In the deepe bosome of the Ocean buried.
Now are our browes bound with victorious wreathes,
Our bruised armes hung vp for monuments,
Our sterne alarmes changd to merry meetings,
Our dreadfull marches to delightfull measures.
Grim-visagde warre, hath smoothde his wrinkled front,
And now in steed of mounting barbed steedes,
To fright the soules of fearefull aduersaries.
He capers nimbly in a Ladies chamber,
To the lasciuious pleasing of a loue.
But I that am not shapte for sportiue trickes,
Nor made to court an amorous looking glasse,
I that am rudely stampt and want loues maiesty,
To strut before a wanton ambling Nymph:
I that am curtaild of this faire proportion,
Cheated of feature by dissembling nature,
Deformd, vnfinisht, sent before my time
Into this breathing world scarce halfe made vp,
And that so lamely and vnfashionable,
That dogs barke at me as I halt by them:
Why I in this weake piping time of peace
Haue no delight to passe away the time,
Vnlesse to spie my shadow in the sunne,
And descant on mine owne deformity:
And therefore since I cannot prooue a louer
To entertaine these faire well spoken daies,

I am

The opening soliloquy, in the earliest printed version (1597) of
the play

The Tragedy of Richard the Third

King Edward IV
Edward, Prince of Wales, afterwards King Edward V ⎫ sons of
Richard, Duke of York ⎭ the King
George, Duke of Clarence ⎫ brothers of
Richard, Duke of Gloucester, afterwards King ⎬ the King
   Richard III ⎭
A young son of Clarence (Edward)
Henry, Earl of Richmond, afterwards King Henry VII
Cardinal Bourchier, Archbishop of Canterbury
Thomas Rotherham, Archbishop of York
John Morton, Bishop of Ely
Duke of Buckingham
Duke of Norfolk
Earl of Surrey, his son
Anthony Woodville, Earl Rivers, brother of Queen Elizabeth
Marquis of Dorset and Lord Grey, sons of Queen Elizabeth
Earl of Oxford
Lord Stanley, called also Earl of Derby
Lord Hastings

Lord Woodville	Sir Richard Ratcliffe
Lord Scales	Sir James Tyrrel
Lord Lovell	Sir James Blunt
Sir Robert Brakenbury,	Sir Walter Herbert
· Lieutenant of the Tower	Sir William Brandon
Sir Thomas Vaughan	William Catesby

Lord Mayor of London
Christopher Urswick, a chaplain
Tressel and Barkley, gentlemen attending on Lady Anne
Queen Elizabeth, wife of King Edward IV
Queen Margaret, widow of King Henry VI
Duchess of York, mother of King Edward IV, Clarence, and
   Gloucester
Lady Anne, widow of Edward Prince of Wales, son of King
   Henry VI; afterwards married to Richard
A young daughter of Clarence (Margaret)
Ghosts of Richard's victims, Lords and other Attendants, Bishops,
   Priest, Sheriff, Keeper, Two Murderers, Pursuivant, Scrivener,
   Page, Citizens, Messengers, Soldiers, &c.

Scene: England]

The Tragedy of Richard the Third

ACT 1

Scene 1. [*London. A street.*]

Enter Richard, Duke of Gloucester, solus.°1

Richard. Now is the winter of our discontent
  Made glorious summer by this sun° of York;
  And all the clouds that loured upon our house
  In the deep bosom of the ocean buried.
  Now are our brows bound with victorious wreaths,   5
  Our bruisèd arms hung up for monuments,°
  Our stern alarums° changed to merry meetings,
  Our dreadful marches to delightful measures.°
  Grim-visaged War hath smoothed his wrinkled
    front,°
  And now, instead of mounting barbèd° steeds   10
  To fright the souls of fearful adversaries,
  He capers nimbly in a lady's chamber
  To the lascivious pleasing of a lute.
  But I, that am not shaped for sportive tricks
  Nor made to court an amorous looking glass;   15

---

¹ The degree sign (°) indicates a footnote, which is keyed to the text by line number. Text references are printed in **boldface** type; the annotation follows in roman type.
1.1. s.d. **solus** alone   2 **sun** (1) emblem of King Edward (2) son
6 **monuments** memorials   7 **alarums** calls to arms   8 **measures** dances   9 **front** forehead   10 **barbèd** armored

I, that am rudely stamped, and want° love's
   majesty
To strut before a wanton ambling nymph;
I, that am curtailed of this fair proportion,
Cheated of feature° by dissembling Nature,
20   Deformed, unfinished, sent before my time
Into this breathing world scarce half made up,
And that so lamely and unfashionable
That dogs bark at me as I halt° by them;
Why, I, in this weak piping time° of peace,
25   Have no delight to pass away the time,
Unless to spy my shadow in the sun
And descant° on mine own deformity.
And therefore, since I cannot prove a lover
To entertain° these fair well-spoken days,
30   I am determinèd to prove a villain
And hate the idle pleasures of these days.
Plots have I laid, inductions° dangerous,
By drunken prophecies, libels, and dreams,
To set my brother Clarence and the King
35   In deadly hate the one against the other;
And if King Edward be as true and just
As I am subtle, false, and treacherous,
This day should Clarence closely be mewed up°
About a prophecy which says that G
40   Of Edward's heirs the murderer shall be.
Dive, thoughts, down to my soul. Here Clarence
   comes.

Enter Clarence, guarded, and Brakenbury,
        [Lieutenant of the Tower].

Brother, good day. What means this armèd guard
That waits upon your Grace?

Clarence.   His Majesty,
Tend'ring° my person's safety, hath appointed
45   This conduct° to convey me to the Tower.

16 **want** lack   19 **feature** good shape   23 **halt** limp   24 **piping
time** i.e., time when shepherds play their pipes   27 **descant** comment
29 **entertain** while away   32 **inductions** first steps   38 **mewed up**
caged in prison   44 **Tend'ring** taking care of   45 **conduct** escort

Richard. Upon what cause?

Clarence.　　　　　　　　Because my name is George.

Richard. Alack, my lord, that fault is none of yours;
　　He should for that commit your godfathers.
　　O, belike° his Majesty hath some intent
　　That you should be new christ'ned in the Tower.　　　50
　　But what's the matter, Clarence? May I know?

Clarence. Yea, Richard, when I know; for I protest
　　As yet I do not. But, as I can learn,
　　He harkens after prophecies and dreams,
　　And from the crossrow° plucks the letter *G,*　　　55
　　And says a wizard told him that by *G*
　　His issue disinherited should be;
　　And, for° my name of George begins with *G,*
　　It follows in his thought that I am he.
　　These (as I learn) and suchlike toys° as these　　　60
　　Hath moved his Highness to commit me now.

Richard. Why, this it is when men are ruled by
　　　women.
　　'Tis not the King that sends you to the Tower.
　　My Lady Grey his wife, Clarence, 'tis she
　　That tempers° him to this extremity.°　　　65
　　Was it not she, and that good man of worship,°
　　Anthony Woodeville° her brother there,
　　That made him send Lord Hastings to the Tower,
　　From whence this present day he is deliverèd?
　　We are not safe, Clarence, we are not safe.　　　70

Clarence. By heaven, I think there is no man secure
　　But the Queen's kindred, and night-walking
　　　heralds°
　　That trudge betwixt the King and Mistress Shore.°

---

49 **belike** probably　55 **crossrow** alphabet　58 **for** because　60 **toys** trifles　65 **tempers** persuades　65 **extremity** extreme severity　66 **good man of worship** (play on "goodman," common man, raised to "worship," honor, as Earl Rivers　67 **Woodeville** (trisyllabic, play on "would evil")　72 **heralds** king's messengers (ironic)　73 **Mistress Shore** Jane Shore, wife of a London citizen; Edward IV's mistress

Heard you not what an humble suppliant
75 Lord Hastings was to her for his delivery?

Richard. Humbly complaining to her deity
Got my Lord Chamberlain his liberty.
I'll tell you what, I think it is our way,
If we will keep in favor with the King,
80 To be her men and wear her livery.
The jealous o'erworn widow° and herself,
Since that our brother dubbed them gentlewomen,
Are mighty gossips° in our monarchy.

Brakenbury. I beseech your Graces both to pardon me.
85 His Majesty hath straitly° given in charge
That no man shall have private conference,
Of what degree° soever, with your brother.

Richard. Even so? And° please your worship, Braken-
bury,
You may partake of anything we say.
90 We speak no treason, man; we say the King
Is wise and virtuous, and his noble queen
Well struck° in years, fair, and not jealous;
We say that Shore's wife hath a pretty foot,
A cherry lip, a bonny eye, a passing pleasing
tongue;
95 And that the Queen's kindred are made gentlefolks.
How say you, sir? Can you deny all this?

Brakenbury. With this, my lord, myself have nought
to do.

Richard. Naught° to do with Mistress Shore! I tell
thee, fellow,
He that doth naught with her, excepting one,
100 Were best to do it secretly alone.

Brakenbury. What one, my lord?

Richard. Her husband, knave. Wouldst thou betray
me?

81 **widow** Queen Elizabeth, widow of Sir John Grey   83 **gossips** chattering women, busybodies 85 **straitly** strictly 87 **degree** rank
88 **And** if   92 **struck** advanced   98 **Naught** evil

Brakenbury. I beseech your Grace to pardon me, and
  withal°
  Forbear your conference with the noble Duke.

Clarence. We know thy charge, Brakenbury, and will
  obey.   *105*

Richard. We are the Queen's abjects,° and must obey.
  Brother, farewell. I will unto the King;
  And whatsoe'er you will employ me in,
  Were it to call King Edward's widow sister,
  I will perform it to enfranchise° you.-   *110*
  Meantime, this deep disgrace in brotherhood
  Touches me deeper than you can imagine.

Clarence. I know it pleaseth neither of us well.

Richard. Well, your imprisonment shall not be long;
  I will deliver you, or else lie for° you.   *115*
  Meantime, have patience.

Clarence.   I must perforce. Farewell.
      Exit Clarence, [with Brakenbury and Guard].

Richard. Go tread the path that thou shalt ne'er
  return.
  Simple plain Clarence, I do love thee so
  That I will shortly send thy soul to heaven,
  If heaven will take the present at our hands.   *120*
  But who comes here? The new-delivered Hastings!

                  Enter Lord Hastings.

Hastings. Good time of day unto my gracious lord.

Richard. As much unto my good Lord Chamberlain.
  Well are you welcome to the open air.
  How hath your lordship brooked° imprisonment?   *125*

Hastings. With patience, noble lord, as prisoners must.
  But I shall live, my lord, to give them thanks
  That were the cause of my imprisonment.

103 **withal** moreover 106 **abjects** abject slaves 110 **enfranchise**
set free 115 **lie for** (1) go to prison instead of (2) tell lies about
125 **brooked** endured

Richard. No doubt, no doubt; and so shall Clarence
too,
130   For they that were your enemies are his
And have prevailed as much on him as you.

Hastings. More pity that the eagles should be mewed
Whiles kites° and buzzards prey at liberty.

Richard. What news abroad?

135   *Hastings.* No news so bad abroad as this at home:
The King is sickly, weak, and melancholy,
And his physicians fear° him mightily.

Richard. Now, by Saint John, that news is bad in-
deed.
O, he hath kept an evil diet° long
140   And overmuch consumed his royal person.
'Tis very grievous to be thought upon.
What, is he in his bed?

Hastings. He is.

Richard. Go you before, and I will follow you.
                                    Exit Hastings.
145   He cannot live, I hope, and must not die
Till George be packed with post horse° up to
heaven.
I'll in to urge his hatred more to Clarence
With lies well steeled° with weighty arguments;
And, if I fail not in my deep intent,
150   Clarence hath not another day to live.
Which done, God take King Edward to his mercy
And leave the world for me to bustle in!
For then I'll marry Warwick's youngest daughter.°
What though I killed her husband and her father?°
155   The readiest way to make the wench amends
Is to become her husband and her father.
The which will I, not all so much for love

133 **kites** birds of the hawk family   137 **fear** fear for   139 **diet** way
of living   146 **packed with post horse** sent off in a hurry   148
steeled reinforced   153 **Warwick's youngest daughter** Lady Anne
154 **father** father-in-law (Henry VI)

As for another secret close intent
By marrying her which I must reach unto.
But yet I run before my horse to market.   160
Clarence still breathes, Edward still lives and reigns;
When they are gone, then must I count my gains.

                                 Exit.

Scene 2. [*A street.*]

   Enter the corse° of Henry the Sixth, with Hal-
berds° to guard it, Lady Anne being the mourner.

original stage direction

Anne. Set down, set down your honorable load—
  If honor may be shrouded in a hearse—
  Whilst I awhile obsequiously° lament
  Th' untimely fall of virtuous Lancaster.
             [*The Bearers set down the hearse.*]
  Poor key-cold figure of a holy king,   5
  Pale ashes of the house of Lancaster,
  Thou bloodless remnant of that royal blood,
  Be it lawful that I invocate thy ghost
  To hear the lamentations of poor Anne,
  Wife to thy Edward, to thy slaught'red son,   10
  Stabbed by the selfsame hand that made these
    wounds!
  Lo, in these windows that let forth thy life
  I pour the helpless° balm of my poor eyes.
  O, cursèd be the hand that made these holes!
  Cursèd the heart that had the heart to do it!   15
  Cursèd the blood that let this blood from hence!
  More direful hap betide° that hated wretch
  That makes us wretched by the death of thee
  Than I can wish to wolves, to spiders, toads,

1.2.s.d. **corse** corpse   s.d. **Halberds** guards armed with long poleaxes
3 **obsequiously** like a mourner at a funeral   13 **helpless** unavailing
17 **hap betide** fortune happen to

20   Or any creeping venomed thing that lives!
      If ever he have child, abortive be it,
      Prodigious,° and untimely brought to light,
      Whose ugly and unnatural aspect
      May fright the hopeful mother at the view,
25   And that be heir to his unhappiness!°
      If ever he have wife, let her be made
      More miserable by the life of him
      Than I am made by my young lord and thee!
      Come, now towards Chertsey with your holy load,
30   Taken from Paul's° to be interrèd there;
                  [*The Bearers take up the hearse.*]
      And still as° you are weary of this weight,
      Rest you, whiles I lament King Henry's corse.

           Enter Richard, Duke of Gloucester.

Richard. Stay, you that bear the corse, and set it
    down.

Anne. What black magician conjures up this fiend
35   To stop devoted charitable deeds?

Richard. Villains, set down the corse, or, by Saint
    Paul,
    I'll make a corse of him that disobeys.

Gentleman. My lord, stand back and let the coffin
    pass.

Richard. Unmannered dog, stand° thou when I com-
    mand!
40   Advance thy halberd higher than my breast,
      Or, by Saint Paul, I'll strike thee to my foot
      And spurn° upon thee, beggar, for thy boldness.
                  [*The Bearers set down the hearse.*]

Anne. What, do you tremble? Are you all afraid?
      Alas, I blame you not, for you are mortal,
45   And mortal eyes cannot endure the devil.
      Avaunt,° thou dreadful minister of hell!

22 **Prodigious** monstrous   25 **unhappiness** wickedness   30 **Paul's**
St. Paul's Cathedral   31 **still as** whenever   39 **stand** halt   42 **spurn**
trample   46 **Avaunt** begone

Thou hadst but power over his mortal body,
His soul thou canst not have; therefore, begone.

Richard. Sweet saint, for charity, be not so curst.°

Anne. Foul devil, for God's sake hence, and trouble
    us not,   50
For thou hast made the happy earth thy hell,
Filled it with cursing cries and deep exclaims.
If thou delight to view thy heinous deeds,
Behold this pattern° of thy butcheries.
O gentlemen, see, see dead Henry's wounds   55
Open their congealed mouths and bleed afresh!
Blush, blush, thou lump of foul deformity,
For 'tis thy presence that exhales° this blood
From cold and empty veins where no blood dwells.
Thy deed inhuman and unnatural   60
Provokes this deluge most unnatural.
O God, which this blood mad'st, revenge his death!
O earth, which this blood drink'st, revenge his
    death!
Either heav'n, with lightning strike the murd'rer
    dead,
Or earth, gape open wide and eat him quick,°   65
As thou dost swallow up this good king's blood
Which his hell-governed arm hath butcherèd!

Richard. Lady, you know no rules of charity,
    Which renders good for bad, blessings for curses.

Anne. Villain, thou know'st nor law of God nor man.   70
    No beast so fierce but knows some touch of pity.

Richard. But I know none, and therefore am no beast.

Anne. O wonderful, when devils tell the truth!

Richard. More wonderful, when angels are so angry.
    Vouchsafe, divine perfection of a woman,   75
    Of these supposèd crimes to give me leave
    By circumstance° but to acquit myself.

---

49 curst sharp-tongued   **54 pattern** example   **58 exhales** causes to
flow   **65 quick** alive   **77 By circumstance** in detail

Anne. Vouchsafe, diffused° infection of a man,
　　Of these known evils but to give me leave
80　By circumstance to accuse thy cursèd self.

Richard. Fairer than tongue can name thee, let me have
　　Some patient leisure to excuse myself.

Anne. Fouler than heart can think thee, thou canst make
　　No excuse current° but to hang thyself.

85　*Richard.* By such despair I should accuse myself.

Anne. And by despairing shalt thou stand excusèd
　　For doing worthy vengeance on thyself
　　That didst unworthy slaughter upon others.

Richard. Say that I slew them not?

Anne.　　　　　　　　Then say they were not slain.
90　But dead they are, and, devilish slave, by thee.

Richard. I did not kill your husband.

Anne.　　　　　　　　　　Why, then he is alive.

Richard. Nay, he is dead, and slain by Edward's hands.

Anne. In thy foul throat thou li'st! Queen Margaret saw
　　Thy murd'rous falchion° smoking in his blood;
95　The which thou once didst bend against her breast,
　　But that thy brothers beat aside the point.

Richard. I was provokèd by her sland'rous tongue,
　　That laid their guilt upon my guiltless shoulders.

Anne. Thou wast provokèd by thy bloody mind,
100　That never dream'st on aught but butcheries.
　　Didst thou not kill this king?

Richard.　　　　　　　　I grant ye.

---

78 **diffused** shapeless　84 **current** genuine　94 **falchion** curved
sword

Anne. Dost grant me, hedgehog? Then God grant me
 too
 Thou mayst be damnèd for that wicked deed!
 O, he was gentle, mild, and virtuous!

Richard. The better for the King of heaven that hath
 him.   105

Anne. He is in heaven, where thou shalt never come.

Richard. Let him thank me that holp° to send him
 thither;
 For he was fitter for that place than earth.

Anne. And thou unfit for any place but hell.

Richard. Yes, one place else, if you will hear me name
 it.   110

Anne. Some dungeon.

Richard.   Your bedchamber.

Anne. Ill rest betide the chamber where thou liest!

Richard. So will it, madam, till I lie with you.

Anne. I hope so.

Richard.   I know so. But, gentle Lady Anne,
 To leave this keen encounter of our wits   115
 And fall something into a slower method,
 Is not the causer of the timeless° deaths
 Of these Plantagenets, Henry and Edward,
 As blameful as the executioner?

Anne. Thou wast the cause and most accursed effect.° 120

Richard. Your beauty was the cause of that effect;
 Your beauty, that did haunt me in my sleep
 To undertake the death of all the world,
 So I might live one hour in your sweet bosom.

Anne. If I thought that, I tell thee, homicide,   125

107 **holp** helped   117 **timeless** untimely   120 **effect** effective agent

These nails should rend that beauty from my
cheeks.

Richard. These eyes could not endure that beauty's
wrack.°
You should not blemish it if I stood by.
As all the world is cheerèd by the sun,
130 So I by that; it is my day, my life.

Anne. Black night o'ershade thy day, and death thy
life!

Richard. Curse not thyself, fair creature; thou art both.

Anne. I would I were, to be revenged on thee.

Richard. It is a quarrel most unnatural
135 To be revenged on him that loveth thee.

Anne. It is a quarrel just and reasonable
To be revenged on him that killed my husband.

Richard. He that bereft thee, lady, of thy husband,
Did it to help thee to a better husband.

140 *Anne.* His better doth not breathe upon the earth.

Richard. He lives that loves thee better than he could.

Anne. Name him.

Richard.   Plantagenet.

Anne.   Why, that was he.

Richard. The selfsame name, but one of better nature.

Anne. Where is he?

Richard.   Here.   [*She*] *spits at him.*
Why dost thou spit at me?

145 *Anne.* Would it were mortal poison for thy sake!

Richard. Never came poison from so sweet a place.

Anne. Never hung poison on a fouler toad.
Out of my sight! Thou dost infect mine eyes.

127 **wrack** destruction

Richard. Thine eyes, sweet lady, have infected mine.

Anne. Would they were basilisks° to strike thee dead!	150

Richard. I would they were, that I might die at once;°
For now they kill me with a living death.
Those eyes of thine from mine have drawn salt
    tears,
Shamed their aspect° with store of childish drops,
These eyes which never shed remorseful° tear,	155
No, when my father York and Edward wept
To hear the piteous moan that Rutland° made
When black-faced° Clifford shook his sword at him,
Nor when thy warlike father, like a child,
Told the sad story of my father's death	160
And twenty times made pause to sob and weep,
That all the standers-by had wet their cheeks
Like trees bedashed with rain. In that sad time
My manly eyes did scorn an humble tear;
And what these sorrows could not thence exhale	165
Thy beauty hath, and made them blind with weep-
    ing.
I never sued to friend nor enemy;
My tongue could never learn sweet smoothing°
    word;
But now thy beauty is proposed my fee,
My proud heart sues, and prompts my tongue to
    speak.	170

                    She looks scornfully at him.
Teach not thy lip such scorn, for it was made
For kissing, lady, not for such contempt.
If thy revengeful heart cannot forgive,
Lo, here I lend thee this sharp-pointed sword;
Which if thou please to hide in this true breast	175
And let the soul forth that adoreth thee,
I lay it naked to the deadly stroke

---

150 **basilisks** fabulous monsters believed to kill by a look 151 **at once**
once and for all 154 **aspect** appearance 155 **remorseful** pitying
157 **Rutland** a young brother of Richard (see *3 Henry VI*, 1.3) 158
black-faced cruel-looking 168 **smoothing** flattering

And humbly beg the death upon my knee.

He lays his breast open.
She offers at [it]with his sword.

Nay, do not pause, for I did kill King Henry,
180   But 'twas thy beauty that provokèd me.
Nay, now dispatch; 'twas I that stabbed young Edward,
But 'twas thy heavenly face that set me on.

She falls° the sword.

Take up the sword again, or take up me.

Anne. Arise, dissembler; though I wish thy death,
185   I will not be thy executioner.

Richard. Then bid me kill myself, and I will do it.

Anne. I have already.

Richard.   That was in thy rage.
Speak it again, and even with the word
This hand, which for thy love did kill thy love,
190   Shall for thy love kill a far truer love.
To both their deaths shalt thou be accessary.°

Anne. I would I knew thy heart.

Richard. 'Tis figured° in my tongue.

Anne. I fear me both are false.

195   *Richard.* Then never was man true.

Anne. Well, well, put up your sword.

Richard. Say, then, my peace is made.

Anne. That shalt thou know hereafter.

Richard. But shall I live in hope?

200   *Anne.* All men, I hope, live so.

Richard. Vouchsafe° to wear this ring.

Anne. To take is not to give.

              [*Richard puts the ring on her finger.*]

182 s.d. **falls** lets fall   191 **accessary** sharing in guilt   193 **figured**
pictured   201 **Vouchsafe** consent

Richard. Look how° my ring encompasseth thy finger,
Even so thy breast encloseth my poor heart.
Wear both of them, for both of them are thine.   *205*
And if thy poor devoted servant may
But beg one favor at thy gracious hand,
Thou dost confirm his happiness forever.

Anne. What is it?

Richard. That it may please you leave these sad de-
signs   *210*
To him that hath most cause to be a mourner,
And presently° repair to Crosby House,
Where, after I have solemnly interred
At Chertsey monast'ry this noble king
And wet his grave with my repentant tears,   *215*
I will with all expedient° duty see you.
For divers unknown° reasons, I beseech you,
Grant me this boon.

Anne. With all my heart; and much it joys me too
To see you are become so penitent.   *220*
Tressel and Barkley, go along with me.

Richard. Bid me farewell.

Anne.   'Tis more than you deserve;
But since you teach me how to flatter you,
Imagine I have said farewell already.
                              Exit two with Anne.

Richard. Sirs, take up the corse.

Gentleman.   Towards Chertsey, noble lord? *225*

Richard. No, to Whitefriars; there attend° my coming.
                  Exit [Bearers and Gentlemen with] corse.
Was ever woman in this humor° wooed?
Was ever woman in this humor won?
I'll have her, but I will not keep her long.
What! I that killed her husband and his father   *230*
To take her in her heart's extremest hate,

203 **Look how** just as   212 **presently** immediately   216 **expedient**
speedy   217 **unknown** secret   226 **attend** await   227 **humor** mood

With curses in her mouth, tears in her eyes,
The bleeding witness of my hatred by,
Having God, her conscience, and these bars against
    me,
235 And I no friends to back my suit at all
But the plain devil and dissembling looks,
And yet to win her, all the world to nothing!
Ha!
Hath she forgot already that brave prince,
240 Edward her lord, whom I, some three months since,
Stabbed in my angry mood at Tewkesbury?°
A sweeter and a lovelier gentleman,
Framed in the prodigality° of nature,
Young, valiant, wise, and, no doubt, right royal,
245 The spacious world cannot again afford.°
And will she yet abase her eyes on me,
That cropped the golden prime° of this sweet
    prince
And made her widow to a woeful bed?
On me, whose all not equals Edward's moi'ty?°
250 On me, that halts and am misshapen thus?
My dukedom to a beggarly denier,°
I do mistake my person all this while.
Upon my life, she finds, although I cannot,
Myself to be a marv'lous proper° man.
255 I'll be at charges for° a looking glass
And entertain° a score or two of tailors
To study fashions to adorn my body.
Since I am crept in favor with myself,
I will maintain it with some little cost.
260 But first I'll turn yon fellow in° his grave,
And then return lamenting to my love.
Shine out, fair sun, till I have bought a glass
That I may see my shadow as I pass.   *Exit.*

---

241 **Tewkesbury** scene of a Yorkist victory 243 **prodigality** lavish-
ness 245 **afford** supply 247 **prime** springtime 249 **moi'ty** half
251 **denier** French coin worth a tenth of an English penny 254 **marv'-
lous proper** wonderfully handsome 255 **at charges for** at the expense
of 256 **entertain** engage 260 **in** into

Scene 3. [*The palace.*]

*Enter Queen [Elizabeth,] Lord Rivers, [Dorset,]
and Lord Grey.*

Rivers. Have patience, madam; there's no doubt his Majesty
Will soon recover his accustomed health.

Grey. In that you brook° it ill, it makes him worse.
Therefore for God's sake entertain good comfort
And cheer his Grace with quick and merry eyes.   5

Queen Elizabeth. If he were dead, what would betide on° me?

Grey. No other harm but loss of such a lord.

Queen Elizabeth. The loss of such a lord includes all harms.

Grey. The heavens have blessed you with a goodly son
To be your comforter when he is gone.   10

Queen Elizabeth. Ah, he is young, and his minority
Is put unto the trust of Richard Gloucester,
A man that loves not me, nor none of you.

Rivers. Is it concluded he shall be Protector?

Queen Elizabeth. It is determined, not concluded° yet;   15
But so it must be if the King miscarry.°

Enter Buckingham and [Stanley, Earl of] Derby.

Grey. Here come the lords of Buckingham and Derby.

Buckingham. Good time of day unto your royal Grace!

1.3.3 **brook** endure   6 **betide on** happen to   15 **determined, not concluded** decided, not finally decreed   16 **miscarry** die

Stanley. God make your Majesty joyful as you have
　been!

Queen Elizabeth. The Countess Richmond,° good my
20　　Lord of Derby,
　To your good prayer will scarcely say "Amen."
　Yet, Derby, notwithstanding she's your wife
　And loves not me, be you, good lord, assured
　I hate not you for her proud arrogance.

25　*Stanley.* I do beseech you, either not believe
　The envious slanders of her false accusers,
　Or, if she be accused on true report,
　Bear with her weakness, which I think proceeds
　From wayward sickness and no grounded malice.

Queen Elizabeth. Saw you the King today, my Lord
30　　of Derby?

Stanley. But now° the Duke of Buckingham and I
　Are come from visiting his Majesty.

Queen Elizabeth. What likelihood of his amendment,
　lords?

Buckingham. Madam, good hope; his Grace speaks
　cheerfully.

Queen Elizabeth. God grant him health! Did you con-
35　　fer with him?

Buckingham. Ay, madam; he desires to make atone-
　　ment°
　Between the Duke of Gloucester and your brothers,
　And between them and my Lord Chamberlain,°
　And sent to warn° them to his royal presence.

Queen Elizabeth. Would all were well! But that will
40　　never be.
　I fear our happiness is at the height.

20 **Countess Richmond** Margaret Tudor, mother of the Earl of Richmond (later Henry VII) and wife of Lord Stanley　31 **But now** just
now　36 **atonement** reconciliation　38 **Lord Chamberlain** Hastings
39 **warn** summon

Enter Richard [and Hastings].

Richard. They do me wrong, and I will not endure it!
  Who is it that complains unto the King
  That I, forsooth, am stern, and love them not?
  By holy Paul, they love his Grace but lightly   *45*
  That fill his ears with such dissentious rumors.
  Because I cannot flatter and look fair,
  Smile in men's faces, smooth, deceive, and cog,°
  Duck with French nods and apish courtesy,
  I must be held a rancorous enemy.   *50*
  Cannot a plain man live and think no harm
  But thus his simple truth must be abused
  With silken, sly, insinuating Jacks?°

Grey. To who in all this presence speaks your Grace?

Richard. To thee, that hast nor honesty nor grace.°   *55*
  When have I injured thee? When done thee wrong?
  Or thee? Or thee? Or any of your faction?
  A plague upon you all! His royal Grace—
  Whom God preserve better than you would wish!—
  Cannot be quiet scarce a breathing while°   *60*
  But you must trouble him with lewd° complaints.

Queen Elizabeth. Brother of Gloucester, you mistake
    the matter.
  The King on his own royal disposition,
  And not provoked by any suitor else,
  Aiming, belike, at your interior hatred   *65*
  That in your outward action shows itself
  Against my children, brothers, and myself,
  Makes° him to send that he may learn the ground.

Richard. I cannot tell; the world is grown so bad
  That wrens make prey where eagles dare not perch.   *70*
  Since every Jack became a gentleman,
  There's many a gentle° person made a Jack.

---

48 **cog** fawn   53 **Jacks** knaves   55 **grace** virtue   60 **breathing while**
time to take a breath   61 **lewd** wicked   68 **Makes** (the subject has
shifted from *The King* to *your interior hatred*)   72 **gentle** wellborn

Queen Elizabeth. Come, come, we know your mean-
    ing, brother Gloucester.
  You envy my advancement and my friends'.
75 God grant we never may have need of you!

Richard. Meantime, God grants that I have need of
    you.
  Our brother is imprisoned by your means,
  Myself disgraced, and the nobility
  Held in contempt, while great promotions
80 Are daily given to ennoble those
  That scarce, some two days since, were worth a
    noble.°

Queen Elizabeth. By him that raised me to this care-
    ful° height
  From that contented hap° which I enjoyed,
  I never did incense his Majesty
85 Against the Duke of Clarence, but have been
  An earnest advocate to plead for him.
  My lord, you do me shameful injury
  Falsely to draw me in° these vile suspects.°

Richard. You may deny that you were not the mean
90 Of my Lord Hastings' late imprisonment.

Rivers. She may, my lord, for—

Richard. She may, Lord Rivers! Why, who knows not
    so?
  She may do more, sir, than denying that:
  She may help you to many fair preferments,°
95 And then deny her aiding hand therein
  And lay those honors on your high desert.
  What may she not? She may, ay, marry,° may she!

Rivers. What, marry, may she?

Richard. What, marry, may she! Marry with a king,
100 A bachelor and a handsome stripling too.

---

81 **noble** coin worth a third of a pound 82 **careful** care-filled
83 **hap** fortune 88 **in** into 88 **suspects** suspicions 94 **preferments** promotions 97 **marry** indeed (from "By the Virgin Mary")

Iwis° your grandam had a worser match.

Queen Elizabeth. My Lord of Gloucester, I have too
    long borne
Your blunt upbraidings and your bitter scoffs.
By heaven, I will acquaint his Majesty
Of those gross taunts that oft I have endured.   *105*
I had rather be a country servant maid
Than a great queen with this condition,
To be so baited,° scorned, and stormèd at.

      Enter old Queen Margaret, [behind].

Small joy have I in being England's Queen.

Queen Margaret. [Aside] And less'ned be that small,
    God I beseech him!   *110*
Thy honor, state, and seat is due to me.

Richard. What! Threat you me with telling of the
    King?
Tell him and spare not. Look what° I have said
I will avouch in presence of the King.
I dare adventure to be sent to th' Tow'r.   *115*
'Tis time to speak; my pains° are quite forgot.

Queen Margaret. [Aside] Out, devil! I do remember
    them too well.
Thou kill'dst my husband Henry in the Tower
And Edward, my poor son, at Tewkesbury.

Richard. Ere you were queen, ay, or your husband
    king,   *120*
I was a packhorse in his great affairs,
A weeder-out of his proud adversaries,
A liberal rewarder of his friends;
To royalize his blood I spent mine own.

Queen Margaret. [Aside] Ay, and much better blood
    than his or thine.   *125*

Richard. In all which time you and your husband Grey

---

101 **Iwis** certainly 108 **baited** tormented 113 **Look what** whatever 116 **pains** efforts

Were factious for the house of Lancaster;
And, Rivers, so were you. Was not your husband
In Margaret's battle° at Saint Albans slain?
130 Let me put in your minds, if you forget,
What you have been ere this, and what you are;
Withal, what I have been, and what I am.

Queen Margaret. [*Aside*] A murd'rous villain, and so
still thou art.

Richard. Poor Clarence did forsake his father° Warwick;
135 Ay, and forswore himself—which Jesu pardon!—

Queen Margaret. [*Aside*] Which God revenge!

Richard. To fight on Edward's party for the crown;
And for his meed,° poor lord, he is mewèd up.
I would to God my heart were flint like Edward's,
140 Or Edward's soft and pitiful like mine.
I am too childish-foolish for this world.

Queen Margaret. [*Aside*] Hie thee to hell for shame
and leave this world,
Thou cacodemon!° There thy kingdom is.

Rivers. My Lord of Gloucester, in those busy days
145 Which here you urge to prove us enemies,
We followed then our lord, our sovereign king.
So should we you, if you should be our king.

Richard. If I should be! I had rather be a peddler.
Far be it from my heart, the thought thereof!

150 *Queen Elizabeth.* As little joy, my lord, as you suppose
You should enjoy were you this country's king,
As little joy you may suppose in me
That I enjoy, being the queen thereof.

Queen Margaret. [*Aside*] A little joy enjoys the queen
thereof;
155 For I am she, and altogether joyless.
I can no longer hold me patient. [*Comes forward.*]

129 **battle** army 134 **father** father-in-law 138 **meed** reward 143 **cacodemon** evil spirit

Hear me, you wrangling pirates, that fall out
In sharing that which you have pilled° from me!
Which of you trembles not that looks on me?
If not, that I am queen, you bow like subjects,   160
Yet that,° by you deposed, you quake like rebels.
Ah, gentle° villain, do not turn away!

Richard. Foul wrinkled witch, what mak'st thou° in
  my sight?

Queen Margaret. But repetition of what thou hast
  marred;
That will I make before I let thee go.   165

Richard. Wert thou not banishèd on pain of death?

Queen Margaret. I was; but I do find more pain in
  banishment
Than death can yield me here by my abode.
A husband and a son thou ow'st to me;
And thou a kingdom; all of you allegiance.   170
This sorrow that I have, by right is yours,
And all the pleasures you usurp are mine.

Richard. The curse my noble father laid on thee
When thou didst crown his warlike brows with
  paper
And with thy scorns drew'st rivers from his eyes   175
And then to dry them gav'st the Duke a clout°
Steeped in the faultless blood of pretty Rutland,
His curses then from bitterness of soul
Denounced against thee are all fall'n upon thee;
And God, not we, hath plagued thy bloody deed.   180

Queen Elizabeth. So just is God to right the innocent.

Hastings. O, 'twas the foulest deed to slay that babe
And the most merciless that e'er was heard of!

Rivers. Tyrants themselves wept when it was reported.

Dorset. No man but prophesied revenge for it.   185

158 **pilled** plundered   160–61 **that ... that** because ... because   162
gentle (1) wellborn (2) kindly (ironic)   163 **mak'st thou** are you
doing   176 **clout** piece of cloth

Buckingham. Northumberland, then present, wept to
    see it.

Queen Margaret. What! Were you snarling all before I
    came,
    Ready to catch each other by the throat,
    And turn you all your hatred now on me?
    Did York's dread curse prevail so much with
190   heaven
    That Henry's death, my lovely Edward's death,
    Their kingdom's loss, my woeful banishment,
    Should all but answer° for that peevish° brat?
    Can curses pierce the clouds and enter heaven?
    Why then, give way, dull clouds, to my quick°
195   curses!
    Though not by war, by surfeit die your king,
    As ours by murder, to make him a king!
    Edward thy son, that now is Prince of Wales,
    For Edward our son, that was Prince of Wales,
200   Die in his youth by like untimely violence!
    Thyself a queen, for me that was a queen,
    Outlive thy glory like my wretched self!
    Long mayst thou live to wail thy children's death
    And see another, as I see thee now,
205   Decked in thy rights as thou art stalled° in mine!
    Long die thy happy days before thy death,
    And, after many length'ned hours of grief,
    Die neither mother, wife, nor England's Queen!
    Rivers and Dorset, you were standers-by,
210   And so wast thou, Lord Hastings, when my son
    Was stabbed with bloody daggers. God I pray him
    That none of you may live his natural age,
    But by some unlooked accident cut off!

Richard. Have done thy charm,° thou hateful withered
    hag!

Queen Margaret. And leave out thee? Stay, dog, for
215   thou shalt hear me.

---

193 **but answer** only pay back   193 **peevish** foolish   195 **quick** full
of life   205 **stalled** installed   214 **charm** spell, curse

If heaven have any grievous plague in store
Exceeding those that I can wish upon thee,
O let them keep it till thy sins be ripe
And then hurl down their indignation
On thee, the troubler of the poor world's peace!   220
The worm of conscience still begnaw thy soul!
Thy friends suspect for traitors while thou liv'st,
And take deep traitors for thy dearest friends!
No sleep close up that deadly eye of thine,
Unless it be while some tormenting dream   225
Affrights thee with a hell of ugly devils!
Thou elvish-marked,° abortive, rooting hog!°
Thou that wast sealed° in thy nativity
The slave of nature and the son of hell!
Thou slander of thy heavy° mother's womb!   230
Thou loathèd issue of thy father's loins!
Thou rag of honor! Thou detested—

Richard. Margaret.

Queen Margaret.   Richard!

Richard.   Ha?

Queen Margaret.   I call thee not.

Richard. I cry thee mercy° then, for I did think
That thou hadst called me all these bitter names.   235

Queen Margaret. Why, so I did, but looked for no
reply.
O, let me make the period° to my curse!

Richard. 'Tis done by me, and ends in "Margaret."

Queen Elizabeth. Thus have you breathed your curse
against yourself.

Queen Margaret. Poor painted° queen, vain flourish°
of my fortune,   240
Why strew'st thou sugar on that bottled° spider

227 **elvish-marked** disfigured by evil fairies   227 **hog** (the boar was
Richard's emblem)   228 **sealed** marked   230 **heavy** sorrowful   234
cry thee mercy beg your pardon   237 **period** end   240 **painted**
unreal   240 **vain flourish** useless decoration   241 **bottled** swollen

Whose deadly web ensnareth thee about?
Fool, fool, thou whet'st a knife to kill thyself.
The day will come that thou shalt wish for me
To help thee curse this poisonous bunch-backed
245   toad.

Hastings. False-boding woman, end thy frantic curse,
Lest to thy harm thou move our patience.

Queen Margaret. Foul shame upon you! You have all
moved mine.

Rivers. Were you well served, you would be taught
250   your duty.

Queen Margaret. To serve me well, you all should do
me duty,
Teach me to be your queen and you my subjects.
O, serve me well and teach yourselves that duty!

Dorset. Dispute not with her; she is lunatic.

Queen Margaret. Peace, Master Marquis, you are
malapert.°
255   Your fire-new stamp° of honor is scarce current.
O that your young nobility could judge
What 'twere to lose it and be miserable!
They that stand high have many blasts to shake
them,
And if they fall, they dash themselves to pieces.

Richard. Good counsel, marry! Learn it, learn it, Mar-
260   quis.

Dorset. It touches you, my lord, as much as me.

Richard. Ay, and much more; but I was born so high.
Our aerie° buildeth in the cedar's top
And dallies with the wind and scorns the sun.

Queen Margaret. And turns the sun to shade, alas!
265   alas!
Witness my son, now in the shade of death,

254 **malapert** impudent 255 **fire-new stamp** newly coined title
263 **aerie** brood of eagles

Whose bright outshining beams thy cloudy wrath
Hath in eternal darkness folded up.
Your aerie buildeth in our aerie's nest.
O God, that seest it, do not suffer it!   270
As it is won with blood, lost be it so!

Buckingham. Peace, peace, for shame, if not for
    charity.

Queen Margaret. Urge neither charity nor shame to
    me.
Uncharitably with me have you dealt,
And shamefully my hopes by you are butchered.   275
My charity is outrage, life my shame,
And in that shame still live my sorrow's rage!

Buckingham. Have done, have done.

Queen Margaret. O princely Buckingham, I'll kiss thy
    hand
In sign of league and amity with thee.   280
Now fair befall thee and thy noble house!
Thy garments are not spotted with our blood,
Nor thou within the compass of my curse.

Buckingham. Nor no one here; for curses never pass
The lips of those that breathe them in the air.   285

Queen Margaret. I will not think but they ascend the
    sky
And there awake <u>God's gentle-sleeping peace</u>.
O Buckingham, take heed of yonder dog!
Look when° he fawns he bites; and when he bites,
His venom tooth will rankle to the death.   290
Have not to do with him, beware of him.
Sin, death, and hell have set their marks on him
And all their ministers attend on him.

Richard. What doth she say, my Lord of Buckingham?

Buckingham. Nothing that I respect,° my gracious
    lord.   295

289 **Look when** whenever   295 **respect** pay heed to

Queen Margaret. What, dost thou scorn me for my
    gentle counsel
    And soothe the devil that I warn thee from?
    O, but remember this another day,
    When he shall split thy very heart with sorrow,
300   And say poor Margaret was a prophetess.
    Live each of you the subjects to his hate,
    And he to yours, and all of you to God's!   *Exit.*

Buckingham. My hair doth stand on end to hear her
    curses. *the mocker, but also chilled*

Rivers. And so doth mine. I muse° why she's at
    liberty.

305 *Richard.* I cannot blame her. By God's holy mother,
    She hath had too much wrong, and I repent
    My part thereof that I have done to her.

Queen Elizabeth. I never did her any to my knowl-
    edge.

Richard. Yet you have all the vantage of her wrong:
310   I was too hot to do somebody good
    That is too cold in thinking of it now.
    Marry, as for Clarence, he is well repaid;
    He is franked up° to fatting for his pains.
    God pardon them that are the cause thereof!

315 *Rivers.* A virtuous and a Christianlike conclusion,
    To pray for them that have done scathe° to us.

Richard. So do I ever—[*speaks to himself*] being well
    advised;
    For had I cursed now, I had cursed myself.

Enter Catesby.

Catesby. Madam, his Majesty doth call for you;
320   And for your Grace; and yours, my gracious lord.

Queen Elizabeth. Catesby, I come. Lords, will you go
    with me?

304 **muse** wonder 313 **franked up** shut up (like an animal to be
slaughtered) 316 **scathe** harm

Rivers. We wait upon your Grace.
                    Exeunt all but [Richard of] Gloucester.

Richard. I do the wrong, and first begin to brawl.
    The secret mischiefs that I set abroach°
    I lay unto the grievous charge of others.   325
    Clarence, who I indeed have cast in darkness,
    I do beweep to many simple gulls,°
    Namely to Derby, Hastings, Buckingham,
    And tell them 'tis the Queen and her allies°
    That stir the King against the Duke my brother.   330
    Now they believe it, and withal whet me
    To be revenged on Rivers, Dorset, Grey.
    But then I sigh, and with a piece of Scripture
    Tell them that God bids us do good for evil;
    And thus I clothe my naked villainy   335
    With odd old ends stol'n forth of holy writ,
    And seem a saint when most I play the devil.

                    Enter two Murderers.

    But soft! Here come my executioners.
    How now, my hardy, stout-resolvèd mates!
    Are you now going to dispatch this thing?   340

First Murderer. We are, my lord, and come to have
        the warrant
    That we may be admitted where he is.

Richard. Well thought upon; I have it here about me.
                    [*Gives the warrant.*]
    When you have done, repair to Crosby Place.
    But, sirs, be sudden in the execution,   345
    Withal obdurate, do not hear him plead;
    For Clarence is well-spoken, and perhaps
    May move your hearts to pity if you mark him.

First Murderer. Tut, tut, my lord, we will not stand
        to prate.
    Talkers are no good doers; be assured   350
    We go to use our hands and not our tongues.

---

324 **set abroach** originate   327 **gulls** dupes   329 **allies** kindred

Richard. Your eyes drop millstones when fools' eyes
    fall° tears.
  I like you, lads; about your business straight.°
  Go, go, dispatch.

First Murderer.   We will, my noble lord.   *Exeunt.*

Scene 4. [*The Tower.*]

Enter Clarence and Keeper.

Keeper. Why looks your Grace so heavily° today?

Clarence. O, I have passed a miserable night,
  So full of fearful dreams, of ugly sights,
  That, as I am a Christian faithful man,
5 I would not spend another such a night
  Though 'twere to buy a world of happy days,
  So full of dismal terror was the time.

Keeper. What was your dream, my lord? I pray you
  tell me.

Clarence. Methoughts° that I had broken from the
  Tower
10 And was embarked to cross to Burgundy,
  And in my company my brother Gloucester,
  Who from my cabin tempted me to walk
  Upon the hatches. Thence we looked toward Eng-
  land
  And cited up a thousand heavy times,
15 During the wars of York and Lancaster,
  That had befall'n us. As we paced along
  Upon the giddy footing of the hatches,
  Methought that Gloucester stumbled, and in falling
  Struck me (that thought to stay° him) overboard

352 **fall** let fall   353 **straight** at once   1.4.1 **heavily** sadly   9 **Me-thoughts** it seemed to me   19 **stay** support

Into the tumbling billows of the main.°   20
O Lord, methought what pain it was to drown!
What dreadful noise of water in mine ears!
What sights of ugly death within mine eyes!
Methoughts I saw a thousand fearful wracks;
A thousand men that fishes gnawed upon;   25
Wedges of gold, great anchors, heaps of pearl,
Inestimable stones, unvalued° jewels,
All scatt'red in the bottom of the sea.
Some lay in dead men's skulls, and in the holes
Where eyes did once inhabit there were crept,   30
As 'twere in scorn of eyes, reflecting gems
That wooed the slimy bottom of the deep
And mocked the dead bones that lay scatt'red by.

Keeper. Had you such leisure in the time of death
To gaze upon these secrets of the deep?   35

Clarence. Methought I had; and often did I strive
To yield the ghost, but still the envious flood
Stopped in my soul and would not let it forth
To find the empty, vast, and wand'ring air,
But smothered it within my panting bulk,°   40
Who almost burst to belch it in the sea.

Keeper. Awaked you not in this sore agony?

Clarence. No, no, my dream was lengthened after life.
O, then began the tempest to my soul!
I passed, methought, the melancholy flood,   45
With that sour ferryman° which poets write of,
Unto the kingdom of perpetual night.
The first that there did greet my stranger soul
Was my great father-in-law, renownèd Warwick,
Who spake aloud, "What scourge for perjury   50
Can this dark monarchy afford false Clarence?"
And so he vanished. Then came wand'ring by
A shadow like an angel, with bright hair
Dabbled in blood, and he shrieked out aloud,

20 **main** ocean   27 **unvaluèd** priceless   40 **bulk** body   46 **ferry-man** Charon, who ferried the dead across the Styx

"Clarence is come, false, fleeting,° perjured Clar-
55   ence,
That stabbed me in the field by Tewkesbury.
Seize on him, Furies, take him unto torment!"
With that, methought, a legion of foul fiends
Environed me and howlèd in mine ears
60   Such hideous cries that with the very noise
I, trembling, waked, and for a season after
Could not believe but that I was in hell,
Such terrible impression made my dream.

Keeper. No marvel, lord, though it affrighted you.
65   I am afraid, methinks, to hear you tell it.

Clarence. Ah, keeper, keeper, I have done these things
That now give evidence against my soul
For Edward's sake, and see how he requites me!
O God! If my deep pray'rs cannot appease thee,
70   But thou wilt be avenged on my misdeeds,
Yet execute thy wrath in me alone.
O, spare my guiltless wife and my poor children!
Keeper, I prithee sit by me awhile.
My soul is heavy, and I fain would sleep.

Keeper. I will, my lord. God give your Grace good
75   rest!   [*Clarence sleeps.*]

Enter Brakenbury, the Lieutenant.

Brakenbury. Sorrow breaks seasons and reposing
hours,
Makes the night morning and the noontide night.
Princes have but their titles for their glories,
An outward honor for an inward toil,
80   And for unfelt imaginations°
They often feel a world of restless cares;
So that between their titles and low name
There's nothing differs but the outward fame.

Enter two Murderers.

First Murderer. Ho! Who's here?

55 **fleeting** fickle   80 **unfelt imaginations** pleasures imagined but not
felt

Brakenbury. What wouldst thou, fellow? And how
   cam'st thou hither?   *85*

First Murderer. I would speak with Clarence, and I
   came hither on my legs.

Brakenbury. What, so brief?

Second Murderer. 'Tis better, sir, than to be tedious.
   Let him see our commission, and talk no more.   *90*
                      [*Brakenbury*] *reads* [*it*].

Brakenbury. I am in this commanded to deliver
   The noble Duke of Clarence to your hands.
   I will not reason what is meant hereby,
   Because I will be guiltless from the meaning.
   There lies the Duke asleep, and there the keys.   *95*
   I'll to the King and signify to him
   That thus I have resigned to you my charge.

First Murderer. You may, sir, 'tis a point of wisdom.
   Fare you well.
                 Exit [*Brakenbury with Keeper*].

Second Murderer. What, shall we stab him as he   *100*
   sleeps?

First Murderer. No, he'll say 'twas done cowardly
   when he wakes.

Second Murderer. Why, he shall never wake until the
   great Judgment Day.   *105*

First Murderer. Why, then he'll say we stabbed him
   sleeping.

Second Murderer. The urging of that word "judgment"
   hath bred a kind of remorse in me.

First Murderer. What, art thou afraid?   *110* .

Second Murderer. Not to kill him, having a warrant;
   but to be damned for killing him, from the which
   no warrant can defend me.

First Murderer. I thought thou hadst been resolute.

115 *Second Murderer.* So I am—to let him live.

First Murderer. I'll back to the Duke of Gloucester and tell him so.

Second Murderer. Nay, I prithee stay a little. I hope this passionate humor° of mine will change; it was 120 wont to hold me but while one tells° twenty.

First Murderer. How dost thou feel thyself now?

Second Murderer. Faith, some certain dregs of conscience are yet within me.

First Murderer. Remember our reward when the 125 deed's done.

Second Murderer. Zounds,° he dies! I had forgot the reward.

First Murderer. Where's thy conscience now?

Second Murderer. O, in the Duke of Gloucester's 130 purse.

First Murderer. When he opens his purse to give us our reward, thy conscience flies out.

Second Murderer. 'Tis no matter, let it go. There's few or none will entertain it.

135 *First Murderer.* What if it come to thee again?

Second Murderer. I'll not meddle with it; it makes a man a coward. A man cannot steal, but it accuseth him; a man cannot swear, but it checks him; a man cannot lie with his neighbor's wife, but it detects 140 him. 'Tis a blushing shamefaced spirit that mutinies in a man's bosom. It fills a man full of obstacles. It made me once restore a purse of gold that, by chance, I found. It beggars any man that keeps it. It is turned out of town and cities for a dangerous 145 thing, and every man that means to live well endeavors to trust to himself and live without it.

119 **passionate humor** compassionate mood   120 **tells** counts   126 **Zounds** (an oath, from "By God's wounds")

First Murderer. Zounds, 'tis even now at my elbow, persuading me not to kill the Duke.

Second Murderer. Take the devil in thy mind, and believe him° not. He would insinuate with thee but to make thee sigh. 150

First Murderer. I am strong-framed; he cannot prevail with me.

Second Murderer. Spoke like a tall° man that respects thy reputation. Come, shall we fall to work? 155

First Murderer. Take him on the costard° with the hilts of thy sword, and then throw him into the malmsey butt° in the next room.

Second Murderer. O excellent device! And make a sop° of him. 160

First Murderer. Soft, he wakes.

Second Murderer. Strike!

First Murderer. No, we'll reason° with him.

Clarence. Where art thou, keeper? Give me a cup of wine.

Second Murderer. You shall have wine enough, my lord, anon. 165

Clarence. In God's name, what art thou?

First Murderer. A man, as you are.

Clarence. But not as I am, royal.

First Murderer. Nor you as we are, loyal.

Clarence. Thy voice is thunder, but thy looks are humble. 170

First Murderer. My voice is now the King's, my looks mine own.

150 **him** i.e., conscience 154 **tall** brave 156 **costard** head 158 **malmsey butt** cask of malmsey, a Greek wine 160 **sop** piece of bread soaked in wine 163 **reason** talk

Clarence. How darkly and how deadly dost thou
    speak!
  Your eyes do menace me. Why look you pale?
  Who sent you hither? Wherefore do you come?

175 *Second Murderer.* To, to, to—

Clarence. To murder me?

Both. Ay, ay.

Clarence. You scarcely have the hearts to tell me so,
  And therefore cannot have the hearts to do it.
180   Wherein, my friends, have I offended you?

First Murderer. Offended us you have not, but the
    King.

Clarence. I shall be reconciled to him again.

Second Murderer. Never, my lord; therefore prepare
    to die.

Clarence. Are you drawn forth among a world of men
185   To slay the innocent? What is my offense?
  Where is the evidence that doth accuse me?
  What lawful quest° have given their verdict up
  Unto the frowning judge? Or who pronounced
  The bitter sentence of poor Clarence' death?
190   Before I be convict by course of law,
  To threaten me with death is most unlawful.
  I charge you, as you hope to have redemption
  By Christ's dear blood shed for our grievous sins,
  That you depart, and lay no hands on me.
195   The deed you undertake is damnable.°

First Murderer. What we will do, we do upon com-
    mand.

Second Murderer. And he that hath commanded is our
    king.

Clarence. Erroneous vassals! The great King of kings
  Hath in the table of his law commanded
200   That thou shalt do no murder. Will you then

187 **quest** jury   195 **damnable** i.e., one which will damn your souls

Spurn at his edict and fulfill a man's?
Take heed; for he holds vengeance in his hand
To hurl upon their heads that break his law.

Second Murderer. And that same vengeance doth he
  hurl on thee
For false forswearing and for murder too.   205
Thou didst receive the sacrament to fight
In quarrel of the house of Lancaster.

First Murderer. And like a traitor to the name of God
  Didst break that vow, and with thy treacherous
    blade
Unrip'st the bowels of thy sov'reign's son.   210

Second Murderer. Whom thou wast sworn to cherish
  and defend.

First Murderer. How canst thou urge God's dreadful
  law to us
When thou hast broke it in such dear° degree?

Clarence. Alas! For whose sake did I that ill deed?
For Edward, for my brother, for his sake.   215
He sends you not to murder me for this,
For in that sin he is as deep as I.
If God will be avengèd for the deed,
O, know you yet he doth it publicly.
Take not the quarrel from his pow'rful arm.   220
He needs no indirect or lawless course
To cut off those that have offended him.

First Murderer. Who made thee then a bloody min-
  ister
When gallant-springing brave Plantagenet,
That princely novice,° was struck dead by thee?   225

Clarence. My brother's love, the devil, and my rage.

First Murderer. Thy brother's love, our duty, and thy
  faults
Provoke us hither now to slaughter thee.

Clarence. If you do love my brother, hate not me.

213 **dear** high   225 **princely novice** young prince

230 I am his brother, and I love him well.
    If you are hired for meed,° go back again,
    And I will send you to my brother Gloucester,
    Who shall reward you better for my life
    Than Edward will for tidings of my death.

Second Murderer. You are deceived; your brother
235   Gloucester hates you.

Clarence. O, no, he loves me and he holds me dear.
    Go you to him from me.

First Murderer.   Ay, so we will.

Clarence. Tell him, when that our princely father York
    Blessed his three sons with his victorious arm
240 And charged us from his soul to love each other,
    He little thought of this divided friendship.
    Bid Gloucester think on this, and he will weep.

First Murderer. Ay, millstones, as he lessoned° us to
    weep.

Clarence. O, do not slander him, for he is kind.

First Murderer. Right as° snow in harvest. Come, you
245   deceive yourself.
    'Tis he that sends us to destroy you here.

Clarence. It cannot be, for he bewept my fortune
    And hugged me in his arms and swore with sobs
    That he would labor° my delivery.

250 *First Murderer.* Why so he doth, when he delivers you
    From this earth's thralldom to the joys of heaven.

Second Murderer. Make peace with God, for you must
    die, my lord.

Clarence. Have you that holy feeling in your souls
    To counsel me to make my peace with God,
255 And are you yet to your own souls so blind
    That you will war with God by murd'ring me?

231 **meed** reward 243 **lessoned** taught 245 **Right as** just like
249 **labor** work for

O, sirs, consider, they that set you on
To do this deed will hate you for the deed.

Second Murderer. What shall we do?

Clarence.   Relent, and save your souls.

First Murderer. Relent! No. 'Tis cowardly and woman-
    ish.   260

Clarence. Not to relent is beastly, savage, devilish.
    [*To Second Murderer*] My friend, I spy some pity
        in thy looks.
    O, if thine eye be not a flatterer,
    Come thou on my side and entreat for me.
    A begging prince what beggar pities not?   265
    Which of you, if you were a prince's son,
    Being pent from liberty as I am now,
    If two such murderers as yourselves came to you,
    Would not entreat for life? As you would beg,
    Were you in my distress—   270

Second Murderer. Look behind you, my lord!

First Murderer. Take that! And that! (*Stabs him.*) If
    all this will not do,
    I'll drown you in the malmsey butt within.
                                Exit [*with the body*].

Second Murderer. A bloody deed and desperately
    dispatched!
    How fain, like Pilate, would I wash my hands   275
    Of this most grievous murder!

                Enter First Murderer.

First Murderer. How now? What mean'st thou that
    thou help'st me not?
    By heaven, the Duke shall know how slack you
        have been.

Second Murderer. I would he knew that I had saved
    his brother!
    Take thou the fee, and tell him what I say,   280
    For I repent me that the Duke is slain.   *Exit.*

First Murderer. So do not I. Go, coward as thou art.
 Well, I'll go hide the body in some hole
 Till that the Duke give order for his burial;
285 And when I have my meed, I will away,
 For this will out, and then I must not stay. *Exit.*

ACT 2

Scene 1. [*The palace.*]

Flourish.° Enter the King, sick, the Queen, Lord
    Marquis Dorset, [Grey,] Rivers, Hastings,
    Catesby, Buckingham, Woodville, [and Scales].

King Edward. Why, so. Now have I done a good day's
    work.
You peers, continue this united league.
I every day expect an embassage
From my Redeemer to redeem me hence;
And more in peace my soul shall part to heaven,   *5*
Since I have made my friends at peace on earth.
Rivers and Hastings, take each other's hand;
Dissemble° not your hatred, swear your love.

Rivers. By heaven, my soul is purged from grudging
    hate,
And with my hand I seal my true heart's love.   *10*

Hastings. So thrive I as I truly swear the like!

King Edward. Take heed you dally° not before your
    king,
Lest he that is the supreme King of kings

2.1.s.d. **Flourish** fanfare of trumpets 8 **Dissemble** disguise by false
pretense 12 **dally** trifle

Confound your hidden falsehood and award
15 Either of you to be the other's end.

Hastings. So prosper I as I swear perfect love!

Rivers. And I as I love Hastings with my heart!

King Edward. Madam, yourself is not exempt from this;
Nor you, son Dorset; Buckingham, nor you;
20 You have been factious one against the other.
Wife, love Lord Hastings, let him kiss your hand,
And what you do, do it unfeignedly.

Queen Elizabeth. There, Hastings. I will never more remember
Our former hatred, so thrive I and mine!

King Edward. Dorset, embrace him; Hastings, love
25 Lord Marquis.

Dorset. This interchange of love, I here protest,
Upon my part shall be inviolable.

Hastings. And so swear I.

King Edward. Now, princely Buckingham, seal thou this league
30 With thy embracements to my wife's allies,
And make me happy in your unity.

Buckingham. [*To the Queen*] Whenever Buckingham doth turn his hate
Upon your Grace, but° with all duteous love
Doth cherish you and yours, God punish me
35 With hate in those where I expect most love!
When I have most need to employ a friend,
And most assurèd that he is a friend,
Deep, hollow, treacherous, and full of guile
Be he unto me! This do I beg of God,
40 When I am cold in zeal to you or yours.   *Embrace.*

King Edward. A pleasing cordial, princely Buckingham,

33 **but** (the meaning calls for "and not")

Is this thy vow unto my sickly heart.
There wanteth now our brother Gloucester here
To make the blessèd period° of this peace.

Buckingham. And in good time,   45
Here comes Sir Richard Ratcliffe and the Duke.

Enter Ratcliffe and [Richard, Duke of] Gloucester.

Richard. Good morrow to my sovereign king and
    queen;
And, princely peers, a happy time of day!

King Edward. Happy indeed, as we have spent the
    day.
Gloucester, we have done deeds of charity,   50
Made peace of enmity, fair love of hate,
Between these swelling wrong-incensèd peers.

Richard. A blessèd labor, my most sovereign lord.
Among this princely heap° if any here
By false intelligence or wrong surmise   55
Hold me a foe;
If I unwittingly, or in my rage,
Have aught committed that is hardly borne°
By any in this presence, I desire
To reconcile me to his friendly peace.   60
'Tis death to me to be at enmity;
I hate it, and desire all good men's love.
First, madam, I entreat true peace of you,
Which I will purchase with my duteous service;
Of you, my noble cousin Buckingham,   65
If ever any grudge were lodged between us;
Of you and you, Lord Rivers and of Dorset,
That all without desert° have frowned on me;
Of you, Lord Woodville, and, Lord Scales,° of you;
Dukes, earls, lords, gentlemen; indeed, of all.   70
I do not know that Englishman alive
With whom my soul is any jot at odds

44 **period** conclusion   54 **heap** company, group   58 **hardly borne**
resented   68 **all without desert** wholly without my deserving
it   69 **Lord Woodville, and, Lord Scales** (historically, these are both
other titles of Anthony Woodville, Earl Rivers)

More than the infant that is born tonight.
I thank my God for my humility.

Queen Elizabeth. A holy day shall this be kept here-
75   after.
I would to God all strifes were well compounded.°
My sovereign lord, I do beseech your Highness
To take our brother Clarence to your Grace.

Richard. Why, madam, have I off'red love for this,
80   To be so flouted in this royal presence?
Who knows not that the gentle Duke is dead?

                                   They all start.
You do him injury to scorn his corse.

King Edward. Who knows not he is dead! Who knows
he is?

Queen Elizabeth. All-seeing heaven, what a world is
this!

85   *Buckingham.* Look I so pale, Lord Dorset, as the rest?

Dorset. Ay, my good lord; and no man in the presence
But his red color hath forsook his cheeks.

King Edward. Is Clarence dead? The order was reversed.

Richard. But he, poor man, by your first order died,
90   And that a wingèd Mercury did bear;
Some tardy cripple bare the countermand,
That came too lag° to see him burièd.
God grant that some, less noble and less loyal,
Nearer in bloody thoughts, and° not in blood,
95   Deserve not worse than wretched Clarence did,
And yet go current from° suspicion!

          Enter [Lord Stanley,] Earl of Derby.

Stanley. A boon, my sovereign, for my service done!

King Edward. I prithee peace. My soul is full of
sorrow.

76 **compounded** settled   92 **lag** late   94 **and** if   96 **go current
from** are taken at face value without

Stanley. I will not rise unless your Highness hear me.

King Edward. Then say at once what is it thou re-
quests.   *100*

Stanley. The forfeit, sovereign, of my servant's life,°
Who slew today a riotous gentleman
Lately attendant on the Duke of Norfolk.

King Edward. Have I a tongue to doom my brother's
death,
And shall that tongue give pardon to a slave?   *105*
My brother killed no man, his fault was thought,
And yet his punishment was bitter death.
Who sued to me for him? Who, in my wrath,
Kneeled at my feet and bid me be advised?°
Who spoke of brotherhood? Who spoke of love?   *110*
Who told me how the poor soul did forsake
The mighty Warwick and did fight for me?
Who told me, in the field at Tewkesbury
When Oxford had me down, he rescuèd me
And said, "Dear brother, live, and be a king"?   *115*
Who told me, when we both lay in the field
Frozen almost to death, how he did lap° me
Even in his garments, and did give himself
All thin and naked, to the numb-cold night?
All this from my remembrance brutish wrath   *120*
Sinfully plucked, and not a man of you
Had so much grace to put it in my mind.
But when your carters or your waiting vassals
Have done a drunken slaughter and defaced
The precious image of our dear Redeemer,   *125*
You straight are on your knees for "Pardon,
pardon!"
And I, unjustly too, must grant it you.

                         [Stanley rises.]
But for my brother not a man would speak,
Nor I, ungracious, speak unto myself
For him, poor soul. The proudest of you all   *130*
Have been beholding to him in his life;

---

101 **forfeit . . . life** i.e., forfeited life   109 **be advised** consider carefully   117 **lap** wrap

    Yet none of you would once beg for his life.
    O God, I fear thy justice will take hold
    On me and you, and mine and yours, for this!
    Come, Hastings, help me to my closet.° Ah, poor
135   Clarence!   *Exeunt some with King and Queen.*

Richard. This is the fruits of rashness. Marked you not
    How that the guilty kindred of the Queen
    Looked pale when they did hear of Clarence'
      death?
    O, they did urge it still unto the King!
140   God will revenge it. Come, lords, will you go
    To comfort Edward with our company?

Buckingham. We wait upon your Grace.   *Exeunt.*

Scene 2. [*The palace.*]

*Enter the old Duchess of York, with the two Children
of Clarence.*

Boy. Good grandam, tell us, is our father dead?

Duchess of York. No, boy.

Daughter. Why do you weep so oft, and beat your
    breast,
    And cry, "O Clarence, my unhappy son"?

5 *Boy.* Why do you look on us, and shake your head,
    And call us orphans, wretches, castaways,
    If that our noble father were alive?

Duchess of York. My pretty cousins,° you mistake me
    both.
    I do lament the sickness of the King,
10   As loath to lose him, not your father's death.
    It were lost sorrow to wail one that's lost.

135 **closet** private room   2.2.8 **cousins** relatives

Boy. Then you conclude, my grandam, he is dead.
  The King mine uncle is too blame° for it.
  God will revenge it, whom I will importune
  With earnest prayers all to that effect.   15

Daughter. And so will I.

Duchess of York. Peace, children, peace! The King
    doth love you well.
  Incapable° and shallow innocents,
  You cannot guess who caused your father's death.

Boy. Grandam, we can; for my good uncle Gloucester   20
  Told me the King, provoked to it by the Queen,
  Devised impeachments° to imprison him;
  And when my uncle told me so, he wept,
  And pitied me, and kindly kissed my cheek;
  Bade me rely on him as on my father,   25
  And he would love me dearly as a child.

Duchess of York. Ah, that deceit should steal such
    gentle shape°
  And with a virtuous visor° hide deep vice!
  He is my son, ay, and therein my shame;
  Yet from my dugs he drew not this deceit.   30

Boy. Think you my uncle did dissemble, grandam?

Duchess of York. Ay, boy.

Boy. I cannot think it. Hark! What noise is this?

  *Enter the Queen, [Elizabeth,] with her hair about
      her ears, Rivers and Dorset after her.*

Queen Elizabeth. Ah, who shall hinder me to wail and
    weep,
  To chide my fortune, and torment myself?   35
  I'll join with black despair against my soul
  And to myself become an enemy.

Duchess of York. What means this scene of rude im-
    patience?

13 **too blame** too blameworthy   18 **Incapable** unable to understand
22 **impeachments** accusations   27 **shape** disguise   28 **visor** mask

Queen Elizabeth. To make an act of tragic violence.
40   Edward, my lord, thy son, our king, is dead!
        Why grow the branches when the root is gone?
        Why wither not the leaves that want their sap?
        If you will live, lament; if die, be brief,
        That our swift-wingèd souls may catch the King's,
45   Or like obedient subjects follow him
        To his new kingdom of ne'er-changing night.

Duchess of York. Ah, so much interest° have I in thy
          sorrow
        As I had title° in thy noble husband!
        I have bewept a worthy husband's death,
50   And lived with looking on his images;°
        But now two mirrors of his princely semblance°
        Are cracked in pieces by malignant death,
        And I for comfort have but one false glass
        That grieves me when I see my shame in him.
55   Thou art a widow, yet thou art a mother
        And hast the comfort of thy children left;
        But death hath snatched my husband from mine
          arms
        And plucked two crutches from my feeble hands,
        Clarence and Edward. O, what° cause have I,
60   Thine being but a moi'ty of my moan,°
        To overgo thy woes and drown thy cries!

Boy. Ah, aunt, you wept not for our father's death.
        How can we aid you with our kindred tears?

Daughter. Our fatherless distress was left unmoaned;
65   Your widow-dolor likewise be unwept!

Queen Elizabeth. Give me no help in lamentation;
        I am not barren to bring forth complaints.
        All springs reduce° their currents to mine eyes,
        That I, being governed by the watery moon,
70   May send forth plenteous tears to drown the world.
        Ah for my husband, for my dear lord Edward!

47 **interest** share 48 **title** legal right 50 **images** i.e., children
51 **semblance** appearance 59 **what** how much 60 **moi'ty of my
moan** half of my grief 68 **reduce** bring

Children. Ah for our father, for our dear lord Clarence!

Duchess of York. Alas for both, both mine, Edward and Clarence!

Queen Elizabeth. What stay° had I but Edward? And he's gone.

Children. What stay had we but Clarence? And he's gone.   75

Duchess of York. What stays had I but they? And they are gone.

Queen Elizabeth. Was never widow had so dear a loss.

Children. Were never orphans had so dear a loss.

Duchess of York. Was never mother had so dear a loss.
   Alas, I am the mother of these griefs!   80
   Their woes are parceled,° mine is general.
   She for an Edward weeps, and so do I;
   I for a Clarence weep, so doth not she.
   These babes for Clarence weep, and so do I;
   I for an Edward weep, so do not they.   85
   Alas, you three on me, threefold distressed,
   Pour all your tears! I am your sorrow's nurse,
   And I will pamper it with lamentation.

Dorset. Comfort, dear mother; God is much displeased
   That you take with unthankfulness his doing.   90
   In common worldly things 'tis called ungrateful
   With dull unwillingness to repay a debt
   Which with a bounteous hand was kindly lent;
   Much more to be thus opposite with° heaven
   For° it requires the royal debt it lent you.   95

Rivers. Madam, bethink you like a careful mother
   Of the young prince your son. Send straight for him;

74 **stay** support 81 **parceled** particular 94 **opposite with** opposed
to 95 **For** because

Let him be crowned; in him your comfort lives.
Drown desperate sorrow in dead Edward's grave
100 And plant your joys in living Edward's throne.

Enter Richard, Buckingham, [Stanley, Earl of]
Derby, Hastings, and Ratcliffe.

Richard. Sister, have comfort. All of us have cause
To wail the dimming of our shining star;
But none can help our harms by wailing them.
Madam, my mother, I do cry you mercy;
105 I did not see your Grace. Humbly on my knee
I crave your blessing.

Duchess of York. God bless thee, and put meekness
in thy breast,
Love, charity, obedience, and true duty!

Richard. Amen! [*Aside*] And make me die a good old
man!
110 That is the butt-end of a mother's blessing;
I marvel that her Grace did leave it out.

Buckingham. You cloudy princes and heart-sorrowing
peers
That bear this heavy mutual load of moan,
Now cheer each other in each other's love.
115 Though we have spent our harvest of this king,
We are to reap the harvest of his son.
The broken rancor of your high-swol'n hates,
But lately splintered,° knit, and joined together,
Must gently be preserved, cherished, and kept.°
120 Me seemeth° good that with some little train
Forthwith from Ludlow the young prince be fet°
Hither to London, to be crowned our king.

Rivers. Why with some little train, my Lord of Buckingham?

Buckingham. Marry, my lord, lest by a multitude

---

118 **splintered** set in splints 119 **Must ... kept** (the subject has
shifted from *rancor* to its opposite) 120 **Me seemeth** it seems to
me 121 **fet** fetched

The new-healed wound of malice should break out,   125
Which would be so much the more dangerous
By how much the estate is green° and yet un-
    governed.
Where every horse bears his commanding rein
And may direct his course as please himself,
As well the fear of harm as harm apparent,°   130
In my opinion, ought to be prevented.

Richard. I hope the King made peace with all of us;
And the compact is firm and true in me.

Rivers. And so in me; and so (I think) in all.
Yet, since it is but green, it should be put   135
To no apparent likelihood of breach,
Which haply° by much company might be urged.
Therefore I say with noble Buckingham
That it is meet° so few should fetch the Prince.

Hastings. And so say I.   140

Richard. Then be it so; and go we to determine
Who they shall be that straight shall post to Lud-
    low.
Madam, and you, my sister, will you go
To give your censures° in this business?

Queen and Duchess of York. With all our hearts.   145
            Exeunt. Manet° Buckingham and Richard.

Buckingham. My lord, whoever journeys to the
    Prince,
For God sake let not us two stay at home;
For by the way I'll sort occasion,°
As index° to the story we late talked of,
To part the Queen's proud kindred from the Prince.   150

Richard. My other self, my counsel's consistory,°

127 **estate is green** regime is new   130 **apparent** seen clearly 137 **haply** perhaps   139 **meet** fitting   144 **censures** judgments   145 s.d. **Manet** (Latin for "remains." The third person plural is *manent*, but the Elizabethans commonly used the third person singular—like "exit"—for the plural)   148 **sort occasion** contrive opportunity   149 **index** preface   151 **consistory** council chamber

My oracle, my prophet, my dear cousin,
I, as a child, will go by thy direction.
Toward Ludlow then, for we'll not stay behind.

Exeunt.

Scene 3. [*A street.*]

*Enter one Citizen at one door and another at the
other.*

First Citizen. Good morrow, neighbor. Whither away
so fast?

Second Citizen. I promise you, I scarcely know myself.
Hear you the news abroad?

First Citizen.   Yes, that the King is dead.

Second Citizen. Ill news, by'r Lady; seldom comes the
better.°
5   I fear, I fear 'twill prove a giddy world.

Enter another Citizen.

Third Citizen. Neighbors, Godspeed!

First Citizen.   Give you good morrow, sir.

Third Citizen. Doth the news hold of good King Edward's death?

Second Citizen. Ay, sir, it is too true, God help the
while!

Third Citizen. Then, masters, look to see a troublous
world.

First Citizen. No, no; by God's good grace his son
10   shall reign.

2.3.4 **seldom comes the better** change for the better is rare (a proverb)

Third Citizen. Woe to that land that's governed by a
  child!

Second Citizen. In him there is a hope of government,
  Which in his nonage counsel° under him,
  And, in his full and ripened years, himself,
  No doubt shall then and till then govern well.   *15*

First Citizen. So stood the state when Henry the Sixth
  Was crowned in Paris but at nine months old.

Third Citizen. Stood the state so? No, no, good
  friends, God wot!°
  For then this land was famously enriched
  With politic grave counsel; then the King   *20*
  Had virtuous uncles to protect his Grace.

First Citizen. Why, so hath this, both by his father and
  mother.

Third Citizen. Better it were they all came by his
  father,
  Or by his father there were none at all;
  For emulation° who shall now be nearest   *25*
  Will touch us all too near, if God prevent not.
  O, full of danger is the Duke of Gloucester,
  And the Queen's sons and brothers haught° and
  proud!
  And were they to be ruled,° and not to rule,
  This sickly land might solace° as before.   *30*

First Citizen. Come, come, we fear the worst. All will
  be well.

Third Citizen. When clouds are seen, wise men put on
  their cloaks;
  When great leaves fall, then winter is at hand;
  When the sun sets, who doth not look for night?
  Untimely storms makes men expect a dearth.°   *35*
  All may be well; but if God sort° it so,

12–13 **In him ... counsel** there is hope of good rule in him, during
whose minority advisers 18 **wot** knows 25 **emulation** rivalry
28 **haught** haughty 29 **were they to be ruled** if they could be controlled 30 **solace** take comfort 35 **dearth** famine 36 **sort** arrange

'Tis more than we deserve or I expect.

Second Citizen. Truly, the hearts of men are full of
    fear.
    You cannot reason,° almost, with a man
40 That looks not heavily and full of dread.

Third Citizen. Before the days of change, still is it so.
    By a divine instinct men's minds mistrust
    Ensuing danger, as by proof° we see
    The water swell before a boist'rous storm.
45 But leave it all to God. Whither away?

Second Citizen. Marry, we were sent for to the justices.

Third Citizen. And so was I. I'll bear you company.
                                              Exeunt.

Scene 4. [*The palace.*]

*Enter [the] Archbishop [of York], [the] young
    [Duke of] York, the Queen, [Elizabeth,] and
    the Duchess [of York].*

Archbishop. Last night, I hear, they lay at Stony
    Stratford;
    And at Northampton they do rest tonight;
    Tomorrow or next day they will be here.

Duchess of York. I long with all my heart to see the
    Prince.
5   I hope he is much grown since last I saw him.

Queen Elizabeth. But I hear no; they say my son of
    York
    Has almost overta'en him in his growth.

York. Ay, mother, but I would not have it so.

39 **reason** talk   43 **proof** experience

Duchess of York. Why, my good cousin? It is good to grow.

York. Grandam, one night as we did sit at supper,   10
My uncle Rivers talked how I did grow
More than my brother. "Ay," quoth my uncle Gloucester,
"Small herbs ·have grace,° great weeds do grow apace."°
And since, methinks, I would not grow so fast,
Because sweet flow'rs are slow and weeds make haste.   15

Duchess of York. Good faith, good faith, the saying did not hold
In him that did object° the same to thee.
He was the wretched'st thing when he was young,
So long a-growing and so leisurely,
That, if his rule were true, he should be gracious.°   20

Archbishop. And so no doubt he is, my gracious madam.

Duchess of York. I hope he is; but yet let mothers doubt.

York. Now, by my troth, if I had been remem'bred,°
I could have given my uncle's grace a flout°
To touch his growth nearer than he touched mine.   25

Duchess of York. How, my young York? I prithee let me hear it.

York. Marry, they say, my uncle grew so fast
That he could gnaw a crust at two hours old.
'Twas full two years ere I could get a tooth.
Grandam, this would have been a biting jest.   30

Duchess of York. I prithee, pretty York, who told thee this?

York. Grandam, his nurse.

2.4.13 **grace** virtue   13 **apace** quickly   17 **object** bring as a reproach   20 **gracious** virtuous   23 **been remem'bred** thought 24 **flout** taunt

Duchess of York. His nurse! Why, she was dead ere thou wast born.

York. If 'twere not she, I cannot tell who told me.

Queen Elizabeth. A parlous° boy! Go to, you are too
35   shrewd.°

Duchess of York. Good madam, be not angry with the child.

Queen Elizabeth. Pitchers have ears.°

Enter a Messenger.

Archbishop. Here comes a messenger. What news?

Messenger. Such news, my lord, as grieves me to report.

Queen Elizabeth. How doth the Prince?

40   *Messenger.*   Well, madam, and in health.

Duchess of York. What is thy news?

Messenger. Lord Rivers and Lord Grey are sent to Pomfret,
And with them Sir Thomas Vaughan, prisoners.

Duchess of York. Who hath committed them?

Messenger.   The mighty dukes,
Gloucester and Buckingham.

45   *Archbishop.*   For what offense?

Messenger. The sum of all I can I have disclosed.
Why or for what the nobles were committed
Is all unknown to me, my gracious lord.

Queen Elizabeth. Ay me! I see the ruin of my house.
50   The tiger now hath seized the gentle hind;°
Insulting tyranny begins to jut°
Upon the innocent and aweless° throne.
Welcome destruction, blood, and massacre!

---

35 **parlous** terribly quick-witted 35 **shrewd** sharp-tongued 37
Pitchers have ears (a proverb: small pitchers have great ears) 50 **hind**
doe 51 **jut** encroach 52 **aweless** inspiring no awe

I see, as in a map, the end of all.

Duchess of York. Accursèd and unquiet wrangling days,   55
  How many of you have mine eyes beheld!
  My husband lost his life to get the crown,
  And often up and down my sons were tossed
  For me to joy and weep their gain and loss;
  And being seated, and domestic broils°   60
  Clean overblown, themselves, the conquerors,
  Make war upon themselves, brother to brother,
  Blood to blood, self against self. O preposterous°
  And frantic outrage, end thy damnèd spleen,°
  Or let me die, to look on death no more!   65

Queen Elizabeth. Come, come, my boy; we will to sanctuary.°
  Madam, farewell.

Duchess of York. Stay, I will go with you.

Queen Elizabeth. You have no cause.

Archbishop.   [*To the Queen*] My gracious lady, go,
  And thither bear your treasure and your goods.
  For my part, I'll resign unto your Grace   70
  The seal I keep; and so betide to me
  As well I tender° you and all of yours!
  Go, I'll conduct you to the sanctuary.   *Exeunt.*

---

60 **domestic broils** civil wars 63 **preposterous** inverting natural order 64 **spleen** malice 66 **sanctuary** refuge on church property 72 **tender** care for

ACT 3

Scene 1. [*A street.*]

The trumpets sound. Enter [the] young Prince,
the Dukes of Gloucester and Buckingham,
Lord Cardinal, [Catesby,] with others.

Buckingham. Welcome, sweet Prince, to London, to
your chamber.°

Richard. Welcome, dear cousin, my thoughts' sovereign.
The weary way hath made you melancholy.

Prince Edward. No, uncle, but our crosses° on the
way
5   Have made it tedious, wearisome, and heavy.
I want° more uncles here to welcome me.

Richard. Sweet Prince, the untainted virtue of your
years
Hath not yet dived into the world's deceit;
Nor more can you distinguish of a man
10   Than of his outward show, which, God he knows,
Seldom or never jumpeth° with the heart.
Those uncles which you want were dangerous;

3.1.1 **chamber** capital   4 **crosses** vexations   6 **want** (1) lack (2) wish
for   11 **jumpeth** agrees

Your Grace attended to their sug'red words
But looked not on the poison of their hearts.
God keep you from them, and from such false
    friends!

15

Prince Edward. God keep me from false friends!
    But they were none.

Richard. My lord, the Mayor of London comes to
    greet you.

Enter Lord Mayor [and Citizens].

Lord Mayor. God bless your Grace with health and
    happy days!

Prince Edward. I thank you, good my lord, and thank
    you all.   [*Mayor and Citizens stand aside.*]
I thought my mother and my brother York
Would long ere this have met us on the way.
Fie, what a slug° is Hastings that he comes not
To tell us whether they will come or no!

20

Enter Lord Hastings.

Buckingham. And in good time here comes the sweat-
    ing lord.

Prince Edward. Welcome, my lord. What, will our
    mother come?

25

Hastings. On what occasion° God he knows, not I,
The Queen your mother and your brother York
Have taken sanctuary. The tender Prince
Would fain have come with me to meet your Grace,
But by his mother was perforce° withheld.

30

Buckingham. Fie, what an indirect and peevish°
    course
Is this of hers! Lord Cardinal, will your Grace
Persuade the Queen to send the Duke of York
Unto his princely brother presently?°

22 **slug** sluggard   26 **On what occasion** for what cause   30 **perforce**
by force   31 **indirect and peevish** devious and obstinate   34 **presently** at once

35   If she deny, Lord Hastings, go with him
     And from her jealous° arms pluck him perforce.

Cardinal. My Lord of Buckingham, if my weak or-
     atory
     Can from his mother win the Duke of York,
     Anon expect him here; but if she be obdurate
40   To mild entreaties, God in heaven forbid
     We should infringe the holy privilege
     Of blessèd sanctuary! Not for all this land
     Would I be guilty of so deep a sin.

Buckingham. You are too senseless-obstinate, my lord,
45   Too ceremonious° and traditional.
     Weigh it but with the grossness° of this age,
     You break not sanctuary in seizing him.
     The benefit thereof is always granted
     To those whose dealings have deserved the place
50   And those who have the wit to claim the place.
     This prince hath neither claimed it nor deserved it,
     And therefore, in mine opinion, cannot have it.
     Then, taking him from thence that is not there,
     You break no privilege nor charter there.
55   Oft have I heard of sanctuary men,
     But sanctuary children ne'er till now.

Cardinal. My lord, you shall o'errule my mind for
     once.
     Come on, Lord Hastings, will you go with me?

Hastings. I go, my lord.

Prince Edward. Good lords, make all the speedy haste
60   you may.   *Exit Cardinal and Hastings.*
     Say, uncle Gloucester, if our brother come,
     Where shall we sojourn till our coronation?

Richard. Where it seems best unto your royal self.
     If I may counsel you, some day or two
65   Your Highness shall repose you at the Tower;
     Then where you please, and shall be thought most
     fit

36 **jealous** suspicious 45 **ceremonious** punctilious 46 **grossness**
coarseness

For your best health and recreation.

Prince Edward. I do not like the Tower, of any place.°
Did Julius Caesar build that place, my lord?

Buckingham. He did, my gracious lord, begin that
place,   70
Which since succeeding ages have re-edified.°

Prince Edward. Is it upon record, or else reported
Successively from age to age, he built it?

Buckingham. Upon record, my gracious lord.

Prince Edward. But say, my lord, it were not reg-
ist'red,   75
Methinks the truth should live from age to age,
As 'twere retailed° to all posterity,
Even to the general all-ending day.

Richard. [*Aside*] So wise so young, they say do ne'er
live long.

Prince Edward. What say you, uncle?   80

Richard. I say, without characters° fame lives long.
[*Aside*] Thus, like the formal° Vice,° Iniquity,
I moralize° two meanings in one word.

Prince Edward. That Julius Caesar was a famous man.
With what° his valor did enrich his wit,   85
His wit set down to make his valor live.
Death makes no conquest of this conqueror,
For now he lives in fame, though not in life.
I'll tell you what, my cousin Buckingham—

Buckingham. What, my gracious lord?   90

Prince Edward. And if I live until I be a man,
I'll win our ancient right in France again
Or die a soldier as I lived a king.

---

68 **of any place** of all places   71 **re-edified** rebuilt   77 **retailed**
reported   81 **characters** written letters   82 **formal** careful to observe
forms (i.e., hypocritical)   82 **Vice** mischief-maker in a morality
play   83 **moralize** interpret   85 **With what** that with which

Richard. [*Aside*] Short summers lightly have a forward spring.°

  Enter [*the*] *young* [*Duke of*] *York, Hastings, and Cardinal.*

Buckingham. Now in good time here comes the Duke
95 of York.

Prince Edward. Richard of York, how fares our loving
brother?

York. Well, my dread° lord—so must I call you now.

Prince Edward. Ay, brother, to our grief, as it is yours.
Too late° he died that might have kept that title,
100 Which by his death hath lost much majesty.

Richard. How fares our cousin, noble Lord of York?

York. I thank you, gentle uncle. O, my lord,
You said that idle° weeds are fast in growth.
The Prince my brother hath outgrown me far.

Richard. He hath, my lord.

105 *York.*   And therefore is he idle?

Richard. O my fair cousin, I must not say so.

York. Then he is more beholding to you than I.

Richard. He may command me as my sovereign,
But you have power in me as in a kinsman.

110 *York.* I pray you, uncle, give me this dagger.

Richard. My dagger, little cousin? With all my heart.

Prince Edward. A beggar, brother?

York. Of my kind uncle, that I know will give,
And being but a toy,° which is no grief to give.

115 *Richard.* A greater gift than that I'll give my cousin.

---

94 **Short ... spring** i.e., the short-lived are usually (*lightly*) precocious 97 **dread** revered 99 **late** recently 103 **idle** useless 114 **toy** trifle

York. A greater gift? O, that's the sword to it.

Richard. Ay, gentle cousin, were it light enough.

York. O, then I see you will part but with light° gifts!
In weightier things you'll say a beggar nay.

Richard. It is too heavy for your Grace to wear.   120

York. I weigh° it lightly, were it heavier.

Richard. What, would you have my weapon, little
lord?

York. I would, that I might thank you as you call me.

Richard. How?

York. Little.   125

Prince Edward. My Lord of York will still be cross°
in talk.
Uncle, your Grace knows how to bear with him.

York. You mean, to bear me, not to bear with me.
Uncle, my brother mocks both you and me;
Because that I am little, like an ape,   130
He thinks that you should bear me on your
shoulders.°

Buckingham. [*Aside*] With what a sharp, provided°
wit he reasons!
To mitigate the scorn he gives his uncle
He prettily and aptly taunts himself.
So cunning and so young is wonderful.   135

Richard. My lord, will't please you pass along?
Myself and my good cousin Buckingham
Will to your mother, to entreat of her
To meet you at the Tower and welcome you.

York. What, will you go unto the Tower, my lord?   140

---

118 **light** slight 121 **weigh** value 126 **still be cross** always be contrary 131 **bear me on your shoulders** i.e., carry me on your hunch-
back 132 **provided** ready

Prince Edward. My Lord Protector needs will have it
    so.

York. I shall not sleep in quiet at the Tower.

Richard. Why, what should you fear?

York. Marry, my uncle Clarence' angry ghost.
145   My grandam told me he was murd'red there.

Prince Edward. I fear no uncles dead.

Richard. Nor none that live, I hope.

Prince Edward. And if they live, I hope I need not
    fear.
    But come, my lord; with a heavy heart,
150   Thinking on them, go I unto the Tower.
      A sennet.° Exeunt Prince [Edward], York, Hastings,
               [Cardinal, and others]. Manet Richard,
                       Buckingham, and Catesby.

Buckingham. Think you, my lord, this little prating
    York
    Was not incensed° by his subtle mother
    To taunt and scorn you thus opprobriously?

Richard. No doubt, no doubt. O, 'tis a parlous boy,
155   Bold, quick, ingenious, forward, capable:
    He is all the mother's, from the top to toe.

Buckingham. Well, let them rest. Come hither,
    Catesby.
    Thou art sworn as deeply to effect° what we in-
    tend
    As closely to conceal what we impart.
160   Thou knowest our reasons urged upon the way.
    What thinkest thou? Is it not an easy matter
    To make William Lord Hastings of our mind
    For the installment° of this noble duke
    In the seat royal of this famous isle?

165 *Catesby.* He for his father's sake so loves the Prince

150 s.d. **sennet** trumpet signal   152 **incensèd** stirred up   158 **effect**
carry out   163 **installment** installation as a king

That he will not be won to aught against him.

Buckingham. What thinkest thou then of Stanley?
      What will he?

Catesby. He will do all in all as Hastings doth.

Buckingham. Well then, no more but this: go, gentle
      Catesby,
   And, as it were far off, sound thou Lord Hastings   *170*
   How he doth stand affected° to our purpose,
   And summon him tomorrow to the Tower
   To sit° about the coronation.
   If thou dost find him tractable to us,
   Encourage him, and tell him all our reasons.   *175*
   If he be leaden, icy-cold, unwilling,
   Be thou so too, and so break off the talk,
   And give us notice of his inclination;
   For we tomorrow hold divided councils,°
   Wherein thyself shalt highly be employed.   *180*

Richard. Commend me to Lord William. Tell him,
      Catesby,
   His ancient knot° of dangerous adversaries
   Tomorrow are let blood at Pomfret Castle,
   And bid my lord, for joy of this good news,
   Give Mistress Shore one gentle kiss the more.   *185*

Buckingham. Good Catesby, go effect this business
      soundly.

Catesby. My good lords both, with all the heed I can.

Richard. Shall we hear from you, Catesby, ere we
      sleep?

Catesby. You shall, my lord.

Richard. At Crosby House, there shall you find us
      both.   *190*
                                        Exit Catesby.

171 **affected** inclined   173 **sit** meet with the council   179 **divided
councils** i.e., meetings of the council in two separate groups   182
ancient knot long-standing clique

Buckingham. Now, my lord, what shall we do if we
  perceive
  Lord Hastings will not yield to our complots?°

Richard. Chop off his head. Something we will determine.
  And look when° I am king, claim thou of me
195 The earldom of Hereford and all the movables°
  Whereof the King my brother was possessed.

Buckingham. I'll claim that promise at your Grace's
  hand.

Richard. And look° to have it yielded with all kindness.
  Come, let us sup betimes,° that afterwards
200 We may digest° our complots in some form.

                                             Exeunt.

          Scene 2. [*Before Lord Hastings' house.*]

          Enter a Messenger to the door of Hastings.

Messenger. My lord! My lord!

Hastings. [*Within*] Who knocks?

Messenger. One from the Lord Stanley.

Hastings. [*Within*] What is't o'clock?

5 *Messenger.* Upon the stroke of four.

                  Enter Lord Hastings.

Hastings. Cannot my Lord Stanley sleep these tedious
  nights?

Messenger. So it appears by that I have to say:

192 **complots** plots 194 **look when** whenever 195 **movables** goods
198 **look** expect 199 **betimes** early 200 **digest** arrange

First, he commends him to your noble self.

Hastings. What then?

Messenger. Then certifies your lordship that this night   10
    He dreamt the boar had rasèd off his helm.°
    Besides, he says there are two councils kept,
    And that may be determined at the one
    Which may make you and him to rue at th' other.
    Therefore he sends to know your lordship's
        pleasure,   15
    If you will presently take horse with him
    And with all speed post with him toward the
        north
    To shun the danger that his soul divines.

Hastings. Go, fellow, go return unto thy lord;
    Bid him not fear the separated council.   20
    His honor and myself are at the one,
    And at the other is my good friend Catesby;
    Where nothing can proceed that toucheth us
    Whereof I shall not have intelligence.
    Tell him his fears are shallow, without instance;°   25
    And for his dreams, I wonder he's so simple
    To trust the mock'ry of unquiet slumbers.
    To fly the boar before the boar pursues
    Were to incense the boar to follow us
    And make pursuit where he did mean no chase.   30
    Go bid thy master rise and come to me,
    And we will both together to the Tower,
    Where he shall see the boar will use us kindly.

Messenger. I'll go, my lord, and tell him what you
    say.   *Exit.*

                Enter Catesby.

Catesby. Many good morrows to my noble lord!   35

Hastings. Good morrow, Catesby; you are early stir-
    ring.
    What news, what news, in this our tott'ring state?

3.2.11 **the boar ... helm** i.e., Richard had cut off his head   25
instance cause

Catesby. It is a reeling world indeed, my lord,
    And I believe will never stand upright
40   Till Richard wear the garland of the realm.

Hastings. How! Wear the garland! Dost thou mean
    the crown?

Catesby. Ay, my good lord.

Hastings. I'll have this crown of mine cut from my
    shoulders
    Before I'll see the crown so foul misplaced.
45   But canst thou guess that he doth aim at it?

Catesby. Ay, on my life, and hopes to find you
    forward
    Upon his party° for the gain thereof;
    And thereupon he sends you this good news,
    That this same very day your enemies,
50   The kindred of the Queen, must die at Pomfret.

Hastings. Indeed I am no mourner for that news,
    Because they have been still my adversaries;
    But that I'll give my voice on Richard's side
    To bar my master's heirs in true descent,
55   God knows I will not do it, to the death!

Catesby. God keep your lordship in that gracious°
    mind!

Hastings. But I shall laugh at this a twelvemonth
    hence,
    That they which brought me in my master's hate,
    I live to look upon their tragedy.
60   Well, Catesby, ere a fortnight make me older,
    I'll send some packing° that yet think not on't.

Catesby. 'Tis a vile thing to die, my gracious lord,
    When men are unprepared and look not for it.

Hastings. O monstrous, monstrous! And so falls it out
65   With Rivers, Vaughan, Grey; and so 'twill do
    With some men else that think themselves as safe

47 **party** side 56 **gracious** virtuous 61 **send some packing** get rid
of some

As thou and I, who, as thou know'st, are dear
To princely Richard and to Buckingham.

Catesby. The Princes both make high account of
  you—
  [*Aside*] For they account his head upon the Bridge.° 70

Hastings. I know they do, and I have well deserved it.

    Enter Lord Stanley.

Come on, come on! Where is your boarspear, man?
Fear you the boar, and go so unprovided?

Stanley. My lord, good morrow; good morrow,
  Catesby.
You may jest on, but, by the holy rood,°   75
I do not like these several° councils, I.

Hastings. My lord, I hold my life as dear as yours,°
And never in my days, I do protest,
Was it so precious to me as 'tis now.
Think you, but that I know our state° secure,   80
I would be so triumphant as I am?

Stanley. The lords at Pomfret, when they rode from
  London,
Were jocund and supposed their states were sure,
And they indeed had no cause to mistrust;
But yet you see how soon the day o'ercast.   85
This sudden stab of rancor I misdoubt.°
Pray God, I say, I prove a needless coward!
What, shall we toward the Tower? The day is
  spent.°

Hastings. Come, come, have with you. Wot° you what,
  my lord?
Today the lords you talk of are beheaded.   90

Stanley. They, for their truth,° might better wear
  their heads

70 **the Bridge** London Bridge (where traitors' heads were displayed) 75 **rood** cross 76 **several** separate 77 **as yours** i.e., as
you do yours 80 **state** position 86 **misdoubt** have misgivings
about 88 **spent** wasted 89 **Wot** know 91 **truth** loyalty

Than some that have accused them wear their hats.
But come, my lord, let's away.

Enter a Pursuivant.°

Hastings. Go on before. I'll talk with this good fellow.
                    Exit Lord Stanley, and Catesby.
95   How now, sirrah?° How goes the world with thee?

Pursuivant. The better that your lordship please to
ask.

Hastings. I tell thee, man, 'tis better with me now
Than when thou met'st me last where now we meet.
Then was I going prisoner to the Tower
100 By the suggestion° of the Queen's allies;
But now I tell thee—keep it to thyself—
This day those enemies are put to death,
And I in better state than e'er I was.

Pursuivant. God hold it, to your honor's good content!

105 *Hastings.* Gramercy,° fellow; there, drink that for me.
                              Throws him his purse.

Pursuivant. I thank your honor.   *Exit Pursuivant.*

Enter a Priest.

Priest. Well met, my lord; I am glad to see your honor.

Hastings. I thank thee, good Sir° John, with all my
heart.
I am in your debt for your last exercise;°
110 Come the next Sabbath, and I will content° you.
                              He whispers in his ear.

Enter Buckingham.

Buckingham. What, talking with a priest, Lord Chamberlain?
Your friends at Pomfret, they do need the priest;

93 s.d. **Pursuivant** royal messenger with power to execute warrants   95 **sirrah** (common form of address to an inferior)   100 **suggestion** instigation   105 **Gramercy** much thanks   108 **Sir** (used for a
priest, as well as for a knight)   109 **exercise** sermon   110 **content**
reward

Your honor hath no shriving° work in hand.

Hastings. Good faith, and when I met this holy man
The men you talk of came into my mind.   *115*
What, go you toward the Tower?

Buckingham. I do, my lord, but long I cannot stay
there.
I shall return before your lordship thence.

Hastings. Nay, like enough, for I stay dinner there.

Buckingham. [*Aside*] And supper too, although thou
know'st it not.   *120*
Come, will you go?

Hastings.   I'll wait upon your lordship.
                                        Exeunt.

Scene 3. [*Pomfret Castle.*]

*Enter Sir Richard Ratcliffe, with Halberds,
carrying the Nobles, [Rivers, Grey, and
Vaughan,] to death at Pomfret.*

Rivers. Sir Richard Ratcliffe, let me tell thee this:
Today shalt thou behold a subject die
For truth, for duty, and for loyalty.

Grey. God bless the Prince from all the pack of you!
A knot you are of damnèd bloodsuckers.   *5*

Vaughan. You live that shall cry woe for this hereafter.

Ratcliffe. Dispatch; the limit of your lives is out.

Rivers. O Pomfret, Pomfret! O thou bloody prison,
Fatal and ominous to noble peers!
Within the guilty closure° of thy walls   *10*

113 **shriving** confessing   3.3.10 **closure** circuit

Richard the Second here was hacked to death;
And, for more slander° to thy dismal seat,
We give to thee our guiltless blood to drink.

Grey. Now Margaret's curse is fall'n upon our heads,
15   When she exclaimed on Hastings, you, and I,
For standing by when Richard stabbed her son.

Rivers. Then cursed she Richard, then cursed she Buckingham,
Then cursed she Hastings. O, remember, God,
To hear her prayer for them, as now for us!
20   And for my sister and her princely sons,
Be satisfied, dear God, with our true blood,
Which, as thou know'st, unjustly must be spilt.

Ratcliffe. Make haste; the hour of death is expiate.°

Rivers. Come, Grey, come, Vaughan, let us here embrace.
25   Farewell, until we meet again in heaven.   *Exeunt.*

Scene 4. [*The Tower.*]

Enter Buckingham, [Lord Stanley, Earl of]
Derby, Hastings, Bishop of Ely, Norfolk, Rat-
cliffe, Lovell, with others, at a table.

Hastings. Now, noble peers, the cause why we are met
Is to determine of the coronation.
In God's name, speak, when is the royal day?

Buckingham. Is all things ready for the royal time?

5   *Stanley.* It is, and wants but nomination.°

12 **slander** disgrace   23 **expiate** come for suffering   3.4.5 **nomination** naming

Bishop of Ely. Tomorrow then I judge a happy day.

Buckingham. Who knows the Lord Protector's mind
   herein?
   Who is most inward° with the noble Duke?

Bishop of Ely. Your Grace, we think, should soonest
   know his mind.

Buckingham. We know each other's faces; for our
   hearts,   10
   He knows no more of mine than I of yours;
   Or I of his, my lord, than you of mine.
   Lord Hastings, you and he are near in love.

Hastings. I thank his Grace, I know he loves me well;
   But for his purpose in the coronation   15
   I have not sounded him, nor he delivered
   His gracious pleasure any way therein.
   But you, my honorable lords, may name the time,
   And in the Duke's behalf I'll give my voice,
   Which I presume he'll take in gentle part.   20

   Enter [Richard, Duke of] Gloucester.

Bishop of Ely. In happy time here comes the Duke
   himself.

Richard. My noble lords and cousins all, good
   morrow.
   I have been long a sleeper, but I trust
   My absence doth neglect° no great design
   Which by my presence might have been concluded.   25

Buckingham. Had you not come upon your cue, my
   lord,
   William Lord Hastings had pronounced your part,
   I mean your voice for crowning of the King.

Richard. Than my Lord Hastings no man might be
   bolder.
   His lordship knows me well and loves me well.   30
   My Lord of Ely, when I was last in Holborn
   I saw good strawberries in your garden there.

8 **inward** intimate   24 **neglect** cause neglect of

    I do beseech you send for some of them.

Bishop of Ely. Marry, and will, my lord, with all my
    heart.   *Exit Bishop.*

35 *Richard.* Cousin of Buckingham, a word with you.
                                   [Takes him aside.]
    Catesby hath sounded Hastings in our business
    And finds the testy gentleman so hot
    That he will lose his head ere give consent
    His master's child, as worshipfully° he terms it,
40   Shall lose the royalty of England's throne.

Buckingham. Withdraw yourself awhile. I'll go with
    you.   *Exeunt [Richard and Buckingham].*

Stanley. We have not yet set down this day of tri-
    umph.
    Tomorrow, in my judgment, is too sudden;
    For I myself am not so well provided
45   As else I would be, were the day prolonged.°

              Enter the Bishop of Ely.

Bishop of Ely. Where is my lord the Duke of
    Gloucester?
    I have sent for these strawberries.

Hastings. His Grace looks cheerfully and smooth this
    morning;
    There's some conceit° or other likes° him well
50   When that he bids good morrow with such spirit.
    I think there's never a man in Christendom
    Can lesser hide his love or hate than he,
    For by his face straight shall you know his heart.

Stanley. What of his heart perceive you in his face
55   By any livelihood° he showed today?

Hastings. Marry, that with no man here he is offended;
    For were he, he had shown it in his looks.

---

39 **worshipfully** respectfully 45 **prolonged** postponed 49 **conceit**
idea 49 **likes** pleases 55 **livelihood** liveliness

Enter Richard and Buckingham.

Richard. I pray you all, tell me what they deserve
    That do conspire my death with devilish plots
    Of damnèd witchcraft, and that have prevailed   60
    Upon my body with their hellish charms.

Hastings. The tender love I bear your Grace, my lord,
    Makes me most forward in this princely presence
    To doom th' offenders, whosoe'er they be.
    I say, my lord, they have deservèd death.   65

Richard. Then be your eyes the witness of their evil.
    Look how I am bewitched. Behold, mine arm
    Is like a blasted sapling withered up;
    And this is Edward's wife, that monstrous witch,
    Consorted with that harlot strumpet Shore,   70
    That by their witchcraft thus have markèd me.

Hastings. If they have done this deed, my noble lord—

Richard. If! Thou protector of this damnèd strumpet,
    Talk'st thou to me of if's? Thou art a traitor.
    Off with his head! Now by Saint Paul I swear   75
    I will not dine until I see the same.
    Lovell and Ratcliffe, look that it be done.
    The rest that love me, rise and follow me.
                Exeunt. Manet Lovell and Ratcliffe, with
                                    the Lord Hastings.

Hastings. Woe, woe for England, not a whit for me!
    For I, too fond,° might have prevented this.   80
    Stanley did dream the boar did rase our helms,
    And I did scorn it and disdain to fly.
    Three times today my footcloth horse° did stumble,
    And started when he looked upon the Tower,
    As loath to bear me to the slaughterhouse.   85
    O, now I need the priest that spake to me!
    I now repent I told the pursuivant,
    As too triumphing, how mine enemies
    Today at Pomfret bloodily were butchered,

80 **fond** foolish   83 **footcloth horse** richly decorated horse

90   And I myself secure in grace and favor.
        O Margaret, Margaret, now thy heavy curse
        Is lighted on poor Hastings' wretched head!

Ratcliffe. Come, come, dispatch; the Duke would be
        at dinner.
        Make a short shrift;° he longs to see your head.

95   *Hastings.* O momentary grace° of mortal men,
        Which we more hunt for than the grace of God!
        Who builds his hope in air of your good looks
        Lives like a drunken sailor on a mast,
        Ready with every nod to tumble down
100   Into the fatal bowels of the deep.

Lovell. Come, come, dispatch; 'tis bootless° to ex-
        claim.

Hastings. O bloody Richard! Miserable England!
        I prophesy the fearful'st time to thee
        That ever wretched age hath looked upon.
105   Come, lead me to the block; bear him my head.
        They smile at me who shortly shall be dead.
                                                Exeunt.

        [Scene 5. *The Tower walls.*]

        Enter Richard, [Duke of Gloucester,] and Buck-
        ingham, in rotten° armor, marvelous ill-favored.°

Richard. Come, cousin, canst thou quake and change
        thy color,
        Murder thy breath in middle of a word,
        And then again begin, and stop again,
        As if thou wert distraught and mad with terror?

---

94 **shrift** confession   95 **grace** favor   101 **bootless** useless   3.5.s.d.
rotten worn-out   s.d.   **ill-favored** bad-looking

Buckingham. Tut, I can counterfeit the deep tra-
   gedian,   5
  Speak and look back, and pry on every side,
  Tremble and start at wagging of a straw,
  Intending° deep suspicion. Ghastly looks
  Are at my service, like enforcèd smiles;
  And both are ready in their offices°   10
  At any time to grace my stratagems.
  But what, is Catesby gone?

Richard. He is; and see, he brings the Mayor along.

        Enter the Mayor and Catesby.

Buckingham. Lord Mayor—

Richard. Look to the drawbridge there!   15

Buckingham. Hark! A drum.

Richard. Catesby, o'erlook° the walls.

Buckingham. Lord Mayor, the reason we have sent—

Richard. Look back, defend thee! Here are enemies.

Buckingham. God and our innocency defend and
   guard us!   20

    Enter Lovell and Ratcliffe, with Hastings' head.

Richard. Be patient, they are friends, Ratcliffe and
   Lovell.

Lovell. Here is the head of that ignoble traitor,
  The dangerous and unsuspected Hastings.

Richard. So dear I loved the man that I must weep:
  I took him for the plainest harmless creature   25
  That breathed upon the earth a Christian;
  Made him my book,° wherein my soul recorded
  The history of all her secret thoughts.
  So smooth he daubed° his vice with show of virtue
  That, his apparent open guilt omitted,   30

---

8 **Intending** pretending   10 **offices** functions   17 **o'erlook** watch
over   27 **book** notebook   29 **daubed** whitewashed

I mean his conversation° with Shore's wife,
He lived from all attainder of suspects.°

Buckingham. Well, well, he was the covert'st° shelt'red traitor
That ever lived.

35 Would you imagine, or almost believe,
Were't not that by great preservation
We live to tell it, that the subtle traitor
This day had plotted, in the council house,
To murder me and my good Lord of Gloucester?

40 *Mayor.* Had he done so?

Richard. What! Think you we are Turks or infidels?
Or that we would, against the form of law,
Proceed thus rashly in the villain's death
But that the extreme peril of the case,

45 The peace of England, and our persons' safety
Enforced us to this execution?

Mayor. Now fair befall you! He deserved his death,
And your good Graces both have well proceeded
To warn false traitors from the like attempts.

50 *Buckingham.* I never looked for better at his hands
After he once fell in with Mistress Shore.
Yet had we not determined he should die
Until your lordship came to see his end,
Which now the loving haste of these our friends,

55 Something against our meanings, have prevented;°
Because, my lord, I would have had you heard
The traitor speak, and timorously confess
The manner and the purpose of his treasons,
That you might well have signified the same

60 Unto the citizens, who haply may
Misconster° us in him and wail his death.

Mayor. But, my good lord, your Grace's words shall serve
As well as I had seen and heard him speak;

31 **conversation** intercourse 32 **from ... suspects** free from all stain
of suspicions 33 **covert'st** most secret 55 **prevented** forestalled
61 **Misconster** misjudge

And do not doubt, right noble princes both,
But I'll acquaint our duteous citizens   65
With all your just proceedings in this case.

Richard. And to that end we wished your lordship
    here,
T' avoid the censures of the carping world.

Buckingham. Which,° since you come too late of° our
    intent,
Yet witness what you hear we did intend.   70
And so, my good Lord Mayor, we bid farewell.

                                    Exit Mayor.

Richard. Go after, after, cousin Buckingham.
The Mayor towards Guildhall° hies him in all
    post.°
There, at your meetest° vantage of the time,
Infer° the bastardy of Edward's children.   75
Tell them how Edward put to death a citizen
Only for saying he would make his son
Heir to the Crown, meaning indeed his house,
Which by the sign thereof was termèd so.
Moreover, urge his hateful luxury°   80
And bestial appetite in change of lust,
Which stretched unto their servants, daughters,
    wives,
Even where his raging eye or savage heart,
Without control, lusted to make a prey.
Nay, for a need, thus far come near my person: 85
Tell them, when that my mother went with child
Of that insatiate Edward, noble York
My princely father then had wars in France,
And by true computation of the time
Found that the issue was not his begot;   90
Which well appearèd in his lineaments,
Being nothing like the noble Duke my father.
Yet touch this sparingly, as 'twere far off,
Because, my lord, you know my mother lives.

69 **Which** as to which   69 **of** for   73 **Guildhall** the city hall of London   73 **post** haste   74 **meetest** fittest   75 **Infer** bring forward as an argument   80 **luxury** lechery

95   *Buckingham.* Doubt not, my lord, I'll play the orator
      As if the golden fee for which I plead
      Were for myself; and so, my lord, adieu.

      Richard. If you thrive well, bring them to Baynard's
         Castle,
      Where you shall find me well accompanied
100   With reverend fathers and well-learnèd bishops.

      Buckingham. I go; and towards three or four o'clock
      Look for the news that the Guildhall affords.
                                        Exit Buckingham.

      Richard. Go, Lovell, with all speed to Doctor Shaw.
      [*To Catesby*] Go thou to Friar Penker. Bid them
         both
105   Meet me within this hour at Baynard's Castle.
                          Exeunt [*Lovell, Catesby, and Ratcliffe*].
      Now will I go to take some privy order°
      To draw the brats of Clarence out of sight,
      And to give order that no manner° person
      Have any time recourse unto the Princes.   *Exit.*

                    [Scene 6. *A street.*]

              Enter a Scrivener [*with a paper in his hand*].

      Scrivener. Here is the indictment of the good Lord
         Hastings,
      Which in a set° hand fairly is engrossed°
      That it may be today read o'er in Paul's.°
      And mark how well the sequel hangs together:
5   Eleven hours I have spent to write it over,
      For yesternight by Catesby was it sent me;
      The precedent° was full as long a-doing;

   106 **privy order** secret arrangement   108 **no manner** no sort of
   3.6.2 **set** formal   2 **fairly is engrossed** is written clearly   3 **Paul's** St.
   Paul's   7 **precedent** original draft

And yet within these five hours Hastings lived,
Untainted,° unexamined, free, at liberty.
Here's a good world the while! Who is so gross°   10
That cannot see this palpable device?°
Yet who so bold but says he sees it not?
Bad is the world, and all will come to nought
When such ill dealing must be seen in thought.°

                                        Exit.

[Scene 7. *Baynard's Castle.*]

Enter Richard, [Duke of Gloucester,] and Buck-
ingham at several° doors.

Richard. How now, how now? What say the citizens?

Buckingham. Now, by the holy Mother of our Lord,
    The citizens are mum, say not a word.

Richard. Touched you the bastardy of Edward's
    children?

Buckingham. I did, with his contract with Lady Lucy°   5
    And his contract by deputy° in France;
    Th' insatiate greediness of his desire
    And his enforcement of the city wives;
    His tyranny for trifles; his own bastardy,
    As being got,° your father then in France,   10
    And his resemblance,° being not like the Duke.
    Withal I did infer your lineaments,
    Being the right idea° of your father
    Both in your form and nobleness of mind;
    Laid open all your victories in Scotland,   15

9 **Untainted** not accused   10 **gross** dull   11 **palpable device** obvious
trick   14 **in thought** i.e., in silence   3.7. s.d. **several** separate   5
Lady Lucy Elizabeth Lucy (whose betrothal to Edward was never
proved)   6 **by deputy** (Edward had sent Warwick to arrange a French
marriage)   10 **got** begotten   11 **resemblance** appearance   13 **right
idea** exact image

Your discipline in war, wisdom in peace,
Your bounty, virtue, fair humility;
Indeed, left nothing fitting for your purpose
Untouched or slightly handlèd in discourse;
20 And when my oratory drew toward end,
I bid them that did love their country's good
Cry, "God save Richard, England's royal king!"

Richard. And did they so?

Buckingham. No, so God help me, they spake not a
       word,
25 But like dumb statues° or breathing stones
Stared each on other and looked deadly pale.
Which when I saw, I reprehended them
And asked the Mayor what meant this willful
       silence.
His answer was, the people were not usèd
30 To be spoke to but by the Recorder.°
Then he was urged to tell my tale again:
"Thus saith the Duke, thus hath the Duke in-
       ferred";
But nothing spoke in warrant from himself.
When he had done, some followers of mine own
35 At lower end of the hall hurled up their caps,
And some ten voices cried, "God save King
       Richard!"
And thus I took the vantage of those few:
"Thanks, gentle citizens and friends," quoth I.
"This general applause and cheerful shout
40 Argues your wisdom and your love to Richard";
And even here brake off and came away.

Richard. What tongueless blocks were they! Would
       they not speak?
Will not the Mayor then and his brethren come?

Buckingham. The Mayor is here at hand. Intend°
       some fear;
45 Be not you spoke with but by mighty suit;°

25 **statues** (pronounced "stat-u-es") 30 **Recorder** chief legal official
of the city 44 **Intend** pretend 45 **suit** petition

And look you get a prayer your hand
And stand between two ch
For on that ground° I'll make en, good my lord,
And be not easily won to our re descant;°
Play the maid's part: still answ y,° and take it.   50

Richard. I go; and if you plead as we
As I can say nay to thee for myself, them
No doubt we bring it to a happy issue.

Buckingham. Go, go up to the leads. The Lord
   Mayor knocks.   [E. Richard.]

      Enter the Mayor, and Citizens.
Welcome, my lord. I dance attendance here.   55
I think the Duke will not be spoke withal.°

      Enter Catesby.

Now, Catesby, what says your lord to my request?

Catesby. He doth entreat your Grace, my noble lord,
   To visit him tomorrow or next day.
   He is within, with two right reverend fathers,   60
   Divinely bent to meditation,
   And in no worldly suits would he be moved
   To draw him from his holy exercise.°

Buckingham. Return, good Catesby, to the gracious
   Duke.
   Tell him, myself, the Mayor and Aldermen,   65
   In deep designs, in matter of great moment,
   No less importing than our general good,
   Are come to have some conference with his Grace.

Catesby. I'll signify so much unto him straight.   *Exit.*

Buckingham. Ah ha, my lord, this prince is not an
   Edward!   70
   He is not lulling° on a lewd love-bed,

---

48 **ground** (1) melody (2) basis   48 **descant** (1) musical variation (2) argument   50 **still answer nay** always say no (a proverb)   54 **leads** flat roof covered with lead   56 **withal** with   63 **exercise** act of devotion   71 **lulling** lounging

              ditation;
But on his knee race of courtesans,
Not dallying w two deep divines;
But meditatin gross° his idle body,
Not sleeping nrich his watchful soul.
But praying gland, would this virtuous prince
Happy were ace the sovereignty thereof;
Take on hi r we shall not win him to it.
But sure I

Mayor. Ma', God defend° his Grace should say us
     nay!

Buckingho. I fear he will. Here Catesby comes
     agai

Enter Catesby.

Now, Catesby, what says his Grace?

Catesby. He wonders to what end you have assemblèd
     Such troops of citizens to come to him,
     His Grace not being warnèd thereof before.
     He fears, my lord, you mean no good to him.

Buckingham. Sorry I am my noble cousin should
     Suspect me that I mean no good to him.
     By heaven, we come to him in perfect love;
     And so once more return and tell his Grace.

                       Exit [Catesby].

When holy and devout religious men
Are at their beads, 'tis much° to draw them thence,
So sweet is zealous contemplation.

     Enter Richard aloft, between two Bishops.
         [Catesby returns.]

Mayor. See where his Grace stands 'tween two
     clergymen!

Buckingham. Two props of virtue for a Christian
     prince,
     To stay him from the fall° of vanity;
     And see, a book of prayer in his hand—

---

75 **engross** make fat   80 **defend** forbid   92 **much** hard   96 **fall** falling into sin

True ornaments to know a holy man.
Famous Plantagenet, most gracious Prince,
Lend favorable ear to our requests,　　　　　　　　　　*100*
And pardon us the interruption
Of thy devotion and right Christian zeal.

Richard. My lord, there needs no such apology.
I do beseech your Grace to pardon me,
Who, earnest in the service of my God,　　　　　　　　*105*
Deferred the visitation of my friends.
But, leaving this, what is your Grace's pleasure?

Buckingham. Even that, I hope, which pleaseth God
　　above
And all good men of this ungoverned isle.

Richard. I do suspect I have done some offense　　　*110*
That seems disgracious° in the city's eye,
And that you come to reprehend my ignorance.

Buckingham. You have, my lord. Would it might
　　please your Grace,
On our entreaties, to amend your fault!

Richard. Else wherefore breathe I in a Christian
　　land?　　　　　　　　　　　　　　　　　　　　　　*115*

Buckingham. Know then it is your fault that you
　　resign
The supreme seat, the throne majestical,
The scept'red office of your ancestors,
Your state° of fortune and your due of birth,
The lineal glory of your royal house,　　　　　　　　*120*
To the corruption of a blemished stock;
Whiles, in the mildness of your sleepy thoughts,
Which here we waken to our country's good,
The noble isle doth want his proper limbs;
His face defaced with scars of infamy,　　　　　　　　*125*
His royal stock graft° with ignoble plants,
And almost should'red in° the swallowing gulf
Of dark forgetfulness and deep oblivion.

111 **disgracious** displeasing　119 **state** high position　126 **graft**
grafted　127 **should'red in** jostled into

Which to recure,° we heartily solicit
130 Your gracious self to take on you the charge
And kingly government of this your land;
Not as protector, steward, substitute,
Or lowly factor° for another's gain,
But as successively,° from blood to blood,
135 Your right of birth, your empery,° your own.
For this, consorted with the citizens,
Your very worshipful and loving friends,
And by their vehement instigation,
In this just cause come I to move your Grace.

140 *Richard.* I cannot tell if to depart in silence
Or bitterly to speak in your reproof
Best fitteth my degree° or your condition.°
If not to answer, you might haply think
Tongue-tied ambition, not replying, yielded
145 To bear the golden yoke of sovereignty
Which fondly you would here impose on me.
If to reprove you for this suit of yours,
So seasoned° with your faithful love to me,
Then, on the other side, I checked° my friends.
150 Therefore, to speak, and to avoid the first,
And then, in speaking, not to incur the last,
Definitively° thus I answer you.
Your love deserves my thanks, but my desert
Unmeritable shuns your high request.
155 First, if all obstacles were cut away
And that my path were even° to the crown
As the ripe revenue and due of birth,
Yet so much is my poverty of spirit,°
So mighty and so many my defects,
160 That I would rather hide me from my greatness,
Being a bark to brook° no mighty sea,
Than in my greatness covet to be hid
And in the vapor of my glory smothered.

129 **recure** remedy   133 **factor** agent   134 **successively** by inheritance   135 **empery** supreme power   142 **degree** rank   142 **condition** status   148 **seasoned** given relish   149 **checked** should be
rebuking   152 **Definitively** once and for all   156 **even** clear   158
poverty of spirit lack of self-confidence   161 **bark to brook** small
ship able to endure

But, God be thanked, there is no need of me,
And much I need° to help you, were there need.   165
The royal tree hath left us royal fruit,
Which, mellowed by the stealing hours of time,
Will well become the seat of majesty
And make, no doubt, us happy by his reign.
On him I lay that you would lay on me,   170
The right and fortune of his happy stars,
Which God defend° that I should wring from him!

Buckingham. My lord, this argues conscience in your
    Grace,
But the respects thereof are nice° and trivial,
All circumstances well consider̀ed.   175
You say that Edward is your brother's son.
So say we too, but not by Edward's wife;
For first was he contract to Lady Lucy—
Your mother lives a witness to his vow—
And afterward by substitute betrothed   180
To Bona, sister to the King of France.
These both put off, a poor petitioner,
A care-crazed mother to a many sons,
A beauty-waning and distress̀ed widow,
Even in the afternoon of her best days,   185
Made prize and purchase° of his wanton eye,
Seduced the pitch° and height of his degree
To base declension° and loathed bigamy.
By her, in his unlawful bed, he got
This Edward, whom our manners call the Prince.   190
More bitterly could I expostulate,
Save that for reverence to some alive
I give a sparing limit to my tongue.
Then, good my lord, take to your royal self
This proffered benefit of dignity;°   195
If not to bless us and the land withal,
Yet to draw forth your noble ancestry

---

165 **need** lack   172 **defend** forbid   174 **respects thereof are nice**
considerations about it are too scrupulous   186 **purchase** booty   187
pitch high point (of a hawk's flight)   188 **base declension** ignoble
falling low   195 **benefit of dignity** gift of greatness

From the corruption of abusing times
Unto a lineal true-derivèd course.

200 *Mayor.* Do, good my lord; your citizens entreat you.

Buckingham. Refuse not, mighty lord, this proffered
      love.

Catesby. O, make them joyful, grant their lawful suit!

Richard. Alas, why would you heap this care on me?
      I am unfit for state and majesty.
205   I do beseech you take it not amiss,
      I cannot nor I will not yield to you.

Buckingham. If you refuse it, as in love and zeal
      Loath to depose the child, your brother's son—
      As well we know your tenderness of heart
210   And gentle, kind, effeminate remorse,°
      Which we have noted in you to your kindred
      And egally° indeed to all estates—
      Yet know, whe'r° you accept our suit or no,
      Your brother's son shall never reign our king,
215   But we will plant some other in the throne
      To the disgrace and downfall of your house;
      And in this resolution here we leave you.
      Come, citizens. Zounds, I'll entreat no more!

Richard. O, do not swear, my lord of Buckingham.
                  Exeunt [Buckingham, Mayor, and Citizens].

Catesby. Call him again, sweet Prince, accept their
220   suit.
      If you deny them, all the land will rue it.

Richard. Will you enforce me to a world of cares?
      Call them again. I am not made of stone,
      But penetrable to your kind entreaties,
225   Albeit against my conscience and my soul.

                  Enter Buckingham and the rest.

Cousin of Buckingham, and sage grave men,

210 **effeminate remorse** softhearted pity   212 **egally** equally   213
whe'r whether

Since you will buckle fortune on my back,
To bear her burden, whe'r I will or no,
I must have patience to endure the load;
But if black scandal or foul-faced reproach   230
Attend the sequel of your imposition,°
Your mere enforcement° shall acquittance° me
From all the impure blots and stains thereof;
For God doth know, and you may partly see,
How far I am from the desire of this.   235

Mayor. God bless your Grace! We see it and will say it.

Richard. In saying so you shall but say the truth.

Buckingham. Then I salute you with this royal title:
Long live King Richard, England's worthy king!

All. Amen.   240

Buckingham. Tomorrow may it please you to be crowned?

Richard. Even when you please, for you will have it so.

Buckingham. Tomorrow then we will attend your Grace,
And so most joyfully we take our leave.

Richard. [*To the Bishops*] Come, let us to our holy work again.   245
Farewell, my cousin; farewell, gentle friends.

                                        Exeunt.

---

231 **imposition** laying on the burden   232 **Your mere enforcement** the simple fact of your compulsion   232 **acquittance** release

ACT 4

Scene 1. [*Before the Tower.*]

*Enter the Queen, [Elizabeth,] the Duchess of
York, and Marquis [of] Dorset [at one door];
Anne, Duchess of Gloucester, [with Clarence's
daughter, at another door].*

Duchess of York. Who meets us here? My niece°
    Plantagenet,
Led in the hand of her kind aunt of Gloucester!
Now, for my life, she's wand'ring to the Tower
On pure heart's love to greet the tender Prince.
Daughter, well met.

5   *Anne.*   God give your Graces both
    A happy and a joyful time of day!

Queen Elizabeth. As much to you, good sister!
    Whither away?

Anne. No farther than the Tower, and, as I guess,
    Upon the like devotion° as yourselves,
10 To gratulate° the gentle princes there.

Queen Elizabeth. Kind sister, thanks. We'll enter all
    together.

4.1.1.**niece** granddaughter 9 **devotion** purpose 10 **gratulate** greet
with joy

Enter the Lieutenant [Brakenbury].

And in good time here the Lieutenant comes.
Master Lieutenant, pray you, by your leave,
How doth the Prince, and my young son of York?

Lieutenant. Right well, dear madam. By your patience,   15
I may not suffer you to visit them;
The King hath strictly charged the contrary.

Queen Elizabeth. The King? Who's that?

Lieutenant.   I mean the Lord Protector.

Queen Elizabeth. The Lord protect him from that
    kingly title!
Hath he set bounds between their love and me?   20
I am their mother; who shall bar me from them?

Duchess of York. I am their father's mother; I will
    see them.

Anne. Their aunt I am in law, in love their mother.
Then bring me to their sights; I'll bear thy blame
And take thy office° from thee on my peril.   25

Lieutenant. No, madam, no; I may not leave° it so.
I am bound by oath, and therefore pardon me.
                                        Exit Lieutenant.

Enter Stanley, [Earl of Derby].

Stanley. Let me but meet you, ladies, one hour hence,
And I'll salute your Grace of York as mother
And reverend looker-on of two fair queens.   30
[*To Anne*] Come, madam, you must straight to
    Westminster,
There to be crownèd Richard's royal queen.

Queen Elizabeth. Ah, cut my lace° asunder,
That my pent heart may have some scope to beat,
Or else I swoon with this dead-killing news!   35

Anne. Despiteful° tidings! O unpleasing news!

25 **take thy office** take over your duty   26 **leave** abandon   33 **lace**
bodice string   36 **Despiteful** cruel

Dorset. Be of good cheer; mother, how fares your
  Grace?

Queen Elizabeth. O Dorset, speak not to me, get thee
    gone!
  Death and destruction dogs thee at thy heels;
40 Thy mother's name is ominous to children.
  If thou wilt outstrip death, go cross the seas
  And live with Richmond, from° the reach of hell.
  Go hie thee, hie thee from this slaughterhouse,
  Lest thou increase the number of the dead
45 . And make me die the thrall° of Margaret's curse,
  Nor mother, wife, nor England's counted queen.°

Stanley. Full of wise care is this your counsel, madam.
  Take all the swift advantage of the hours.
  You shall have letters from me to my son°
50 In your behalf, to meet you on the way.
  Be not ta'en tardy° by unwise delay.

Duchess of York. O ill-dispersing° wind of misery!
  O my accursèd womb, the bed of death!
  A cockatrice° hast thou hatched to the world,
55 Whose unavoided eye is murderous.

Stanley. Come, madam, come; I in all haste was sent.

Anne. And I with all unwillingness will go.
  O, would to God that the inclusive verge°
  Of golden metal that must round° my brow
60 Were red-hot steel to sear me to the brains!
  Anointed let me be with deadly venom
  And die ere men can say, "God save the Queen!"

Queen Elizabeth. Go, go, poor soul! I envy not thy
    glory.
  To feed my humor° wish thyself no harm.

65 *Anne.* No? Why, when he that is my husband now

42 **from** away from 45 **thrall** slave 46 **England's counted queen**
regarded as Queen of England 49 **son** i.e., his wife's son,
Richmond 51 **ta'en tardy** caught napping 52 **ill-dispersing** scat-
tering evil 54 **cockatrice** fabulous monster, basilisk (see 1.2.150)
58 **inclusive verge** enclosing rim 59 **round** encircle 64 **feed my
humor** satisfy my mood

Came to me as I followed Henry's corse,
When scarce the blood was well washed from his
   hands
Which issuèd from my other angel husband
And that dear saint which then I weeping fol-
   lowed—
O, when, I say, I looked on Richard's face,   70
This was my wish: "Be thou," quoth I, "accursed
For making me, so young, so old a widow!°
And when thou wed'st, let sorrow haunt thy bed;
And be thy wife, if any be so mad,
More miserable by the life of thee   75
Than thou hast made me by my dear lord's death!"
Lo, ere I can repeat this curse again,
Within so small a time, <u>my woman's heart</u>   *
Grossly grew captive to his <u>honey words</u>
And proved the subject of mine own soul's curse,   80
Which hitherto hath held mine eyes from rest;
For never yet one hour in his bed
Did I enjoy the golden dew of sleep,
But with his timorous dreams was still° awaked.
Besides, he hates me for my father Warwick,   85
And will, no doubt, shortly be rid of me.

Queen Elizabeth. Poor heart, adieu! I pity thy complaining.

Anne. No more than with my soul I mourn for yours.

Dorset. Farewell, thou woeful welcomer of glory!

Anne. Adieu, poor soul that tak'st thy leave of it!   90

Duchess of York. [*To Dorset*] Go thou to Richmond,
   and good fortune guide thee!
   [*To Anne*] Go thou to Richard, and good angels
   tend thee!
   [*To Queen Elizabeth*] Go thou to sanctuary, and
   good thoughts possess thee!
   I to my grave, where peace and rest lie with me!
   Eighty odd years of sorrow have I seen,   95

72 **so old a widow** a widow so aged by grief   84 **still** continually

And each hour's joy wracked° with a week of teen.°

Queen Elizabeth. Stay, yet look back with me unto the
Tower.
Pity, you ancient stones, those tender babes
Whom envy hath immured within your walls,
100   Rough cradle for such little pretty ones!
Rude ragged nurse, old sullen playfellow
For tender princes, use my babies well!
So foolish sorrow bids your stones farewell.   *Exeunt.*

Scene 2. [*The palace.*]

*Sound a sennet. Enter Richard, in pomp, Buck-
ingham, Catesby, Ratcliffe, Lovell, [a Page, and
others].*

King Richard. Stand all apart. Cousin of Buckingham!

Buckingham. My gracious sovereign?

King Richard. Give me thy hand.
                    Sound. [He ascends the throne.]
                        Thus high, by thy advice
And thy assistance, is King Richard seated.
5   But shall we wear these glories for a day?
Or shall they last, and we rejoice in them?

Buckingham. Still live they, and forever let them last!

King Richard. Ah, Buckingham, now do I play the
touch°
To try if thou be current gold indeed.
Young Edward lives—think now what I would
10   speak.

Buckingham. Say on, my loving lord.

96 **wracked** ruined   96 **teen** grief   4.2.8 **touch** touchstone (used to
test gold)

King Richard. Why, Buckingham, I say I would be
  king.

Buckingham. Why, so you are, my thrice-renownèd
  lord.

King Richard. Ha! Am I king? 'Tis so; but Edward
  lives.

Buckingham. True, noble Prince.

King Richard.   O bitter consequence,°   15
  That Edward still should live true noble prince!
  Cousin, thou wast not wont to be so dull.
  Shall I be plain? I wish the bastards dead,
  And I would have it suddenly performed.
  What say'st thou now? Speak suddenly, be brief.   20

Buckingham. Your Grace may do your pleasure.

King Richard. Tut, tut, thou art all ice, thy kindness
  freezes.
  Say, have I thy consent that they shall die?

Buckingham. Give me some little breath, some pause,
  dear lord,
  Before I positively speak in this.   25
  I will resolve° you herein presently.
                              Exit Buckingham.

Catesby. [*Aside to another*] The King is angry. See,
  he gnaws his lip.

King Richard. I will converse° with iron-witted° fools
  And unrespective° boys. None are for me
  That look into me with considerate° eyes.   30
  High-reaching Buckingham grows circumspect.
  Boy!

Page. My lord?

King Richard. Know'st thou not any whom corrupting
  gold

15 **consequence** sequel   26 **resolve** answer   28 **converse** keep company   28 **iron-witted** dull-witted   29 **unrespective** heedless   30
considerate thoughtful

35   Will tempt unto a close exploit° of death?

Page. I know a discontented gentleman
Whose humble means match not his haughty spirit.
Gold were as good as twenty orators
And will, no doubt, tempt him to anything.

King Richard. What is his name?

40   *Page.*   His name, my lord, is Tyrrel.

King Richard. I partly know the man. Go call him
hither, boy.   *Exit [Page].*
The deep-revolving witty° Buckingham
No more shall be the neighbor to my counsels.
45   Hath he so long held out° with me, untired,
And stops he now for breath? Well, be it so.

Enter Stanley, [Earl of Derby].

How now, Lord Stanley? What's the news?

Stanley.   Know, my loving lord,
The Marquis Dorset, as I hear, is fled
To Richmond in the parts where he abides.
                                       [Stands aside.]

King Richard. Come hither, Catesby. Rumor it abroad
50   That Anne my wife is very grievous sick;
I will take order for her keeping close.
Inquire me out some mean poor gentleman,
Whom I will marry straight to Clarence' daughter.
The boy is foolish,° and I fear not him.
55   Look how thou dream'st! I say again, give out
That Anne my queen is sick and like to die.
About it; for it stands me much upon°
To stop all hopes whose growth may damage me.
                                       [Exit Catesby.]
I must be married to my brother's daughter,
60   Or else my kingdom stands on brittle glass.
Murder her brothers and then marry her!

35 **close exploit** secret deed 42 **deep-revolving witty** deeply-
pondering clever 44 **held out** kept up 54 **foolish** an idiot 57
stands me much upon is very important to me

Uncertain way of gain! But I am in
So far in blood that sin will pluck on sin.
Tear-falling pity dwells not in this eye.

Enter Tyrrel.

Is thy name Tyrrel?   65

Tyrrel. James Tyrrel, and your most obedient subject.

King Richard. Art thou indeed?

Tyrrel.   Prove me, my gracious lord.

King Richard. Dar'st thou resolve to kill a friend of
    mine?

Tyrrel. Please° you;
    But I had rather kill two enemies.   70

King Richard. Why, there thou hast it! Two deep
    enemies,
Foes to my rest and my sweet sleep's disturbers,
Are they that I would have thee deal upon.
Tyrrel, I mean those bastards in the Tower.

Tyrrel. Let me have open means to come to them,   75
    And soon I'll rid you from the fear of them.

King Richard. Thou sing'st sweet music. Hark, come
    hither, Tyrrel.
Go, by this token. Rise, and lend thine ear. *Whispers.*
There is no more but so. Say it is done,
And I will love thee and prefer° thee for it.   80

Tyrrel. I will dispatch it straight.   *Exit.*

Enter Buckingham.

Buckingham. My lord, I have considered in my mind
    The late request that you did sound me in.

King Richard. Well, let that rest. Dorset is fled to
    Richmond.

Buckingham. I hear the news, my lord.   85

69 **Please** If it pleases   80 **prefer** advance

King Richard. Stanley, he is your wife's son. Well,
   look unto it.

Buckingham. My lord, I claim the gift, my due by
   promise,
   For which your honor and your faith is pawned:°
   Th' earldom of Hereford and the movables
90   Which you have promisèd I shall possess.

King Richard. Stanley, look to your wife; if she convey
   Letters to Richmond, you shall answer it.

Buckingham. What says your Highness to my just
   request?

King Richard. I do remember me, Henry the Sixth
95   Did prophesy that Richmond should be king
   When Richmond was a little peevish° boy.
   A king! Perhaps, perhaps.

Buckingham. My lord!

King Richard. How chance the prophet could not at
   that time
100   Have told me, I being by, that I should kill him?

Buckingham. My lord, your promise for the earldom!

King Richard. Richmond! When last I was at Exeter,
   The Mayor in courtesy showed me the castle,
   And called it Rugemont; at which name I started,
105   Because a bard of Ireland told me once
   I should not live long after I saw Richmond.

Buckingham. My lord!

King Richard. Ay, what's o'clock?

Buckingham. I am thus bold to put your Grace in
   mind
   Of what you promised me.

110 *King Richard.*   Well, but what's o'clock?

Buckingham. Upon the stroke of ten.

88 **pawned** pledged 96 **peevish** childish

King Richard.   Well, let it strike.

Buckingham. Why let it strike?

King Richard. Because that like a Jack° thou keep'st
   the stroke°
Betwixt thy begging and my meditation.
I am not in the giving vein today.   *115*

Buckingham. May it please you to resolve me in my
   suit.

King Richard. Thou troublest me; I am not in the vein.
       Exit [King Richard, and all but Buckingham].

Buckingham. And is it thus? Repays he my deep
   service
With such contempt? Made I him king for this?
O, let me think on Hastings, and be gone   *120*
To Brecknock while my fearful head is on!   *Exit.*

[Scene 3. *The palace.*]

Enter Tyrrel.

Tyrrel. The tyrannous and bloody act is done,
   The most arch° deed of piteous massacre
   That ever yet this land was guilty of.
   Dighton and Forrest, who I did suborn
   To do this piece° of ruthful° butchery,   *5*
   Albeit they were fleshed° villains, bloody dogs,
   Melted with tenderness and mild compassion,
   Wept like to children in their death's sad story.
   "O thus," quoth Dighton, "lay the gentle babes."
   "Thus, thus," quoth Forrest, "girdling one another   *10*

---

113 **Jack** (1) figure of a man on a clock, striking the hour (2) knave
113 **thou keep'st the stroke** you keep on making a noise   4.3.2
arch extreme 5 **piece** masterpiece 5 **ruthful** piteous 6 **fleshed**
experienced

Within their alabaster innocent arms.
Their lips were four red roses on a stalk
And in their summer beauty kissed each other.
A book of prayers on their pillow lay,
Which once," quoth Forrest, "almost changed my
15   mind;
But O, the devil"—there the villain stopped;
When Dighton thus told on: "We smotherèd
The most replenishèd° sweet work of Nature
That from the prime° creation e'er she framèd."
20 Hence both are gone with conscience and remorse
They° could not speak; and so I left them both,
To bear this tidings to the bloody King.

Enter [King] Richard.

And here he comes. All health, my sovereign lord!

King Richard. Kind Tyrrel, am I happy in thy news?

25 *Tyrrel.* If to have done the thing you gave in charge
Beget° your happiness, be happy then,
For it is done.

King Richard.   But didst thou see them dead?

Tyrrel. I did, my lord.

King Richard.   And buried, gentle Tyrrel?

Tyrrel. The chaplain of the Tower hath buried them;
30 But where (to say the truth) I do not know.

King Richard. Come to me, Tyrrel, soon at after-
supper,°
When thou shalt tell the process° of their death.
Meantime, but think how I may do thee good
And be inheritor of thy desire.
Farewell till then.

35 *Tyrrel.*   I humbly take my leave.   *[Exit.]*

King Richard. The son of Clarence have I pent up
close;

18 **replenishèd** complete   19 **prime** first   21 **They** i.e., which they
26 **Beget** cause   31 **aftersupper** late supper   32 **process** story

His daughter meanly have I matched in marriage;
The sons of Edward sleep in Abraham's bosom,°
And Anne my wife hath bid this world good night.
Now, for° I know the Britain° Richmond aims   40
At young Elizabeth, my brother's daughter,
And by that knot° looks proudly on the crown,
To her go I, a jolly thriving wooer.

Enter Ratcliffe.

Ratcliffe. My lord!

King Richard. Good or bad news, that thou com'st in
    so bluntly?   45

Ratcliffe. Bad news, my lord. Morton is fled to Rich-
    mond,
And Buckingham, backed with the hardy Welsh-
    men,
Is in the field, and still his power increaseth.

King Richard. Ely with Richmond troubles me more
    near
Than Buckingham and his rash-levied° strength.   50
Come, I have learned that fearful commenting°
Is leaden servitor to dull delay;
Delay leads impotent and snail-paced beggary.°
Then fiery expedition° be my wing,
Jove's Mercury, and herald for a king!   55
Go muster men. My counsel is my shield;
We must be brief when traitors brave the field.
                      Exeunt.

---

38 **Abraham's bosom** paradise   40 **for** because   40 **Britain** Breton
42 **knot** marriage tie   50 **rash-levied** hastily raised   51 **fearful com-
menting** timorous meditating   53 **beggary** bankruptcy   54 **expedition** speed

[Scene 4. *The palace.*]

Enter old Queen Margaret.

Queen Margaret. So now prosperity begins to mellow
And drop into the rotten mouth of death.
Here in these confines slily have I lurked
To watch the waning of mine enemies.
5   A dire induction° am I witness to,
And will to France, hoping the consequence°
Will prove as bitter, black, and tragical.
Withdraw thee, wretched Margaret. Who comes
    here?   [*Retires.*]

Enter Duchess [of York] and Queen [Elizabeth].

Queen Elizabeth. Ah, my poor princes, ah, my tender
    babes!
10   My unblown° flow'rs, new-appearing sweets!
If yet your gentle souls fly in the air
And be not fixed in doom perpetual,
Hover about me with your airy wings
And hear your mother's lamentation!

Queen Margaret. [*Aside*] Hover about her, say that
15   right for right
Hath dimmed your infant morn to agèd night.

Duchess of York. So many miseries have crazed° my
    voice
That my woe-wearied tongue is still and mute.
Edward Plantagenet, why art thou dead?

Queen Margaret. [*Aside*] Plantagenet doth quit°
20   Plantagenet,

4.4.5 **induction** opening scene   6 **consequence** following part   10
unblown unblossomed   17 **crazed** cracked   20 **quit** make up for

Edward for Edward pays a dying debt.

Queen Elizabeth. Wilt thou, O God, fly from such
gentle lambs
And throw them in the entrails of the wolf?
When didst thou sleep when such a deed was done?

Queen Margaret. [*Aside*] When holy Harry died, and
my sweet son.   25

Duchess of York. Dead life, blind sight, poor mortal
living ghost,
Woe's scene, world's shame, grave's due by life
usurped,
Brief abstract° and record of tedious days,
Rest thy unrest on England's lawful earth,
                                              [*Sits down.*]
Unlawfully made drunk with innocent blood!   30

Queen Elizabeth. Ah that thou wouldst as soon afford
a grave
As thou canst yield a melancholy seat!
Then would I hide my bones, not rest them here.
Ah, who hath any cause to mourn but we?
                                         [*Sits down by her.*]

Queen Margaret. [*Comes forward*] If ancient sorrow
be most reverend,   35
Give mine the benefit of seniory°
And let my griefs frown on the upper hand.°
If sorrow can admit society, [*Sits down with them.*]
Tell° o'er your woes again by viewing mine.
I had an Edward, till a Richard killed him;   40
I had a husband, till a Richard killed him.
Thou hadst an Edward, till a Richard killed him;
Thou hadst a Richard, till a Richard killed him.

Duchess of York. I had a Richard too, and thou didst
kill him;
I had a Rutland too, thou holp'st° to kill him.   45

28 **abstract** summary   36 **seniory** seniority   37 **on the upper hand**
i.e., above all others   39 **Tell** count   45 **holp'st** helpedst

Queen Margaret. Thou hadst a Clarence too, and
    Richard killed him.
    From forth the kennel of thy womb hath crept
    A hellhound that doth hunt us all to death.
    That dog that had his teeth before his eyes
50   To worry lambs and lap their gentle blood,
    That foul defacer of God's handiwork,
    That excellent grand° tyrant of the earth
    That reigns in gallèd° eyes of weeping souls,
    Thy womb let loose to chase us to our graves.
55   O upright, just, and true-disposing° God,
    How do I thank thee that this carnal° cur
    Preys on the issue of his mother's body
    And makes her pewfellow° with others' moan!

Duchess of York. O Harry's wife, triumph not in my
    woes!
60   God witness with me I have wept for thine.

Queen Margaret. Bear with me; I am hungry for re-
    venge,
    And now I cloy me with beholding it.
    Thy Edward he is dead, that killed my Edward;
    Thy other Edward dead, to quit my Edward;
65   Young York he is but boot,° because both they
    Matched not the high perfection of my loss.
    Thy Clarence he is dead that stabbed my Edward,
    And the beholders of this frantic play,
    Th' adulterate° Hastings, Rivers, Vaughan, Grey,
70   Untimely smothered in their dusky graves.
    Richard yet lives, hell's black intelligencer,°
    Only reserved their factor° to buy souls
    And send them thither. But at hand, at hand,
    Ensues his piteous and unpitied end.
75   Earth gapes, hell burns, fiends roar, saints pray,
    To have him suddenly conveyed from hence.

---

52 **excellent grand** surpassingly chief 53 **gallèd** sore from rub-
bing 55 **true-disposing** justly ordaining 56 **carnal** carnivorous 58
pewfellow companion 65 **but boot** only a makeweight 69 **adul-
terate** adulterous 71 **intelligencer** secret agent 72 **Only reserved
their factor** kept alive merely as agent for the powers of hell

Cancel his bond of life, dear God, I pray,
That I may live and say, "The dog is dead."

Queen Elizabeth. O, thou didst prophesy the time
　would come
That I should wish for thee to help me curse　　80
That bottled spider, that foul bunch-backed toad!

Queen Margaret. I called thee then vain flourish of
　my fortune;
I called thee then poor shadow, painted queen,
The presentation of but° what I was,
The flattering index° of a direful pageant,°　　85
One heaved a-high° to be hurled down below,
A mother only mocked with two fair babes,
A dream of what thou wast, a garish° flag
To be the aim of every dangerous shot,
A sign of dignity, a breath, a bubble,　　90
A queen in jest, only to fill the scene.
Where is thy husband now? Where be thy brothers?
Where be thy two sons? Wherein dost thou joy?
Who sues and kneels and says, "God save the
　Queen"?
Where be the bending peers that flatterèd thee?　　95
Where be the thronging troops that followèd thee?
Decline° all this, and see what now thou art:
For happy wife, a most distressèd widow;
For joyful mother, one that wails the name;
For one being sued to, one that humbly sues;　　100
For queen, a very caitiff° crowned with care;
For she that scorned at me, now scorned of me;
For she being feared of all, now fearing one;
For she commanding all, obeyed of none.
Thus hath the course of justice whirled about　　105
And left thee but a very prey to time,
Having no more but thought of what thou wast
To torture thee the more, being what thou art.

---

84 **presentation of but** image only of　85 **flattering index** deceptive
prologue　85 **pageant** stage show　86 **a-high** on high　88 **garish**
showy　97 **Decline** recite in order　101 **very caitiff** truly unhappy
wretch

Thou didst usurp my place, and dost thou not
110 Usurp the just proportion° of my sorrow?
Now thy proud neck bears half my burdened yoke,
From which even here I slip my wearied head
And leave the burden of it all on thee.
Farewell, York's wife, and queen of sad mischance!
115 These English woes shall make me smile in France.

Queen Elizabeth. Oh thou well skilled in curses, stay
awhile
And teach me how to curse mine enemies!

Queen Margaret. Forbear to sleep the nights, and fast
the days;
Compare dead happiness with living woe;
120 Think that thy babes were sweeter than they were
And he that slew them fouler than he is.
Bett'ring° thy loss makes the bad causer worse;
Revolving° this will teach thee how to curse.

Queen Elizabeth. My words are dull; O, quicken°
them with thine!

Queen Margaret. Thy woes will make them sharp and
125 pierce like mine.   *Exit [Queen] Margaret.*

Duchess of York. Why should calamity be full of
words?

Queen Elizabeth. Windy attorneys to their client's
woes,°
Airy succeeders of intestate joys,°
Poor breathing orators of miseries,
130 Let them have scope! Though what they will impart
Help nothing else, yet do they ease the heart.

Duchess of York. If so, then be not tongue-tied. Go
with me
And in the breath of bitter words let's smother
My damnèd son that thy two sweet sons smothered.

110 **just proportion** exact extent   122 **Bett'ring** magnifying   123
Revolving meditating on   124 **quicken** give life to   127 **attorneys to
their client's woes** spokesmen for the griefs of the one who employs
them (i.e., words)   128 **succeeders of intestate joys** successors of joys
which died without leaving a will

The trumpet sounds. Be copious in exclaims.   *135*

*Enter King Richard and his Train, [marching
with Drums and Trumpets].*

King Richard. Who intercepts me in my expedition?°

Duchess of York. O, she that might have intercepted thee,
By strangling thee in her accursèd womb,
From all the slaughters, wretch, that thou hast done!

Queen Elizabeth. Hid'st thou that forehead with a golden crown   *140*
Where should be branded, if that right were right,
The slaughter of the prince that owed° that crown
And the dire death of my poor sons and brothers?
Tell me, thou villain-slave, where are my children?

Duchess of York. Thou toad, thou toad, where is thy brother Clarence?   *145*
And little Ned Plantagenet, his son?

Queen Elizabeth. Where is the gentle Rivers, Vaughan, Grey?

Duchess of York. Where is kind Hastings?

King Richard. A flourish, trumpets! Strike alarum, drums!
Let not the heavens hear these telltale women   *150*
Rail on the Lord's anointed. Strike, I say!
                    Flourish. Alarums.
Either be patient and entreat me fair,°
Or with the clamorous report of war
Thus will I drown your exclamations.

Duchess of York. Art thou my son?   *155*

King Richard. Ay, I thank God, my father, and yourself.

Duchess of York. Then patiently hear my impatience.

---

136 **expedition** (1) campaign (2) haste   142 **owed** owned   152 **entreat me fair** treat me courteously

King Richard. Madam, I have a touch of your con-
    dition°
    That cannot brook the accent of reproof.

Duchess of York. O, let me speak!

160 *King Richard.*   Do then; but I'll not hear.

Duchess of York. I will be mild and gentle in my
    words.

King Richard. And brief, good mother, for I am in
    haste.

Duchess of York. Art thou so hasty? I have stayed°
    for thee,
    God knows, in torment and in agony.

165 *King Richard.* And came I not at last to comfort you?

Duchess of York. No, by the holy rood, thou know'st
    it well,
    Thou cam'st on earth to make the earth my hell.
    A grievous burden was thy birth to me;
    Tetchy° and wayward was thy infancy;
    Thy schooldays frightful, desp'rate, wild, and furi-
170   ous;
    Thy prime of manhood daring, bold, and venturous;
    Thy age confirmed,° proud, subtle, sly, and bloody,
    More mild, but yet more harmful, kind in hatred.
    What comfortable hour canst thou name
175   That ever graced me with thy company?

King Richard. Faith, none but Humphrey Hour,° that
    called your Grace
    To breakfast once forth of my company.
    If I be so disgracious° in your eye,
    Let me march on and not offend you, madam.
    Strike up the drum.

180 *Duchess of York.*   I prithee hear me speak.

158 **condition** disposition 163 **stayed** waited 169 **Tetchy** fretful
172 **age confirmed** maturity 176 **Humphrey Hour** (apparently the
name of a man, chosen for the play on *comfortable hour*) 178 **disgracious** displeasing

King Richard. You speak too bitterly.

Duchess of York.   Hear me a word;
   For I shall never speak to thee again.

King Richard. So.

Duchess of York. Either thou wilt die by God's just
      ordinance
   Ere from this war thou turn° a conqueror,   185
   Or I with grief and extreme age shall perish
   And never more behold thy face again.
   Therefore take with thee my most grievous curse,
   Which in the day of battle tire thee more
   Than all the complete armor that thou wear'st!   190
   My prayers on the adverse party fight!
   And there the little souls of Edward's children
   Whisper the spirits of thine enemies
   And promise them success and victory!
   Bloody thou art, bloody will be thy end;   195
   Shame serves thy life and doth thy death attend.
                                                        Exit.

Queen Elizabeth. Though far more cause, yet much
      less spirit to curse
   Abides in me. I say amen to her.

King Richard. Stay, madam; I must talk a word with
      you.

Queen Elizabeth. I have no moe° sons of the royal
      blood   200
   For thee to slaughter. For my daughters, Richard,
   They shall be praying nuns, not weeping queens;
   And therefore level° not to hit their lives.

King Richard. You have a daughter called Elizabeth,
   Virtuous and fair, royal and gracious.   205

Queen Elizabeth. And must she die for this? O, let her
      live,
   And I'll corrupt her manners,° stain her beauty,

185 **turn** return   200 **moe** more (in number)   203 **level** aim   207
manners habits

Slander myself as false to Edward's bed,
Throw over her the veil of infamy;
210 So she may live unscarred of bleeding slaughter,
I will confess she was not Edward's daughter.

King Richard. Wrong not her birth; she is a royal
princess.

Queen Elizabeth. To save her life, I'll say she is not so.

King Richard. Her life is safest only in her birth.

Queen Elizabeth. And only in that safety died her
215 brothers.

King Richard. Lo, at their birth good stars were opposite.

Queen Elizabeth. No, to their lives ill friends were
contrary.

King Richard. All unavoided° is the doom° of destiny.

Queen Elizabeth. True, when avoided grace° makes
destiny.
220 My babes were destined to a fairer death
If grace had blessed thee with a fairer life.

King Richard. You speak as if that I had slain my
cousins!

Queen Elizabeth. Cousins indeed, and by their uncle
cozened°
Of comfort, kingdom, kindred, freedom, life.
225 Whose hand soever lanced their tender hearts,
Thy head (all indirectly°) gave direction.
No doubt the murd'rous knife was dull and blunt
Till it was whetted on thy stone-hard heart
To revel in the entrails of my lambs.
230 But that still use° of grief makes wild grief tame,
My tongue should to thy ears not name my boys
Till that my nails were anchored in thine eyes;

218 **unavoided** inevitable 218 **doom** decree 219 **avoided grace**
i.e., the rejection of God's grace (by Richard) 223 **cozened** defrauded
226 **indirectly** underhandedly 230 **still use** continued habit

And I, in such a desp'rate bay of death,
Like a poor bark of sails and tackling reft,
Rush all to pieces on thy rocky bosom.   235

King Richard. Madam, so thrive I in my enterprise
And dangerous success° of bloody wars
As I intend more good to you and yours
Than ever you and yours by me were harmed!

Queen Elizabeth. What good is covered with the face
    of heaven,   240
To be discovered, that can do me good?

King Richard. Th' advancement of your children,
    gentle lady.

Queen Elizabeth. Up to some scaffold, there to lose
    their heads!

King Richard. Unto the dignity and height of fortune,
The high imperial type° of this earth's glory.   245

Queen Elizabeth. Flatter my sorrow with report of it.
Tell me, what state, what dignity, what honor
Canst thou demise° to any child of mine?

King Richard. Even all I have—ay, and myself and all
Will I withal° endow a child of thine,   250
So in the Lethe° of thy angry soul
Thou drown the sad remembrance of those wrongs
Which thou supposest I have done to thee.

Queen Elizabeth. Be brief, lest that the process° of
    thy kindness
Last longer telling than thy kindness' date.°   255

King Richard. Then know that from my soul I love
    thy daughter.

Queen Elizabeth. My daughter's mother thinks it with
    her soul.

---

237 **success** result   245 **type** symbol   248 **demise** convey legally
250 **withal** with   251 **Lethe** river of oblivion   254 **process** story
255 **date** duration

King Richard. What do you think?

Queen Elizabeth. That thou dost love my daughter
from° thy soul.
260 So from thy soul's love didst thou love her brothers,
And from my heart's love I do thank thee for it.

King Richard. Be not so hasty to confound my mean-
ing.
I mean that with my soul I love thy daughter
And do intend to make her Queen of England.

Queen Elizabeth. Well then, who dost thou mean shall
265 be her king?

King Richard. Even he that makes her queen. Who
else should be?

Queen Elizabeth. What, thou?

King Richard.   Even so. How think you of it?

Queen Elizabeth. How canst thou woo her?

King Richard.   That would I learn of you,
As one being best acquainted with her humor.°

Queen Elizabeth. And wilt thou learn of me?

270 *King Richard.*   Madam, with all my heart.

Queen Elizabeth. Send to her by the man that slew her
brothers
A pair of bleeding hearts; thereon engrave
"Edward" and "York." Then haply will she weep;
Therefore present to her—as sometimes° Margaret
275 Did to thy father, steeped in Rutland's blood—
A handkerchief, which, say to her, did drain
The purple sap from her sweet brother's body,
And bid her wipe her weeping eyes withal.°
If this inducement move her not to love,
280 Send her a letter of thy noble deeds:
Tell her thou mad'st away her uncle Clarence,
Her uncle Rivers; ay, and for her sake

259 **from** apart from (i.e., not with) 269 **humor** disposition 274
sometimes once 278 **withal** with (it)

Mad'st quick conveyance° with her good aunt
    Anne.

King Richard. You mock me, madam; this is not the
    way
To win your daughter,

Queen Elizabeth.   There is no other way,   285
Unless thou couldst put on some other shape
And not be Richard that hath done all this.

King Richard. Say that I did all this for love of her.

Queen Elizabeth. Nay, then indeed she cannot choose
    but hate thee,
Having bought love with such a bloody spoil.°   290

King Richard. Look what° is done cannot be now
    amended.
Men shall deal unadvisedly° sometimes,
Which afterhours gives leisure to repent.
If I did take the kingdom from your sons,
To make amends I'll give it to your daughter.   295
If I have killed the issue of your womb,
To quicken your increase° I will beget
Mine issue of your blood upon your daughter.
A grandam's name is little less in love
Than is the doting title of a mother;   300
They are as children but one step below,
Even of your metal,° of your very blood,
Of all one pain, save for a night of groans
Endured of° her for whom you bid° like sorrow.
Your children were vexation to your youth,   305
But mine shall be a comfort to your age.
The loss you have is but a son being king,
And by that loss your daughter is made queen.
I cannot make you what amends I would;
Therefore accept such kindness as I can.   310
Dorset your son, that with a fearful soul

283 **conveyance** (1) carrying off (2) underhand dealing   290 **spoil**
destruction   291 **Look what** whatever   292 **shall deal unadvisedly**
are bound to act thoughtlessly   297 **quicken your increase** give life to
your offspring   302 **metal** substance   304 **of** by   304 **bid** suffered

Leads discontented steps in foreign soil,
This fair alliance° quickly shall call home
To high promotions and great dignity.
315 The king that calls your beauteous daughter wife
Familiarly shall call thy Dorset brother.
Again shall you be mother to a king,
And all the ruins of distressful times
Repaired with double riches of content.
320 What! We have many goodly days to see.
The liquid drops of tears that you have shed
Shall come again, transformed to orient° pearl,
Advantaging their loan with interest
Of ten times double gain of happiness.
325 Go then, my mother, to thy daughter go;
Make bold her bashful years with your experience;
Prepare her ears to hear a wooer's tale.
Put in her tender heart th' aspiring flame
Of golden sovereignty; acquaint the Princess
330 With the sweet silent hours of marriage joys.
And when this arm of mine hath chastisèd
The petty rebel, dull-brained Buckingham,
Bound with triumphant garlands will I come
And lead thy daughter to a conqueror's bed;
335 To whom I will retail° my conquest won,
And she shall be sole victoress, Caesar's Caesar.

Queen Elizabeth. What were I best to say? Her father's
    brother
Would be her lord? Or shall I say her uncle?
Or he that slew her brothers and her uncles?
340 Under what title shall I woo for thee
That God, the law, my honor, and her love
Can make seem pleasing to her tender years?

King Richard. Infer° fair England's peace by this alli-
    ance.

Queen Elizabeth. Which she shall purchase with still-
    lasting war.

313 **alliance** marriage   322 **orient** shining   335 **retail** recount   343
Infer bring forward as an argument

King Richard. Tell her the King, that may command, entreats. 345

Queen Elizabeth. That at her hands which the King's King forbids.

King Richard. Say she shall be a high and mighty queen.

Queen Elizabeth. To wail the title, as her mother doth.

King Richard. Say I will love her everlastingly.

Queen Elizabeth. But how long shall that title "ever" last? 350

King Richard. Sweetly in force unto her fair life's end.

Queen Elizabeth. But how long fairly shall her sweet life last?

King Richard. As long as heaven and nature lengthens it.

Queen Elizabeth. As long as hell and Richard likes of it.

King Richard. Say I, her sovereign, am her subject low. 355

Queen Elizabeth. But she, your subject, loathes such sovereignty.

King Richard. Be eloquent in my behalf to her.

Queen Elizabeth. An honest tale speeds best being° plainly told.

King Richard. Then plainly to her tell my loving tale.

Queen Elizabeth. Plain and not honest is too harsh° a style. 360

King Richard. Your reasons are too shallow and too quick.

---

358 **speeds best being** succeeds best when it is　360 **harsh** discordant

Queen Elizabeth. O no, my reasons are too deep and
    dead;
  Too deep and dead, poor infants, in their graves.

King Richard. Harp not on that string, madam; that
  is past.

Queen Elizabeth. Harp on it still shall I till heart-
365 strings break.

King Richard. Now, by my George, my garter,° and
  my crown—

Queen Elizabeth. Profaned, dishonored, and the third
  usurped.

King Richard. I swear—

Queen Elizabeth.   By nothing, for this is no oath:
  Thy George, profaned, hath lost his lordly honor;
370 Thy garter, blemished, pawned his knightly virtue;
  Thy crown, usurped, disgraced his kingly glory.
  If something thou wouldst swear to be believed,
  Swear then by something that thou hast not
  wronged.

King Richard. Then by myself—

Queen Elizabeth.   Thyself is self-misused.

King Richard. Now by the world—

375 *Queen Elizabeth.*   'Tis full of thy foul wrongs.

King Richard. My father's death—

Queen Elizabeth.   Thy life hath it dishonored.

King Richard. Why then, by God—

Queen Elizabeth.   God's wrong is most of all.
  If thou didst fear to break an oath with him,
  The unity the King my husband made
380 Thou hadst not broken, nor my brothers died.
  If thou hadst feared to break an oath by him,

366 **George ... garter** insignia of the Order of the Garter (a figure of St. George and a velvet ribbon)

Th' imperial metal circling now thy head
Had graced the tender temples of my child,
And both the Princes had been breathing here,
Which now, two tender bedfellows for dust,   *385*
Thy broken faith hath made the prey for worms.
What canst thou swear by now?

King Richard.   The time to come.

Queen Elizabeth. That thou hast wrongèd in the time
    o'erpast;
For I myself have many tears to wash
Hereafter° time, for time past wronged by thee.   *390*
The children live whose fathers thou hast slaugh-
    tered,
Ungoverned° youth, to wail it in their age;
The parents live whose children thou hast butch-
    ered,
Old barren plants, to wail it with their age.
Swear not by time to come, for that thou hast   *395*
Misused ere used, by times ill-used o'erpast.

King Richard. As I intend to prosper and repent,
So thrive I in my dangerous affairs
Of hostile arms! Myself myself confound!°
Heaven and fortune bar me happy hours!   *400*
Day, yield me not thy light, nor, night, thy rest!
Be opposite all planets of good luck
To my proceeding if, with dear heart's love,
Immaculate devotion, holy thoughts,
I tender° not thy beauteous princely daughter!   *405*
In her consists my happiness and thine;
Without her, follows to myself and thee,
Herself, the land, and many a Christian soul,
Death, desolation, ruin, and decay.
It cannot be avoided but by this;   *410*
It will not be avoided but by this.
Therefore, dear mother—I must call you so—
Be the attorney of my love to her.
Plead what I will be, not what I have been;

390 **Hereafter** future 392 **Ungoverned** unguided 399 **confound**
ruin 405 **tender** look after tenderly

415   Not my deserts, but what I will deserve.
             Urge the necessity and state of times,°
             And be not peevish-fond° in great designs.

Queen Elizabeth. Shall I be tempted of the devil thus?

King Richard. Ay, if the devil tempt you to do good.

420   *Queen Elizabeth.* Shall I forget myself to be myself?°

King Richard. Ay, if yourself's remembrance wrong
             yourself.

Queen Elizabeth. Yet thou didst kill my children.

King Richard. But in your daughter's womb I'll bury
             them,
             Where in that nest of spicery° they will breed
425   Selves of themselves, to your recomforture.°

Queen Elizabeth. Shall I go win my daughter to thy
             will?

King Richard. And be a happy mother by the deed.

Queen Elizabeth. I go. Write to me very shortly,
             And you shall understand from me her mind.

King Richard. Bear her my truelove's kiss; and so
430   farewell.
                                        Exit Queen [Elizabeth].
             Relenting fool, and shallow, changing woman!

             Enter Ratcliffe, [Catesby following].

             How now! What news?

Ratcliffe. Most mighty sovereign, on the western coast
             Rideth a puissant° navy; to our shores
435   Throng many doubtful hollow-hearted friends,
             Unarmed, and unresolved° to beat them back.
             'Tis thought that Richmond is their admiral;

416 **state of times** condition of affairs   417 **peevish-fond** obstinately
foolish   420 **myself to be myself** that I am I   424 **nest of spicery**
(alludes to the nest of the phoenix, a bird that periodically returned to its
fragrant nest, where it was consumed in flame and arose renewed)   425
recomforture consolation   434 **puissant** powerful   436 **unresolved**
irresolute

And there they hull,° expecting° but the aid
Of Buckingham to welcome them ashore.

King Richard. Some light-foot friend post° to the
  Duke of Norfolk: *440*
Ratcliffe, thyself—or Catesby; where is he?

Catesby. Here, my good lord.

King Richard.   Catesby, fly to the Duke.

Catesby. I will, my lord, with all convenient° haste.

King Richard. Ratcliffe, come hither. Post to Salisbury.
When thou com'st thither—[*To Catesby*] Dull un-
  mindful villain,   *445*
Why stay'st thou here and go'st not to the Duke?

Catesby. First, mighty liege, tell me your Highness'
  pleasure
What from your Grace I shall deliver to him.

King Richard. O, true, good Catesby. Bid him levy
  straight
The greatest strength and power that he can make *450*
And meet me suddenly at Salisbury.

Catesby. I go.   *Exit.*

Ratcliffe. What, may it please you, shall I do at Salisbury?

King Richard. Why, what wouldst thou do there before I go?

Ratcliffe. Your Highness told me I should post before. *455*

King Richard. My mind is changed.

            Enter Lord Stanley, [*Earl of Derby*].

                    Stanley, what news with you?

Stanley. None good, my liege, to please you with the
  hearing,

438 **hull** drift with the wind   438 **expecting** awaiting   440 **post** has-
ten   443 **convenient** appropriate

Nor none so bad but well may be reported.

King Richard. Hoyday, a riddle! Neither good nor
  bad!
460 What need'st thou run so many miles about
  When thou mayest tell thy tale the nearest way?
  Once more, what news?

Stanley.   Richmond is on the seas.

King Richard. There let him sink, and be the seas on
  him!
  White-livered runagate,° what doth he there?

465 *Stanley.* I know not, mighty sovereign, but by guess.

King Richard. Well, as you guess?

Stanley. Stirred up by Dorset, Buckingham, and Morton,
  He makes for England, here to claim the crown.

King Richard. Is the chair empty? Is the sword un-
  swayed?
470 Is the King dead, the empire unpossessed?
  What heir of York is there alive but we?
  And who is England's King but great York's heir?
  Then tell me, what makes he upon the seas?

Stanley. Unless for that, my liege, I cannot guess.

King Richard. Unless for that he comes to be your
475   liege,
  You cannot guess wherefore the Welshman comes.
  Thou wilt revolt and fly to him, I fear.

Stanley. No, my good lord; therefore mistrust me not.

King Richard. Where is thy power then to beat him
  back?
480 Where be thy tenants and thy followers?
  Are they not now upon the western shore,
  Safe-conducting the rebels from their ships?

464 **runagate** fugitive

Stanley. No, my good lord, my friends are in the
　　north.

King Richard. Cold friends to me! What do they in
　　the north
　　When they should serve their sovereign in the west?　485

Stanley. They have not been commanded, mighty
　　King.
　　Pleaseth your Majesty to give me leave,
　　I'll muster up my friends and meet your Grace
　　Where and what time your Majesty shall please.

King Richard. Ay, thou wouldst be gone to join with
　　Richmond.　　　　　　　　　　　　　　　　　490
　　But I'll not trust thee.

Stanley.　　　　　　　Most mighty sovereign,
　　You have no cause to hold my friendship doubtful.
　　I never was nor never will be false.

King Richard. Go then and muster men; but leave be-
　　hind
　　Your son George Stanley. Look your heart be firm,　495
　　Or else his head's assurance° is but frail.

Stanley. So deal with him as I prove true to you.
　　　　　　　　　　　　　　　　　　Exit Stanley.

　　　　　　　　Enter a Messenger.

First Messenger. My gracious sovereign, now in Dev-
　　onshire,
　　As I by friends am well advertisèd,°
　　Sir Edward Courtney and the haughty prelate,　　500
　　Bishop of Exeter, his elder brother,
　　With many moe confederates, are in arms.

　　　　　　　Enter another Messenger.

Second Messenger. In Kent, my liege, the Guilfords
　　are in arms,

---

496 **assurance** security　499 **advertisèd** informed

And every hour more competitors°
505   Flock to the rebels, and their power grows strong.

Enter another Messenger.

Third Messenger. My lord, the army of great Buckingham—

King Richard. Out on ye, owls! Nothing but songs of
death?   *He striketh him.*
There, take thou that, till thou bring better news.

Third Messenger. The news I have to tell your Maj-
esty
510   Is that by sudden floods and fall of waters
Buckingham's army is dispersed and scattered,
And he himself wand'red away alone,
No man knows whither.

King Richard.   I cry thee mercy.
There is my purse to cure that blow of thine.
515   Hath any well-advisèd friend proclaimed
Reward to him that brings the traitor in?

Third Messenger. Such proclamation hath been made,
my lord.

Enter another Messenger.

Fourth Messenger. Sir Thomas Lovell and Lord Mar-
quis Dorset,
'Tis said, my liege, in Yorkshire are in arms,
520   But this good comfort bring I to your Highness:
The Britain° navy is dispersed by tempest.
Richmond in Dorsetshire sent out a boat
Unto the shore to ask those on the banks
If they were his assistants, yea or no;
525   Who answered him they came from Buckingham
Upon his party. He, mistrusting them,
Hoised° sail and made his course again for Britain.°

---

504 **competitors** associates   521 **Britain** Breton   527 **Hoised** hoisted
527 **Britain** Brittany

King Richard. March on, march on, since we are up
   in arms,
  If not to fight with foreign enemies,
  Yet to beat down these rebels here at home.   *530*

              Enter Catesby.

Catesby. My liege, the Duke of Buckingham is taken.
  That is the best news. That the Earl of Richmond
  Is with a mighty power landed at Milford
  Is colder news, but yet they must be told.

King Richard. Away towards Salisbury! While we rea-
   son here,   *535*
  A royal battle might be won and lost.
  Someone take order Buckingham be brought
  To Salisbury; the rest march on with me.
                    Flourish. Exeunt.

           [Scene 5. *Lord Stanley's house.*]

     *Enter [Lord Stanley, Earl of] Derby, and
     Sir Christopher [Urswick, a chaplain].*

Stanley. Sir Christopher, tell Richmond this from me:
  That in the sty of the most deadly boar
  My son George Stanley is franked up in hold;°
  If I revolt, off goes young George's head;
  The fear of that holds off my present aid.   *5*
  So get thee gone; commend me to thy lord.
  Withal say that the Queen hath heartily consented
  He should espouse Elizabeth her daughter.
  But tell me, where is princely Richmond now?

4.5.3 franked up in hold penned up in custody (*frank*=sty)

Christopher. At Pembroke or at Harfordwest° in
10   Wales.

Stanley. What men of name resort to him?

Christopher. Sir Walter Herbert, a renownèd soldier,
Sir Gilbert Talbot, Sir William Stanley,
Oxford, redoubted Pembroke, Sir James Blunt,
15   And Rice ap Thomas, with a valiant crew,
And many other of great name and worth;
And towards London do they bend their power,
If by the way they be not fought withal.

Stanley. Well, hie thee to thy lord. I kiss his hand;
20   My letter will resolve° him of my mind.
                                        [*Gives letter.*]
      Farewell.   *Exeunt.*

10 **Harfordwest** Haverfordwest   20 **resolve** inform

ACT 5

Scene 1. [*Salisbury. An open place.*]

*Enter Buckingham with [Sheriff and] Halberds,°
led to execution.*

Buckingham. Will not King Richard let me speak with
  him?

Sheriff. No, my good lord; therefore be patient.

Buckingham. Hastings, and Edward's children, Grey
  and Rivers,
  Holy King Henry and thy fair son Edward,
  Vaughan, and all that have miscarrièd   5
  By underhand corrupted foul injustice,
  If that your moody discontented souls
  Do through the clouds behold this present hour,
  Even for revenge mock my destruction!
  This is All Souls' day, fellow, is it not?   10

Sheriff. It is, my lord.

Buckingham. Why, then All Souls' day is my body's
  doomsday.
  This is the day which in King Edward's time
  I wished might fall on me when I was found
  False to his children and his wife's allies.   15

5.1.s.d. **Halberds** guards armed with long poleaxes

This is the day wherein I wished to fall
By the false faith of him whom most I trusted.
This, this All Souls' day to my fearful soul
Is the determined respite of my wrongs.°
20 That high All-seer which I dallied with
Hath turned my feignèd prayer on my head
And given in earnest what I begged in jest.
Thus doth he force the swords of wicked men
To turn their own points in their masters' bosoms.
25 Thus Margaret's curse falls heavy on my neck:
"When he," quoth she, "shall split thy heart with
sorrow,
Remember Margaret was a prophetess."
Come lead me, officers, to the block of shame;
Wrong hath but wrong, and blame the due of
blame.

Exeunt Buckingham with Officers.

Scene 2. [*Camp near Tamworth.*]

*Enter Richmond, Oxford, Blunt, Herbert,
and others, with Drum and Colors.*

Richmond. Fellows in arms and my most loving
friends,
Bruised underneath the yoke of tyranny,
Thus far into the bowels° of the land
Have we marched on without impediment;
5 And here receive we from our father Stanley
Lines of fair comfort and encouragement.
The wretched, bloody, and usurping boar,
That spoiled your summer fields and fruitful vines,
Swills your warm blood like wash, and makes his
trough

19 **determined respite of my wrongs** end of reprieve for my unjust
acts   5.2.3 **bowels** center

In your emboweled° bosoms, this foul swine   10
Is now even in the center of this isle,
Near to the town of Leicester, as we learn.
From Tamworth thither is but one day's march.
In God's name cheerly on, courageous friends,
To reap the harvest of perpetual peace   15
By this one bloody trial of sharp war.

Oxford. Every man's conscience is a thousand men
To fight against this guilty homicide.

Herbert. I doubt not but his friends will turn to us.

Blunt. He hath no friends but what are friends for
fear,   20
Which in his dearest need will fly from him.

Richmond. All for our vantage. Then in God's name
march!
True hope is swift and flies with swallow's wings;
Kings it makes gods, and meaner creatures kings.
                                        Exeunt omnes.

[Scene 3. *Bosworth Field.*]

*Enter King Richard in arms, with Norfolk,
Ratcliffe, and the Earl of Surrey,
[and Soldiers].*

King Richard. Here pitch our tent, even here in Bosworth field.
My Lord of Surrey, why look you so sad?

Surrey. My heart is ten times lighter than my looks.

King Richard. My Lord of Norfolk!

Norfolk.   Here, most gracious liege.

10 **emboweled** ripped up

King Richard. Norfolk, we must have knocks; ha,
5   must we not?

Norfolk. We must both give and take, my loving lord.

King Richard. Up with my tent! Here will I lie to-
        night;
                    [*Soldiers begin to set up the King's tent.*]
        But where tomorrow? Well, all's one for that.
        Who hath descried the number of the traitors?

10 *Norfolk.* Six or seven thousand is their utmost power.

King Richard. Why, our battalia° trebles that account;
        Besides, the King's name is a tower of strength,
        Which they upon the adverse faction want.°
        Up with the tent! Come, noble gentlemen,
15   Let us survey the vantage of the ground.
        Call for some men of sound direction.°
        Let's lack no discipline, make no delay,
        For, lords, tomorrow is a busy day.   *Exeunt.*

        *Enter Richmond, Sir William Brandon, Oxford,
                and Dorset, [Herbert, and Blunt].*

Richmond. The weary sun hath made a golden set
20   And by the bright tract° of his fiery car°
        Gives token of a goodly day tomorrow.
        Sir William Brandon, you shall bear my standard.
        Give me some ink and paper in my tent.
        I'll draw the form and model of our battle,
25   Limit° each leader to his several charge,
        And part in just proportion our small power.
        My Lord of Oxford, you, Sir William Brandon,
        And you, Sir Walter Herbert, stay with me.
        The Earl of Pembroke keeps° his regiment;
30   Good Captain Blunt, bear my good-night to him,
        And by the second hour in the morning
        Desire the Earl to see me in my tent.
        Yet one thing more, good Captain, do for me:

5.3.11 **battalia** army   13 **want** lack   16 **direction** ability to give
orders   20 **tract** track   20 **car** chariot   25 **Limit** assign   29 **keeps**
stays with

Where is Lord Stanley quartered, do you know?

Blunt. Unless I have mista'en his colors much,   35
   Which well I am assured I have not done,
   His regiment lies half a mile at least
   South from the mighty power of the King.

Richmond. If without peril it be possible,
   Sweet Blunt, make some good means to speak with
     him   40
   And give him from me this most needful note.

Blunt. Upon my life, my lord, I'll undertake it;
   And so God give you quiet rest tonight!

Richmond. Good night, good Captain Blunt. [*Exit
   Blunt.*] Come, gentlemen,
   Let us consult upon tomorrow's business.   45
   Into my tent; the dew is raw and cold.
                    They withdraw into the tent.

    *Enter, [to his tent, King] Richard, Ratcliffe,
        Norfolk, and Catesby.*

King Richard. What is't o'clock?

Catesby.   It's suppertime, my lord;
   It's nine o'clock.

King Richard.   I will not sup tonight.
   Give me some ink and paper.
   What, is my beaver° easier than it was?   50
   And all my armor laid into my tent?

Catesby. It is, my liege; and all things are in readiness.

King Richard. Good Norfolk, hie thee to thy charge;
   Use careful watch, choose trusty sentinels.

Norfolk. I go, my lord.   55

King Richard. Stir with the lark tomorrow, gentle
   Norfolk.

Norfolk. I warrant you, my lord.   *Exit.*

50 **beaver** face-guard of a helmet

King Richard. Catesby!

Catesby. My lord?

King Richard.   Send out a pursuivant-at-arms°
60   To Stanley's regiment; bid him bring his power
      Before sunrising, lest his son George fall
      Into the blind cave of eternal night.   [*Exit Catesby.*]
      Fill me a bowl of wine. Give me a watch.°
      Saddle white Surrey° for the field tomorrow.
65   Look that my staves° be sound and not too heavy.
      Ratcliffe!

Ratcliffe. My lord?

King Richard. Saw'st thou the melancholy Lord
      Northumberland?

Ratcliffe. Thomas the Earl of Surrey and himself,
70   Much about cockshut time,° from troop to troop
      Went through the army, cheering up the soldiers.

King Richard. So, I am satisfied. Give me a bowl of
      wine.
      I have not that alacrity of spirit
      Nor cheer of mind that I was wont to have.
                                          [*Wine brought.*]
75   Set it down. Is ink and paper ready?

Ratcliffe. It is, my lord.

King Richard. Bid my guard watch. Leave me. Rat-
      cliffe,
      About the mid of night come to my tent
      And help to arm me. Leave me, I say.
                        Exit Ratcliffe. [*King Richard sleeps.*]

      Enter [*Stanley, Earl of*] *Derby, to Richmond in
      his tent,* [*Lords and Gentlemen attending*].

80   *Stanley.* Fortune and victory sit on thy helm!

---

59 **pursuivant-at-arms** minor herald 63 **watch** timepiece 64 **Surrey** (the name of a horse) 65 **staves** lances 70 **cockshut time** twilight

Richmond. All comfort that the dark night can afford
   Be to thy person, noble father-in-law!
   Tell me, how fares our loving mother?

Stanley. I by attorney bless thee from thy mother,
   Who prays continually for Richmond's good.   *85*
   So much for that. The silent hours steal on
   And flaky° darkness breaks within the east.
   In brief, for so the season° bids us be,
   Prepare thy battle early in the morning
   And put thy fortune to the arbitrament   *90*
   Of bloody strokes and mortal-staring° war.
   I, as I may—that which I would I cannot—
   With best advantage° will deceive the time°
   And aid thee in this doubtful shock of arms.
   But on thy side I may not be too forward,   *95*
   Lest, being seen, thy brother, tender George,
   Be executed in his father's sight.
   Farewell; the leisure° and the fearful time
   Cuts off the ceremonious vows of love
   And ample interchange of sweet discourse   *100*
   Which so long sund'red friends should dwell upon.
   God give us leisure for these rites of love!
   Once more adieu; be valiant, and speed well.

Richmond. Good lords, conduct him to his regiment.
   I'll strive with° troubled thoughts to take a nap,   *105*
   Lest leaden slumber peise° me down tomorrow
   When I should mount with wings of victory.
   Once more, good night, kind lords and gentlemen.
                      Exeunt. Manet Richmond.
   O thou whose captain I account myself,
   Look on my forces with a gracious eye!   *110*
   Put in their hands thy bruising irons of wrath,
   That they may crush down with a heavy fall
   The usurping helmets of our adversaries!
   Make us thy ministers of chastisement,

87 **flaky** streaked with light 88 **season** time 91 **mortal-staring**
fatally glaring 93 **advantage** opportunity 93 **the time** the people of
this time 98 **leisure** time available 105 **with** against 106 **peise**
weigh

115   That we may praise thee in the victory!
     To thee I do commend my watchful soul
     Ere I let fall the windows° of mine eyes.
     Sleeping and waking, O defend me still!   *Sleeps.*

*Enter the Ghost of Prince Edward, son to Henry
the Sixth.*

   Ghost. [*To Richard*] Let me sit heavy on thy soul
     tomorrow!
120   Think how thou stab'st me in my prime of youth
     At Tewkesbury. Despair therefor° and die!
     [*To Richmond*] Be cheerful, Richmond; for the
     wrongèd souls
     Of butchered princes fight in thy behalf.
     King Henry's issue,° Richmond, comforts thee.
                                           [*Exit.*]

Enter the Ghost of Henry the Sixth.

   Ghost. [*To Richard*] When I was mortal, my anointed
125   body
     By thee was punchèd full of deadly holes.
     Think on the Tower and me. Despair and die!
     Harry the Sixth bids thee despair and die!
     [*To Richmond*] Virtuous and holy, be thou con-
     queror!
130   Harry, that prophesied thou shouldst be king,
     Doth comfort thee in thy sleep. Live and flourish!
                                           [*Exit.*]

Enter the Ghost of Clarence.

   Ghost. [*To Richard*] Let me sit heavy in thy soul to-
     morrow,
     I that was washed to death with fulsome wine,
     Poor Clarence, by thy guile betrayed to death.
135   Tomorrow in the battle think on me,
     And fall° thy edgeless sword. Despair and die!

---

117 **windows** eyelids   121 **therefor** because of that   124 **issue** offspring   136 **fall** let fall

(*To Richmond*) Thou offspring of the house of
    Lancaster,
The wrongèd heirs of York do pray for thee.
Good angels guard thy battle! Live and flourish!
                                        [*Exit.*]

Enter the Ghosts of Rivers, Grey, and Vaughan.

Rivers. [*To Richard*] Let me sit heavy in thy soul to-
    morrow,   140
    Rivers, that died at Pomfret! Despair and die!

Grey. Think upon Grey, and let thy soul despair!

Vaughan. Think upon Vaughan and with guilty fear
    Let fall thy lance: despair, and die!

All. (*To Richmond*) Awake, and think our wrongs in
    Richard's bosom   145
    Will conquer him! Awake, and win the day!
                                        [*Exeunt.*]

Enter the Ghost of Hastings.

Ghost. [*To Richard*] Bloody and guilty, guiltily awake,
    And in a bloody battle end thy days!
    Think on Lord Hastings. Despair and die!
    (*To Richmond*) Quiet untroubled soul, awake,
        awake!   150
    Arm, fight, and conquer for fair England's sake!
                                        [*Exit.*]

Enter the Ghosts of the two young Princes.

Ghosts. (*To Richard*) Dream on thy cousins smoth-
    erèd in the Tower.
    Let us be lead within thy bosom, Richard,
    And weigh thee down to ruin, shame, and death.
    Thy nephews' souls bid thee despair and die!   155
    (*To Richmond*) Sleep, Richmond, sleep in peace
        and wake in joy.
    Good angels guard thee from the boar's annoy!°

157 **annoy** disturbance

Live, and beget a happy race of kings!
Edward's unhappy sons do bid thee flourish.

[*Exeunt.*]

Enter the Ghost of Lady Anne his wife.

Ghost. (*To Richard*) Richard, thy wife, that wretched
160   Anne thy wife,
That never slept a quiet hour with thee,
Now fills thy sleep with perturbations.
Tomorrow in the battle think on me,
And fall thy edgeless sword. Despair and die!
(*To Richmond*) Thou quiet soul, sleep thou a quiet
165   sleep.
Dream of success and happy victory!
Thy adversary's wife doth pray for thee.   [*Exit.*]

Enter the Ghost of Buckingham.

Ghost. (*To Richard*) The first was I that helped thee
to the crown;
The last was I that felt thy tyranny.
170 O, in the battle think on Buckingham,
And die in terror of thy guiltiness!
Dream on, dream on, of bloody deeds and death;
Fainting, despair; despairing, yield thy breath!
(*To Richmond*) I died for hope° ere I could lend
thee aid;
175 But cheer thy heart and be thou not dismayed.
God and good angels fight on Richmond's side,
And Richard falls in height of all his pride.   [*Exit.*]

Richard starteth up out of a dream.

King Richard. Give me another horse! Bind up my
wounds!
Have mercy, Jesu! Soft! I did but dream.
180 O coward conscience, how dost thou afflict me!
The lights burn blue. It is now dead midnight.

174 **for hope** because of hope (to help)

Cold fearful drops stand on my trembling flesh.
What do I fear? Myself? There's none else by.
Richard loves Richard: that is, I am I.
Is there a murderer here? No. Yes, I am.   185
Then fly. What, from myself? Great reason why!
Lest I revenge. What, myself upon myself?
Alack, I love myself. Wherefore? For any good
That I myself have done unto myself?
O no! Alas, I rather hate myself   190
For hateful deeds committed by myself.
I am a villain. Yet I lie, I am not.
Fool, of thyself speak well. Fool, do not flatter.
My conscience hath a thousand several° tongues,
And every tongue brings in a several tale,   195
And every tale condemns me for a villain.
Perjury, perjury in the highest degree,
Murder, stern murder in the direst degree,
All several sins, all used in each degree,
Throng to the bar, crying all, "Guilty! Guilty!"   200
I shall despair. There is no creature loves me;
And if I die, no soul will pity me.
Nay, wherefore should they, since that I myself
Find in myself no pity to myself?
Methought the souls of all that I had murdered   205
Came to my tent, and every one did threat
Tomorrow's vengeance on the head of Richard.

Enter Ratcliffe.

Ratcliffe. My lord!

King Richard. Zounds, who is there?

Ratcliffe. Ratcliffe, my lord; 'tis I. The early village
    cock   210
Hath twice done salutation to the morn.
Your friends are up and buckle on their armor.

King Richard. O Ratcliffe, I have dreamed a fearful
    dream!

194 **several** separate

What think'st thou, will our friends prove all true?

Ratcliffe. No doubt, my lord.

215 *King Richard.*   O Ratcliffe, I fear, I fear!

Ratcliffe. Nay, good my lord, be not afraid of shadows.

King Richard. By the apostle Paul, shadows tonight
Have struck more terror to the soul of Richard
Than can the substance of ten thousand soldiers
220   Armèd in proof° and led by shallow Richmond.
'Tis not yet near day. Come, go with me.
Under our tents I'll play the easedropper°
To see if any mean to shrink from me.
                              Exeunt Richard and Ratcliffe.

Enter the Lords to Richmond sitting in his tent.

Lords. Good morrow, Richmond.

Richmond. Cry mercy,° lords and watchful gentle-
225   men,
That you have ta'en a tardy sluggard here.

Lords. How have you slept, my lord?

Richmond. The sweetest sleep and fairest-boding
dreams
That ever ent'red in a drowsy head
230   Have I since your departure had, my lords.
Methought their souls whose bodies Richard mur-
dered
Came to my tent and cried° on victory.
I promise you my heart is very jocund
In the remembrance of so fair a dream.
235   How far into the morning is it, lords?

Lords. Upon the stroke of four.

Richmond. Why, then 'tis time to arm and give direction.

220 **proof** tested armor   222 **easedropper** eavesdropper   225 **Cry
mercy** (I) beg pardon   232 **cried** called aloud

His Oration to his Soldiers.

More than I have said, loving countrymen,
The leisure and enforcement of the time
Forbids to dwell upon; yet remember this: 240
God and our good cause fight upon our side;
The prayers of holy saints and wrongèd souls,
Like high-reared bulwarks, stand before our faces.
Richard except, those whom we fight against
Had rather have us win than him they follow.   245
For what is he they follow? Truly, gentlemen,
A bloody tyrant and a homicide;
One raised in blood and one in blood established;
One that made means° to come by what he hath,
And slaughterèd those that were the means to help
   him;   250
A base foul stone, made precious by the foil°
Of England's chair, where he is falsely set;
One that hath ever been God's enemy.
Then if you fight against God's enemy,
God will in justice ward° you as his soldiers;   255
If you do sweat to put a tyrant down,
You sleep in peace, the tyrant being slain;
If you do fight against your country's foes,
Your country's fat° shall pay your pains the hire;
If you do fight in safeguard of your wives,   260
Your wives shall welcome home the conquerors;
If you do free your children from the sword,
Your children's children quits° it in your age.
Then in the name of God and all these rights,
Advance your standards, draw your willing swords.   265
For me, the ransom° of my bold attempt
Shall be this cold corpse on the earth's cold face;
But if I thrive, the gain of my attempt
The least of you shall share his part thereof.
Sound drums and trumpets boldly and cheerfully;   270
God and Saint George! Richmond and victory!
                                        [*Exeunt.*]

249 **made means** contrived ways   251 **foil** setting for a gem   255
ward protect   259 **fat** abundance   263 **quits** repays   266 **the ran-
som** i.e., the price paid (if defeated)

Enter King Richard, Ratcliffe, and [Soldiers].

King Richard. What said Northumberland as touching
    Richmond?

Ratcliffe. That he was never trainèd up in arms.

King Richard. He said the truth; and what said Sur-
    rey then?

Ratcliffe. He smiled and said, "The better for our pur-
275   pose."

King Richard. He was in the right, and so indeed it is.
                              The clock striketh.
    Tell° the clock there. Give me a calendar.
    Who saw the sun today?

Ratcliffe.   Not I, my lord.

King Richard. Then he disdains to shine; for by the
    book
280 He should have braved° the east an hour ago.
    A black day will it be to somebody.
    Ratcliffe!

Ratcliffe. My lord?

King Richard.   The sun will not be seen today;
    The sky doth frown and lour upon our army.
285 I would these dewy tears were from the ground.
    Not shine today! Why, what is that to me
    More than to Richmond? For the selfsame heaven
    That frowns on me looks sadly upon him.

                    Enter Norfolk.

Norfolk. Arm, arm, my lord; the foe vaunts in the
    field.

King Richard. Come, bustle, bustle. Caparison my
290   horse.
    Call up Lord Stanley, bid him bring his power.
    I will lead forth my soldiers to the plain,
    And thus my battle shall be orderèd:

277 **Tell** count   280 **braved** made glorious

My foreward shall be drawn out all in length,
Consisting equally of horse and foot;   *295*
Our archers shall be placèd in the midst;
John Duke of Norfolk, Thomas Earl of Surrey,
Shall have the leading of this foot and horse.
They thus directed,° we will follow
In the main battle, whose puissance° on either side   *300*
Shall be well wingèd with our chiefest horse.
This, and Saint George to boot!° What think'st
    thou, Norfolk?

Norfolk. A good direction, warlike sovereign.
This found I on my tent this morning.
                              He showeth him a paper.
"Jockey° of Norfolk, be not so bold,   *305*
For Dickon thy master is bought and sold."°

King Richard. A thing devisèd by the enemy.
Go, gentlemen, every man unto his charge.
Let not our babbling dreams affright our souls;
Conscience is but a word that cowards use,   *310*
Devised at first to keep the strong in awe;
Our strong arms be our conscience, swords our
    law!
March on, join bravely, let us to it pell-mell,
If not to heaven, then hand in hand to hell.

                    His Oration to his Army.

What shall I say more than I have inferred?   *315*
Remember whom you are to cope withal,
A sort° of vagabonds, rascals, and runaways,
A scum of Britains and base lackey peasants,
Whom their o'ercloyèd country vomits forth
To desperate ventures and assured destruction.   *320*
You sleeping safe, they bring to you unrest;
You having lands, and blest with beauteous wives,
They would distrain° the one, distain° the other.

---

299 **directed** arranged   300 **puissance** power   302 **to boot** to our
help   305 **Jockey** (nickname for John)   306 **bought and sold** betrayed for a bribe   317 **sort** set   323 **distrain** confiscate   323 **dis-
tain** dishonor

And who doth lead them but a paltry fellow,
325   Long kept in Britain° at our mother's cost,
A milksop, one that never in his life
Felt so much cold as over shoes in snow?
Let's whip these stragglers o'er the seas again,
Lash hence these overweening rags of France,
330   These famished beggars, weary of their lives,
Who, but for dreaming on this fond° exploit,
For want of means, poor rats, had hanged them-
    selves.
If we be conquerèd, let men conquer us,
And not these bastard Britains, whom our fathers
Have in their own land beaten, bobbed, and
335   thumped,
And in record left them the heirs of shame.
Shall these enjoy our lands? Lie with our wives?
Ravish our daughters? (*Drum afar off.*) Hark! I
    hear their drum.
Fight, gentlemen of England! Fight, bold yeomen!
340   Draw, archers, draw your arrows to the head!
Spur your proud horses hard and ride in blood!
Amaze the welkin° with your broken staves!

Enter a Messenger.

What says Lord Stanley? Will he bring his power?

Messenger. My lord, he doth deny to come.

345 *King Richard.* Off with his son George's head!

Norfolk. My lord, the enemy is past the marsh.
After the battle let George Stanley die.

King Richard. A thousand hearts are great within my
    bosom.
Advance our standards, set upon our foes!
350   Our ancient word of courage, fair Saint George,
Inspire us with the spleen° of fiery dragons!
Upon them! Victory sits on our helms.   *Exeunt.*

325 **Britain** Brittany   331 **fond** foolish   342 **welkin** sky   351
spleen fierce spirit

[Scene 4. *Bosworth Field.*]

Alarum; excursions.° Enter Catesby
[and Norfolk].

Catesby. Rescue, my Lord of Norfolk, rescue, rescue!
   The King enacts more wonders than a man,
   Daring an opposite° to every danger.
   His horse is slain, and all on foot he fights,
   Seeking for Richmond in the throat of death.   *5*
   Rescue, fair lord, or else the day is lost!

Alarums. Enter [King] Richard.

King Richard. A horse! A horse! My kingdom for a
   horse!

Catesby. Withdraw, my lord; I'll help you to a horse.

King Richard. Slave, I have set my life upon a cast,°
   And I will stand the hazard° of the die.   *10*
   I think there be six Richmonds in the field;
   Five have I slain today instead of him.
   A horse! A horse! My kingdom for a horse!
                         [Exeunt.]

5.4.s.d. **excursions** sallies 3 **opposite** opponent 9 **cast** throw (of dice) 10 **hazard** chance

[Scene 5. *Bosworth Field.*]

*Alarum. Enter [King] Richard and Richmond;
they fight; Richard is slain.*

*Retreat° and flourish. Enter Richmond, [Stanley,
Earl of] Derby, bearing the crown, with divers
other Lords.*

Richmond. God and your arms be praised, victorious
    friends!
    The day is ours; the bloody dog is dead.

Stanley. Courageous Richmond, well hast thou acquit
    thee.
    Lo, here this long-usurpèd royalty
5   From the dead temples of this bloody wretch
    Have I plucked off, to grace thy brows withal.
    Wear it, enjoy it, and make much of it.

Richmond. Great God of heaven, say amen to all!
    But tell me, is young George Stanley living?

10 *Stanley.* He is, my lord, and safe in Leicester town,
    Whither, if it please you, we may now withdraw us.

Richmond. What men of name° are slain on either
    side?

Stanley. John Duke of Norfolk, Walter Lord Ferrers,
    Sir Robert Brakenbury, and Sir William Brandon.

15 *Richmond.* Inter their bodies as become their births.
    Proclaim a pardon to the soldiers fled
    That in submission will return to us;

5.5.s.d. **Retreat** trumpet signal to recall troops   12 **name** high rank

And then, as we have ta'en the sacrament,°
We will unite the White Rose and the Red.
Smile heaven upon this fair conjunction,°   20
That long have frowned upon their enmity!
What traitor hears me and says not amen?
England hath long been mad and scarred herself;
The brother blindly shed the brother's blood,
The father rashly slaughtered his own son,   25
The son, compelled, been butcher to the sire.
All this divided York and Lancaster,
Divided in their dire division,
O, now let Richmond and Elizabeth,
The true succeeders of each royal house,   30
By God's fair ordinance conjoin together!
And let their heirs, God, if thy will be so,
Enrich the time to come with smooth-faced peace,
With smiling plenty, and fair prosperous days!
Abate the edge° of traitors, gracious Lord,   35
That would reduce° these bloody days again
And make poor England weep in streams of blood!
Let them not live to taste this land's increase
That would with treason wound this fair land's
    peace!
Now civil wounds are stopped, peace lives again;   40
That she may long live here, God say amen!
                                        Exeunt.

                    FINIS

18 **ta'en the sacrament** taken a solemn oath (to marry Elizabeth when
he won the crown) 20 **conjunction** joining in marriage 35 **Abate
the edge** blunt the sharp point 36 **reduce** bring back

Textual Note

Richard III, one of Shakespeare's most popular plays, appeared in eight quarto editions, more than any other Shakespeare play except *Henry IV, Part I*. The First Quarto (Q1) was entered for publication on October 20, 1597, as "The tragedie of kinge Richard the Third with the death of the Duke of Clarence." The actors of Shakespeare's company who reconstructed this text from memory left out over 200 lines and made many changes, but they preserved some lines omitted in the Folio, especially 4.2.98–115. Printers added errors in each of the later quartos, dated 1598, 1602 (Q3), 1605, 1612, 1622 (Q6), 1629, and 1634.

The best text of the play appeared in 1623 in the First Folio (F). The printer, William Jaggard, had his compositors set up *Richard III* from a quarto marked with many corrections from an authentic manuscript. It used to be believed that this quarto was Q6, supplemented by an uncorrected quarto, Q3. In 1955, however, J. K. Walton, in *The Copy for the Folio Text of Richard III*, concluded that Q3, corrected, was the only quarto used for F. My collation of all variants in the first six quartos supports this conclusion. It is possible that both Q3 and Q6 were used, but that remains to be proved.

The present edition follows the readings of the First Folio except for the changes listed below. These changes have been made for definite reasons. First, the part of the Folio text containing 3.1.1–168 seems to have been printed from Q3 without any correction from a manuscript, and the Folio text from 5.3.49 to the end of the play makes very few corrections. These few corrections have been accepted, but the rest of the text in these passages is based on Q1, from which Q3 and F are here derived. For example, the right reading "as" in 3.1.123 appears in Q1, while "as, as," in F derives from the misprint "as as" in Q3. Second, the reading of Q1 is also preferred, in any part of the play, to a different reading which F merely reprints from Q3. Third, the present text accepts 30 lines from Q1 which are not in F. Finally, I have corrected errors and have made a few emendations.

The divisions into acts and scenes include all those in the Folio, translated from Latin, and these further scenes as marked in modern editions: 3.5–7, 4.3, and 5.3–5. Brackets set off these and other editorial additions. Spelling, punctuation, and capitalization are modernized, and speech prefixes are regularized. In the following list of significant changes from the Folio, and from Q1 where it is the basic text, the reading of the present text is given in italics and the alternative reading of the Folio, or of Q1 or Q3, in roman.

1.1.26 *spy* [Q1] see 42 s.d. *Clarence, guarded, and Brakenbury* Clarence, and Brakenbury, guarded 45 *the* [Q1] th' 52 *for* [Q1] but 65 *tempers him to this* [Q1] tempts him to this harsh 75 *to her for his* [Q1] for her 103 *I* [Q1] I do 124 *the* [Q1] this [Q3] 133 *prey* [Q1] play 142 *What* [Q1] Where

1.2.27 *life* death (cf. 4.1.75) 39 *stand* [Q1] Stand'st 60 *deed* [Q1] Deeds 78 *a man* [Q1] man 80 *accuse* curse 154 *aspect* [Q1] Aspects 195 *was man* [Q1] man was [Q3] 201 *Richard* [Q1, not in F] 202 *Anne. To take . . . give* [Q1, not in F] 225 *Richard. Sirs . . . corse* [Q1, not in F] 235 *at all* [Q1] withall [Q3]

1.3.s.d. *Queen* [Q1] the Queene Mother 17 *come the lords* [Q1] comes the Lord 108 s.d. *Enter old Queen Margaret* [after 109] 113 *Tell . . . said* [Q1, not in F] 114 *avouch* [Q1] auouch't 308 *Queen Elizabeth* [Q1 Qu.] Mar. 341, 349, 354 *First Murderer* Vil. 354 s.d. *Exeunt* [Q1 after 353, not in F]

1.4.13 *Thence* [Q1] There 86 *First Murderer* 2 Mur. 89 *Second Murderer* 1 122 *Faith* [Q1, not in F] 126 *Zounds* [Q1] Come 147 *Zounds* [Q1, not in F] 192–93 *to have . . . sins* [Q1] for any goodnesse 240 *And charged . . . other* [Q1, not in F] 266–70 *Which . . . distress* [not in Q; F inserts after 259]

2.1.5 *in* [Q1] to 7 *Rivers and Hastings* [Q1] Dorset and Riuers 39 *God* [Q1] heauen 40 *zeal* [Q1] loue 57 *unwittingly* [Q1] vnwillingly 59 *By* [Q1] To 109 *at* [Q1] and

2.2.1 *Boy* [Q1] Edw. 3 *do you* [Q1] do 47 *have I* [Q1] haue 83 *weep* [Q1] weepes 84–85 *and so . . . Edward weep* [Q1, not in F] 142, 154 *Ludlow* [Q1] London 145 *Queen and Duchess of York. With all our hearts* [Q1, not in F]

2.3.43 *Ensuing* [Q1] Pursuing (catchword "Ensuing")

2.4.1 *hear* [Q1] heard [Q3] 21 *Archbishop* [Q1 Car.] Yor. 65 *death* [Q1] earth

3.1.s.d. *with others* [F] &c [Q1]   9 *Nor* [Q1] No   40 *God in heaven* [Q1]
God [Q3]   43 *deep* [Q1] great [Q3]   56 *ne'er* [F] neuer [Q1]   57 *o'errule*
[F] ouerrule [Q1]   60 s.d. *Exit* [not in Q1; after 59 in Q3 and F]   63 *seems*
[Q1] thinkst [Q3]   78 *all-ending* [Q1] ending [Q3]   79 *ne'er* neuer [Q1
F]   87 *this* [Q1] his [Q3]   94 s.d. *and Cardinal* [F] Cardinall [Q1]   96
loving [Q1] noble [Q3]   97 *dread* [Q1] deare [Q3]   120 *heavy* [Q1]
weightie [Q3]   123 *as* [Q1] as as [Q3]   141 *needs will* [Q1] will [Q3]   145
grandam [F] Granam [Q1]   149 *with* [Q1] and with   150 s.d. *A sennet* [F,
not in Q1] *Hastings* Hast. Dors [Q1] Hastings, and Dorset [F] *and Catesby* [F,
not in Q1]   154 *parlous* perillous [Q1 F]   160 *knowest* [Q1] know'st   161
thinkest [Q1] think'st   167 *thinkest* [Q1] think'st   167 *What will he?* [Q1]
Will not hee?

3.2.110 s.d. *He whispers in his ear* [Q1] Priest. Ile wait vpon your Lordship
[cf. line 121]

3.4.78 s.d. *Exeunt* [after 77]   81 *rase* [Q1] rowse

3.5.4 *wert* [Q1] were   104 *Penker* Peuker   105 s.d. *Exeunt* Exit   109 s.d.
Exit [Q1] Exeunt

3.7.218 *Zounds, I'll* [Q1] we will   219 *Richard. O . . . Buckingham* [Q1, not
in F]   223 *stone* Stones   246 *cousin* [Q1] Cousins

4.1.s.d. *Enter . . . another door* Enter the Queene, Anne Duchesse of
Gloucester, the Duchesse of Yorke, and Marquesse Dorset 103 *sorrow* Sor-
rowes

4.2.71 *there* [Q1] then   89 *Hereford* [Q1] Hertford   97 *Perhaps, perhaps*
[Q1] perhaps   98–115 *Buckingham. My lord . . . vein today* [Q1, not in F]

4.3.15 *once* [Q1] one   31 *at* [Q1] and

4.4.10 *unblown* [Q1] vnblowed   39 *Tell o'er . . . mine* Tell ouer . . . mine
[Q1, not in F]   45 *holp'st* hop'st   52 *That excellent . . . earth* [after 53]   64
Thy [Q1] The   118 *nights . . . days* [Q1] night . . . day [Q3]   128 *intestate*
[Q1] intestine   141 *Where* [Q1] Where't   200 *moe* [Q1] more [Q3]   268
would I [Q1] I would [Q3]   274 *sometimes* [Q1] sometime [Q3]   284 *this is*
[Q1] this   323 *loan* Loue   348 *wail* [Q1] vaile   364 *Harp . . . past* [after
365]   377 *God . . . God's* [Q1] Heauen . . . Heanens (so misprinted)   392 *in*
[Q1] with   396 *o'erpast* [Q1] repast   417 *peevish-fond* peeuish found   423
I'll I   430 s.d. *Exit Queen* [after 429]   431 s.d. *Enter Ratcliffe* [after
"newes"]   444 *Ratcliffe* Catesby

4.5.10 *Harfordwest* [Q1] Hertford-west [Q3]

5.1.11 *It is, my lord* [Q1] It is

5.2.11 *center* [Q1] Centry

5.3.28 *you* your   54 *sentinels* [F] centinell [Q1]   58 *Catesby* [Q1]
Ratcliffe   59 *Catesby* Rat. [Q1]   68 *Saw'st thou* [Q1] Saw'st   80 *sit* [Q3]
set [Q1]   83 *loving* [Q1] noble [Q3]   90 *the* [Q1] th'   101 *sund'red* [F]

sundried [Q1]   105 *thoughts* [Q1] noise   108 s.d. *Manet Richmond* [F, not in Q1]   113 *The* [Q1] Th'   115 *the* [Q1] thy [Q3]   118 s.d. *Enter . . . Sixth* [F] Enter the ghost of young Prince Edward, sonne Harry the sixt, to Ri. [Q1]   126 *deadly holes* [Q1] holes [Q3]   131 *thy sleep* [Q1] sleepe [Q1]   132 *sit* [Q3] set [Q1]   139 s.d. *and Vaughan* [F] Vaughan [Q1]   140 *Rivers* [Q3] King [Q1]   146 *Will* [Q3] Wel [Q1]   146 s.d.–151 *Enter . . . sake* [Q3; after line 159 in Q1]   146 s.d. *Hastings* [Q1] L. Hastings [Q3]   152 *Ghosts* [F] Ghost [Q1]   153 *lead* [Q1] laid [Q3]   155 *souls bid* [Q1] soule bids   159 s.d. *Lady Anne* [Q1] Anne   162 *perturbations* [Q3] preturbations [Q1]   177 *falls* [Q1] fall   177 s.d. *starteth up out of a dream* [Q1] starts out of his dreame   181 *now* [Q1] not [Q3]   184 *I am I* [Q3] I and I [Q1]   197 *Perjury, perjury* [Q1] Periurie [Q3]   197 *highest* [Q1] high'st   198 *direst* [Q1] dyr'st   200 *to the* [Q1] all to'th'   202 *will* [Q1] shall [Q3]   203 *Nay* [F] And [Q1]   209 *Zounds, who is* [Q1] Who's   213–15 *King Richard. O Ratcliffe . . . my lord* [Q1, not in F]   223 *see* [Q1] heare [Q3]   223 s.d. *Exeunt Richard and Ratcliffe* [F] Exeunt [Q1]   223 s.d. *Enter . . . in his tent* [F] Enter the Lordes to Richmond [Q1]   224 *Lords* [Lo. Q1] Richm.   233 *heart* [F] soule [Q1]   251 *foil* [Q1] soile [Q3]   256 *sweat* [Q1] sweare [Q3]   271 s.d. *Ratcliffe, and* [Rat. &c Q1] Ratcliffe, and Catesby   276 s.d. *The clock striketh* [Q1] Clocke strikes   283 *not* [Q3] nor [Q1]   294 *drawn out all* [Q1] drawne [Q3]   298 *this* [Q1] the [Q3]   302 *boot* [Q3] bootes [Q1]   304 s.d. *He . . . paper* [Q1, not in F]   308 *unto* [Q1] to   310 *Conscience is but* [Q1] For Conscience is   313 *to it* [Q1] too't   314 s.d. *His . . . Army* [Q1, not in F]   320 *ventures* aduentures [Q1]   321 *to you* [Q1] you to [Q3]   323 *distrain* restraine [Q1]   336 *in* [Q1] on [Q3]   339 *Fight, gentlemen* [Q1] Right Gentlemen [Q3]   339 *bold* [Q1] boldly [Q3]   342 s.d. *Enter a Messenger* [F, not in Q1]   352 *helms* [Q1] helpes [Q3]   352 s.d. *Exeunt* [Q1, not in F]

5.4.6 s.d. *Alarums.* [F, not in Q1]

5.5.s.d. *Retreat . . . Lords* [F] then retrait being sounded. Enter Richmond, Darby, bearing the crowne, with other Lords, &c [Q1]   4 *this . . . royalty* [Q1] these . . . Royalties   7 *Wear it, enjoy it* [Q1] Weare it [Q3]   11 *if it please you, we may now* [Q1] (if you please) we may   13 *Stanley* [Der. F, not in Q1]   32 *their* [Q1] thy [Q3]   41 s.d. *Exeunt* [F, not in Q1]

The Sources of
Richard the Third

Shakespeare found the fullest account of Richard in Raphael Holinshed's *Chronicles* (second edition, 1587). Holinshed reprinted most of Sir Thomas More's *History of King Richard the Third* (written about 1513–14, printed in 1557) and wove in further information from Polydore Vergil's *Anglica Historia* (1534), Edward Hall's *The Union of the Two Noble and Illustre Families of Lancaster and York* (1548), and Richard Grafton's *Chronicles* of 1543 and 1569. Shakespeare added a few points from his own reading of Hall or Grafton, and a few from "The Tragedy of Clarence" in *The Mirror for Magistrates* (1559). The rest he drew from Holinshed or invented for himself.

The historical Richard was not so black as he was painted; it is still an unsolved question whether he committed any of the murders charged against him by his enemies. But Shakespeare was dramatizing the Richard of the Tudor historians, and they had no doubt that Richard was a murderer and a tyrant. More wrote that he "spared no man's death whose life withstood his purpose"; Hall declared that if he had not usurped the throne, he would have been "much praised and beloved, as he is now abhorred and vilipended." By the time Shakespeare wrote, Richard had already been staged as a Senecan villain in *Richardus Tertius*, a Latin play acted at Cambridge, and in *The True Tragedy of Richard the Third*, which Shakespeare quotes in *Hamlet*. More's vivid history, however, furnished the chief stimulus to Shakespeare's imagination.

The character sketch of Richard by More is here quoted in his own words, which Holinshed borrowed with little change. Holinshed followed More's *History* in the main up to the point where it ended, with the flight of Buckingham, and he used Hall and other authorities to continue the story.

For Shakespeare's use of his source, see Geoffrey Bullough, *Narrative and Dramatic Sources of Shakespeare*, III (1960); Thomas More, *The History of King Richard the Third*, ed. Richard S. Sylvester (1963); and *Shakespeare's Holinshed*, ed. Richard Hosley (1968).

From The History of King Richard the Third

Richard Duke of York ... was with many nobles of the realm at Wakefield slain, leaving three sons, Edward, George, and Richard. ... Edward, revenging his father's death, deprived King Henry and attained the crown. George Duke of Clarence was a goodly noble prince ... heinous treason was there laid to his charge, and finally, were he faulty, were he faultless, attainted was he by Parliament and judged to the death, and thereupon hastily drowned in a butt of malmsey; whose death King Edward (albeit he commanded it), when he wist it was done, piteously bewailed and sorrowfully repented.

Richard, the third son, of whom we now entreat, was in wit and courage equal with either of them, in body and prowess far under them both; little of stature, ill-featured of limbs, crookbacked, his left shoulder much higher than his right, hard-favored of visage, and such as is in states called warly [i.e., in great men called warlike], in other men otherwise; he was malicious, wrathful, envious, and, from afore his birth, ever froward. It is for truth reported that the Duchess his mother had so much ado in her travail that she could not be delivered of him uncut, and that he came into the world with the feet forward, as men be borne outward, and (as the fame runneth) also not untoothed; whether men of hatred report above the truth, or else that nature changed her course in his beginning, which in the course of his life many things unnaturally committed. None evil captain was he in the war, as to which his disposition was more meetly than for peace. Sundry victories had he, and sometimes overthrows, but never in default, as for his own person, either of hardiness or politic order; free was he called of dispense, and somewhat above his power liberal, with large gifts he got him unsteadfast friendship, for which he was fain to pill and spoil in other places and got him steadfast hatred. He was close and secret, a deep dissimuler, lowly of countenance, arrogant of heart, outwardly companiable [i.e., friendly] where he inwardly hated, not letting to kiss whom he thought to kill; dispiteous and cruel, not for evil will alway, but ofter for ambition, and either for the surety or increase of his estate. Friend and foe was much what indifferent, where his advantage grew; he spared no man's death whose life withstood his purpose. He slew with his own hands King Henry the Sixth, being prisoner in the Tower, as men constantly say, and that without commandment or knowledge of the King, which would undoubtedly, if he had intended that thing, have appointed that butcherly office to some other than his own born brother. Some wise men also ween that his drift, covertly conveyed, lacked not in helping forth his brother of Clarence to his death; which he resisted openly, howbeit somewhat (as men deemed) more faintly than he that were heartily minded to his wealth. And they that thus deem think that he long time in King Edward's life forethought to be king in case that the King his brother (whose life he looked that evil diet should shorten) should happen to decease (as in deed he did) while his children were young. And they deem that for this intent he was glad of his brother's death the Duke of Clarence, whose life must needs have hindered him so intending, whether the same Duke of Clarence had kept him true to his nephew the young King, or enterprised to be king himself. But of all this point is there no certainty, and whoso divineth upon conjectures may as well shoot too far as too short.

RAPHAEL HOLINSHED

From Chronicles of England, Scotland, and Ireland

[At Mortimer's Cross in 1461] the sun (as some write) appeared to the Earl of March [Edward] like three suns, and suddenly joined altogether in one. Upon which sight he took such courage that he, fiercely setting on his enemies, put them to flight; and for this cause men imagined that he gave the sun in his full brightness for his badge or cognizance. . . .

[In 1464] it was thought meet by him and those of his council that a marriage were provided for him in some convenient place; and therefore was the Earl of Warwick sent over into France to demand the Lady Bona, daughter to Lewis Duke of Savoy and sister to the Lady Carlot, then Queen of France; which Bona was at that time in the French court.

The Earl of Warwick, coming to the French King, then lying at Tours, was of him honorably received and right courteously entertained. His message was so well liked . . . that the matrimony on that side was clearly assented to. . . . But here consider the old proverb to be true which saith that marriage goeth by destiny. For, during the time that the Earl of Warwick was thus in France and (according to his instructions) brought the effect of his commission to pass, the King, being on hunting in the forest of Wychwood besides Stony Stratford, came for his recreation to the manor of Grafton, where the Duchess of Bedford then sojourned, wife to Sir Richard Woodville Lord Rivers, on whom was then attendant a daughter of hers called the Lady Elizabeth Grey, widow of Sir John Grey, knight, slain at the last battle of St. Albans. . . .

This widow, having a suit to the King for such lands as her

husband had given her in jointure, so kindled the King's affection towards her that he not only favored her suit, but more her person; for she was a woman of a more formal countenance than of excellent beauty, and yet both of such beauty and favor that with her sober demeanor, sweet looks, and comely smiling (neither too wanton, nor too bashful), besides her pleasant tongue and trim wit, she so allured and made subject unto her the heart of that great prince that, after she had denied him to be his paramour, with so good manner and words so well set as better could not be devised, he finally resolved with himself to marry her. . . .

But yet the Duchess of York his mother letted this match as much as in her lay; and when all would not serve, she caused a precontract to be alleged, made by him with Lady Elizabeth Lucy. But all doubts resolved, all things made clear, and all cavilations avoided, privily in a morning he married the said Lady Elizabeth Grey at Grafton beforesaid, where he first began to fancy her. And in the next year after she was with great solemnity crowned queen at Westminster. Her father also was created Earl Rivers and made high constable of England; her brother Lord Anthony was married to the sole heir of Thomas Lord Scales; Sir Thomas Grey, son to Sir John Grey the Queen's first husband, was created Marquis Dorset. . . .

The Earl of Warwick, being a far-casting prince, perceived somewhat in the Duke of Clarence whereby he judged that he bare no great good will towards the King his brother; and thereupon, feeling his mind by such talk as he of purpose ministered, understood how he was bent, and so won him to his purpose; and for better assurance of his faithful friendship he offered him his eldest daughter in marriage. . . . The Duke of Clarence being come to Calais with the Earl of Warwick, after he had sworn on the sacrament to keep his promise and pact made with the said Earl whole and inviolate, he married the Lady Isabel, eldest daughter to the Earl, in Our Lady's Church there. . . .

Edward Prince of Wales wedded Anne, second daughter to the Earl of Warwick. . . .

The Earl of Pembroke . . . brought the child [Henry Tudor] with him to London to King Henry the Sixth; whom when the King had a good while beheld, he said to such princes as were with him: "Lo, surely this is he to whom both we and our adversaries, leaving the possession of all things, shall hereafter give room and place." So this holy man showed before the chance that should happen, that this Earl Henry, so ordained by God, should in time to come (as he did indeed) have and enjoy the kingdom and whole rule of this realm of England. . . .

[Henry VI's son Edward was taken prisoner at the battle of Tewkesbury,] whom incontinently George Duke of Clarence, Richard Duke of Gloucester, Thomas Grey Marquis Dorset, and William Lord Hastings, that stood by, suddenly murdered; for the which cruel act, the more part of the doers in their latter days drank of the like cup, by the righteous justice and due punishment of God. . . .

Moreover, here is to be remembered that poor King Henry the Sixth, a little before deprived (as ye have heard) of his realm and imperial crown, was now in the Tower spoiled of his life, by Richard Duke of Gloucester (as the constant fame ran), who (to the intent that his brother King Edward might reign in more surety) murdered the said King Henry with a dagger. . . .

The dead corpse on the Ascension Even was conveyed with bills and glaives pompously (if you will call that a funeral pomp) from the Tower to the church of St. Paul, and there laid on a bier or coffin barefaced; the same in presence of the beholders did bleed; where it rested the space of one whole day. From thence he was carried to the Blackfriars, and bled there likewise; and on the next day after, it was conveyed in a boat, without priest or clerk, torch or taper, singing or saying, unto the monastery of Chertsey, distant from London fifteen miles, and there was it first buried. . . .

Some have reported that the cause of [the death of Clarence] . . . rose of a foolish prophecy, which was, that after King Edward one should reign whose first letter of his name should be a G. Wherewith the King and Queen were sore troubled and began to conceive a grievous grudge against this duke, and could not be in quiet till they had brought him to his end. And as the devil is wont to encumber the minds of men which delight in such devilish fantasies, they said afterward that that prophecy lost not his effect when, after King Edward, Gloucester usurped his kingdom. . . .

But sure it is that, although King Edward were consenting to his death, yet he much did both lament his infortunate chance and repent his sudden execution; insomuch that when any person sued to him for the pardon of malefactors condemned to death, he would accustomably say and openly speak: "Oh infortunate brother, for whose life not one would make suit." . . .

King Edward in his life, albeit that this dissension between his friends somewhat irked him, yet in his good health he somewhat the less regarded it, because he thought whatsoever business should fall between them, himself should alway be able to rule both the parties.

But in his last sickness, when he perceived his natural strength so sore enfeebled that he despaired all recovery, then he, considering the youth of his children, albeit he nothing less mistrusted than that that happened, yet well foreseeing that many harms might grow by their debate, while the youth of his children should lack discretion of themselves and good counsel of their friends, of which either party should counsel for their own commodity, and rather by pleasant advice to win themselves favor than by profitable advertisement to do the children good, he called some of them before him that were at variance, and in especial the Lord Marquis Dorset, the Queen's son by her first husband.

So did he also William the Lord Hastings, a noble man, then Lord Chamberlain, against whom the Queen specially grudged, for the great favor the King bare him; and also for that she thought him secretly familiar with the King in wanton company. Her kindred also bare him sore, as well for that the King had made him captain of Calais, which office the Lord Rivers, brother to the Queen, claimed of the King's former promise, as for divers other great gifts which he received, that they looked for. When these lords, with divers other of both the parties, were come in presence, the King, lifting up himself, and underset with pillows, as it is reported, on this wise said unto them.

"My lords, my dear kinsmen and allies, in what plight I lie you see, and I feel. . . . Wherefore in these last words that ever I look to speak with you, I exhort you and require you all, for the love that you have ever borne to me, for the love that I have ever borne unto you, for the love that Our Lord beareth to us all, from this time forward (all griefs forgotten) each of you love other. Which I verily trust you will, if ye anything earthly regard, either God or your king, affinity or kindred, this realm, your own country, or your own surety." And therewithal the King, no longer enduring to sit up, laid him down on his right side, his face towards them; and none was there present that could refrain from weeping.

But the lords recomforting him with as good words as they could, and answering for the time as they thought to stand with his pleasure, there in his presence, as by their words appeared, each forgave other and joined their hands together, when (as it after appeared by their deeds) their hearts were far asunder. As soon as the King was departed, the noble Prince his son drew toward London, which at the time of his decease kept his household at Ludlow in Wales. . . .

The Duke of Gloucester soon set on fire them that were of themselves easy to kindle, and in specially twain, Edward Duke of Buckingham and William Lord Hastings then Chamberlain, both men of honor and of great power, the one by long succession from his ancestry, the other by his office and the King's favor. These two, not bearing each to other so much love, as hatred both unto the Queen's part, in this point accorded together with the Duke of Gloucester that they would utterly remove from the King's company all his mother's friends, under the name of their enemies.

Upon this concluded the Duke of Gloucester, understanding that the lords which at that time were about the King intended to bring him up to his coronation accompanied with such power of their friends, that it should be hard for him to bring his purpose to pass without the gathering and great assembly of people and in manner of open war, whereof the end (he wist) was doubtful, and in which, the King being on their side, his part should have the face and name of a rebellion; he secretly therefore by divers means caused the Queen to be persuaded and brought in the mind that it neither were need, and also should be jeopardous, the King to come up strong. . . .

The Queen, being in this wise persuaded, such word sent unto her son, and unto her brother, being about the King; and over that the Duke of Gloucester himself and other lords, the chief of his band, wrote unto the King so reverently and to the Queen's friends there so lovingly that they, nothing earthly mistrusting, brought the King up in great haste, not in good speed, with a sober company. Now was the King in his way to London gone from Northampton, when these Dukes of Gloucester and Buckingham came thither, where remained behind the Lord Rivers, the King's uncle, intending on the morrow to follow the King and to be with him at Stony Stratford. . . .

But even by and by in his presence they picked a quarrel to the Lord Richard Grey, the King's other brother by his mother, saying that he, with the Lord Marquis his brother and the Lord Rivers his uncle, had compassed to rule the King and the realm. . . .

Unto which words the King answered: "What my brother Marquis hath done I cannot say, but in good faith I dare well answer for mine uncle Rivers and my brother here, that they be innocent of any such matter." "Yea, my liege" (quoth the Duke of Buckingham), "they have kept their dealing in these matters far from the knowledge of your good Grace." And forthwith they arrested the Lord Richard and Sir Thomas Vaughan, knight, in the King's presence. . . . The Duke of Gloucester . . . sent the Lord Rivers and the Lord Richard with Sir Thomas Vaughan into the north country into divers places to prison, and afterward all to Pomfret, where they were in conclusion beheaded.

In this wise the Duke of Gloucester took upon himself the order and governance of the young King, whom with much honor and humble reverence he conveyed upward towards the city. But anon the tidings of this matter came hastily to the Queen a little before the midnight following, and that in the sorest wise, that the King her son was taken, her brother, her son, and her other friends arrested, and sent no man wist whither, to be done with God wot what. With which tidings the Queen in great flight and heaviness . . . got herself in all the haste possible with her younger son and her daughters out of the palace of Westminster, in which she then lay, into the Sanctuary, lodging herself and her company there in the Abbot's place. . . .

When the King approached near to the city, Edmund

Shaw, goldsmith, then Mayor, with William White and John Matthew, Sheriffs, and all the other aldermen in scarlet, with five hundred horse of the citizens, in violet, received him reverently at Hornsey, and riding from thence accompanied him into the city, which he entered the fourth day of May, the first and last year of his reign. But the Duke of Gloucester bare him in open sight so reverently to the Prince, with all semblance of lowliness, that from the great obloquy in which he was so late before, he was suddenly fallen in so great trust that at the council next assembled he was made the only man chosen and thought most meet to be Protector of the King and his realm, so that (were it destiny or were it folly) the lamb was betaken to the wolf to keep. . . .

[Richard said to the council:] "Wherefore me thinketh it were not worst to send unto the Queen, for the redress of this matter, some honorable trusty man, such as both tendereth the King's weal and the honor of his council, and is also in favor and credence with her. For all which considerations, none seemeth more meetly than our reverend father here present, my Lord Cardinal. . . . And if she be percase so obstinate, and so precisely set upon her own will, that neither his wise and faithful advertisement cannot move her, nor any man's reason content her, then shall we, by mine advice, by the King's authority fetch him out of that prison and bring him to his noble presence, in whose continual company he shall be so well cherished and so honorably entreated that all the world shall to our honor and her reproach perceive that it was only malice, frowardness, or folly that caused her to keep him there." . . .

[The Archbishop said:] "God forbid that any man should for anything earthly enterprise to break the immunity and liberty of the sacred sanctuary, that hath been the safeguard of so many a good man's life. And I trust (quoth he) with God's grace, we shall not need it. But for any manner need I would not we should do it." . . .

[Buckingham argued that the Prince] "neither is, nor can be, a sanctuary man . . . he must ask it himself that must have it. . . . And verily, I have often heard of sanctuary men, but I never heard erst of sanctuary children." . . .

When the Lord Cardinal, and these other lords with him, had received this young duke, they brought him into the

Star Chamber, where the Protector took him in his arms and kissed him, with these words: "Now welcome, my lord, even with all my very heart." And he said in that of like-lihood as he thought. Thereupon forthwith they brought him unto the King his brother into the Bishop's palace at Paul's, and from thence through the city honorably into the Tower, out of the which after that day they never came abroad. When the Protector had both the children in his hands, he opened himself more boldly, both to certain other men, and also chiefly to the Duke of Buckingham. . . .

Then it was agreed that the Protector should have the Duke's aid to make him King, and that the Protector's only lawful son should marry the Duke's daughter, and that the Protector should grant him the quiet possession of the earldom of Hereford, which he claimed as his inheritance, and could never obtain it in King Edward's time.

Besides these requests of the Duke, the Protector of his own mind promised him a great quantity of the King's trea-sure and of his household stuff. And when they were thus at a point between themselves, they went about to prepare for the coronation of the young King, as they would have it seem. And that they might turn both the eyes and minds of men from perceiving of their drifts otherwhere, the lords being sent for from all parts of the realm came thick to that solemnity. But the Protector and the Duke, after that they had sent the Lord Cardinal, the Archbishop of York then Lord Chancellor, the Bishop of Ely, the Lord Stanley, and the Lord Hastings then Lord Chamberlain, with many other noble men, to commune and devise about the coronation in one place, as fast were they in another place, contriving the contrary, and to make the Protector king.

To which council albeit there were adhibited very few, and they were secret, yet began there, here and there abouts, some manner of muttering among the people, as though all should not long be well, though they neither wist what they feared, nor wherefore; were it that, before such great things, men's hearts of a secret instinct of nature misgive them, as the sea without wind swelleth of himself sometime before a tempest. . . .

The Lord Stanley, that was after Earl of Derby, wisely mistrusted it, and said unto the Lord Hastings that he much misliked these two several councils. "For while we" (quoth he) "talk of one matter in the tone place, little wot we whereof they talk in the tother place."

"My lord" (quoth the Lord Hastings), "on my life never doubt you; for while one man is there, which is never thence, never can there be thing once moved that should sound amiss toward me, but it should be in mine ears ere it were well out of their mouths." This meant he by Catesby, which was of his near secret council. . . . In whom if the Lord Hastings had not put so special trust, the Lord Stanley and he had departed with divers other lords, and broken all the dance, for many ill signs that he saw, which he now construes all to the best. So surely thought he that there could be none harm toward him in that council intended where Catesby was. And of truth the Protector and the Duke of Buckingham made very good semblance unto the Lord Hastings and kept him much in company. And undoubtedly the Protector loved him well and loath was to have lost him, saving for fear lest his life should have quailed their purpose.

For which cause he moved Catesby to prove with some words cast out afar off whether he could think it possible to win the Lord Hastings unto their part. But Catesby . . . reported unto them that he found him so fast, and heard him speak so terrible words, that he durst no further break. . . .

Whereupon soon after . . . many lords assembled in the Tower and there sat in council, devising the honorable solemnity of the King's coronation. . . . These lords so sitting together communing of this matter, the Protector came in amongst them, first about nine of the clock, saluting them courteously and excusing himself that he had been from them so long, saying merrily that he had been a sleeper that day.

After a little talking with them, he said unto the Bishop of Ely: "My lord, you have very good strawberries at your garden in Holborn; I require you let us have a mess of them." "Gladly, my lord" (quoth he), "would God I had some better thing as ready to your pleasure as that!" And therewithal in all the haste he sent his servant for a mess of strawberries. The Protector set the lords fast in communing and thereupon, praying them to spare him for a little while, departed thence. And soon after one hour, between ten and eleven he returned into the chamber amongst them all, changed with a wonderful sour angry countenance, knitting the brows, frowning and fretting, and gnawing on his lips, and so sat him down in his place.

All the lords were much dismayed and sore marveled at this manner of sudden change, and what thing should him ail. Then, when he had sitten still a while, thus he began: "What were they worthy to have that compass and imagine the destruction of me, being so near of blood unto the King, and Protector of his royal person and his realm?" . . . Then the Lord Chamberlain (as he that for the love between them thought he might be boldest with him) answered and said that they were worthy to be punished as heinous traitors, whatsoever they were. And all the other affirmed the same. "That is" (quoth he) "yonder sorceress my brother's wife, and other with her" (meaning the Queen). . . .

Then said the Protector: "Ye shall all see in what wise that sorceress and that other witch of her counsel, Shore's wife, with their affinity, have by their sorcery and witchcraft wasted my body." And therewith he plucked up his doublet sleeve to his elbow upon his left arm, where he showed a wearish withered arm, and small; as it was never other.

Hereupon every man's mind sore misgave them, well perceiving that this matter was but a quarrel. . . . Natheless, the Lord Chamberlain (which from the death of Kind Edward kept Shore's wife . . .) answered and said: "Certainly, my lord, if they have so heinously done, they be worthy heinous punishment."

"What!" (quoth the Protector), "thou servest me, I ween, with ifs and with ands; I tell thee they have so done, and that I will make good on thy body, traitor." . . . And anon the Protector said to the Lord Hastings: "I arrest thee, traitor." "What! me, my lord?" (quoth he). "Yea, thee, traitor," quoth the Protector. . . . whom the Protector bade speed and shrive him apace, "for by St. Paul" (quoth he), "I will not to dinner till I see thy head off." It booted him not to ask why, but heavily took a priest at adventure and made a short shrift. . . .

A marvelous case is it to hear either the warnings of that he should have voided, or the tokens of that he could not void. For the self night next before his death the Lord

Stanley sent a trusty messenger unto him at midnight in all the haste, requiring him to rise and ride away with him, for he was disposed utterly no longer to bide, he had so fearful a dream; in which him thought that a boar with his tusks so rased them both by the heads that the blood ran about both their shoulders. And forsomuch as the Protector gave the boar for his cognizance, this dream made so fearful an impression in his heart that he was thoroughly determined no longer to tarry, but had his horse ready, if the Lord Hastings would go with him, to ride yet so far the same night that they should be out of danger ere day.

"Ha, good Lord!" (quoth the Lord Hastings to this messenger), "leaneth my lord thy master so much to such trifles and hath such faith in dreams . . . ? Tell him it is plain witchcraft to believe in such dreams, which if they were tokens of things to come, why thinketh he not that we might be as likely to make them true by our going, if we were caught and brought back, as friends fail fliers? for then had the boar a cause likely to rase us with his tusks. . . . And therefore go to thy master (man) and commend me to him, and pray him be merry and have no fear; for I ensure him I am as sure of the man that he wotteth of as I am of mine own hand." . . .

Certain is it also that in riding towards the Tower, the same morning in which he was beheaded, his horse twice or thrice stumbled with him, almost to the falling. . . . The same morning, ere he was up, came a knight unto him, as it were of courtesy, to accompany him to the council; but of truth sent by the Protector to haste him thitherwards. . . .

This knight (I say), when it happened the Lord Chamberlain by the way to stay his horse and commune a while with a priest whom he met in the Tower street, brake his tale and said merrily to him: "What, my lord, I pray you come on; whereto talk you so long with that priest? You have no need of a priest yet"; and therewith he laughed upon him, as though he would say, "Ye shall have soon." . . .

Upon the very Tower wharf, so near the place where his head was off soon after, there met he with one Hastings, a pursuivant of his own name. . . . And therefore he said: "Ha, Hastings, art thou remembered when I met thee here once with an heavy heart?" "Yea, my lord" (quoth he), "that remember I well, and thanked be God they got no good nor you no harm thereby." "Thou wouldst say so" (quoth he), "if thou knewest as much as I know, which few know else as yet, and moe shall shortly." That meant he by the lords of the Queen's kindred that were taken before and should that day be beheaded at Pomfret; which he well wist, but nothing ware that the ax hung over his own head. "In faith, man" (quoth he), "I was never so sorry, nor never stood in so great dread in my life, as I did when thou and I met here. And lo how the world is turned: now stand mine enemies in the danger . . . and I never in my life so merry, nor never in so great surety." . . .

Now flew the flame of this lord's death swiftly through the city, and so forth further about like a wind in every man's ear. But the Protector, immediately after dinner, intending to set some color upon the matter, sent in all the haste for many substantial men out of the city into the Tower.

Now at their coming, himself with the Duke of Buckingham stood harnessed in old ill-faring briganders, such as no man should ween that they would vouchsafe to have put upon their backs except that some sudden necessity had constrained them. And then the Protector showed them that the Lord Chamberlain, and other of his conspiracy, had contrived to have suddenly destroyed him and the Duke, there the same day in the council. And what they intended further was as yet not well known. Of which their treason he never had knowledge before ten of the clock the same forenoon, which sudden fear drove them to put on for their defense such harness as came next to hand. And so had God holpen them that the mischief turned upon them that would have done it. And this he required them to report.

Every man answered him fair, as though no man mistrusted the matter, which of truth no man believed. Yet for the further appeasing of the people's minds he sent immediately after dinner in all the haste one herald of arms with a proclamation to be made through the city in the King's name, containing that the Lord Hastings, with divers other of his traitorous purpose, had before conspired the same day to have slain the Lord Protector and the Duke of Buckingham, sitting in the council. . . .

Now was this proclamation made within two hours after that he was beheaded, and it was so curiously indited, and so fair written in parchment, in so well a set hand, and therewith of itself so long a process, that every child might well perceive that it was prepared before. . . .

Now was it so devised by the Protector and his council that the self day in which the Lord Chamberlain was beheaded in the Tower of London, and about the selfsame hour, was there (not without his assent) beheaded at Pomfret the fore-remembered lords and knights that were taken from the King at Northampton and Stony Stratford. Which thing was done in the presence and by the order of Sir Richard Ratcliffe, knight, whose service the Protector specially used in that counsel and in the execution of such lawless enterprises, as a man that had been long secret with him, having experience of the world and a shrewd wit, short and rude in speech, rough and boisterous of behavior, bold in mischief, as far from pity as from all fear of God.

This knight, bringing them out of the prison to the scaffold and showing to the people about that they were traitors, . . . caused them hastily, without judgment, process, or manner of order, to be beheaded, and without other earthly guilt but only that they were good men, too true to the King, and too nigh to the Queen. . . .

Now then . . . it was by the Protector and his council concluded that this Dr. Shaw should in a sermon at Paul's Cross signify to the people that neither King Edward himself, nor the Duke of Clarence, were lawfully begotten, nor were not the very children of the Duke of York. . . . Then showed he that his very right heir of his body lawfully begotten was only the Lord Protector. For he declared then that King Edward was never lawfully married unto the Queen, but was before God husband unto Dame Elizabeth Lucy, and so his children bastards. . . . but the Lord Protector, he said, the very noble Prince, the special pattern of knightly prowess, as well in all princely behavior as in the lineaments and favor of his visage represented the very face of the noble Duke his father. "This is," quoth he, "the father's own figure, this is his own countenance, the very print of his visage, the sure undoubted image, the plain express likeness of that noble Duke." . . .

Then, on the Tuesday following this sermon, there came to the Guildhall in London the Duke of Buckingham, [who urged the citizens] "to make humble petition to the most puissant Prince, the Lord Protector, that it may like his Grace (at our humble request) to take upon him the guiding and governance of this realm. . . ."

When the Duke had said, and looked that the people, whom he hoped that the Mayor had framed before, should, after this proposition made, have cried, "King Richard, King Richard!" all was hushed and mute, and not one word answered thereunto. Wherewith the Duke was marvelously abashed, and, taking the Mayor nearer to him, with other that were about him privy to that matter, said unto them softly, "What meaneth this, that the people be so still?" "Sir" (quoth the Mayor), "percase they perceive you not well" . . . and said that the people had not been accustomed there to be spoken unto, but by the Recorder, which is the mouth of the city, and haply to him they will answer. . . . But the Recorder so tempered his tale that he showed everything as the Duke's words, and no part his own. . . . At the last in the nether end of the hall an ambushment of the Duke's servants . . . began suddenly at men's backs to cry out, as loud as their throats would give, "King Richard, King Richard!" and threw up their caps in token of joy. . . . Now when the Duke and the Mayor saw this manner, they wisely turned it to their purpose and said it was a goodly cry and a joyful, to hear every man with one voice, no man saying nay. . . .

Then, on the morrow after, the Mayor with all the aldermen and chief commoners of the city, in their best manner appareled, assembling themselves together, resorted unto Baynard's Castle, where the Protector lay. To which place repaired also (according to their appointment) the Duke of Buckingham, and divers noble men with him, beside many knights and other gentlemen. And thereupon the Duke sent word unto the Lord Protector of the being there of a great and honorable company to move a great matter unto his Grace. Whereupon the Protector made difficulty to come out unto them, but if he first knew some part of their errand, as though he doubted and partly mistrusted the coming of such a number unto him so suddenly, without any warning or knowledge whether they came for good or harm.

Then the Duke . . . sent unto him by the messenger such loving message again . . . that at the last he came forth of his chamber, and yet not down unto them, but stood above in a gallery over them [Grafton and Hall add: with a bishop on every hand of him], where they might see him and speak to him, as though he would not yet come too near them till he wist what they meant. And thereupon the Duke of Buckingham first made humble petition unto him on the behalf of them all that his Grace would pardon them. . . .

When the Duke had his leave and pardon to speak, then waxed he bold to show him their intent . . . and finally to beseech his Grace that it would like him, of his accustomed goodness and zeal unto the realm, now with his eye of pity to behold the long-continued distress and decay of the same. . . . All which he might well do by taking upon him the crown and governance of this realm, according to his right and title lawfully descended unto him. . . .

When the Protector had heard the proposition, he looked very strangely thereat, and answered: that, all were it that he partly knew the things by them alleged to be true, yet such entire love he bare unto King Edward and his children . . . that he could not find it in his heart in this point to incline to their desire. For in all other nations, where the truth were not well known, it should peradventure be thought that it were his own ambitious mind and device to depose the Prince and take himself the crown. . . .

Upon this answer given, the Duke . . . showed aloud unto the Protector . . . that the realm was appointed King Edward's line should not any longer reign upon them. . . . These words much moved the Protector. . . .

But when he saw there was none other way, but that either he must take it, or else he and his both go from it, he said unto the lords and commons: "Sith we perceive well that all the realm is so set . . . we be content and agree favorably to incline to your petition and request, and (according to the same) here we take upon us the royal estate . . ."

With this there was a great shout, crying, "King Richard, King Richard!" . . .

King Richard, after his coronation, . . . sent one John Greene (whom he specially trusted) unto Sir Robert Braken-bury, Constable of the Tower, with a letter, and credence also, that the same Sir Robert should in any wise put the two children to death. . . . Who plainly answered that he would never put them to death, to die therefor. With which answer John Greene, returning, recounted the same to King Richard at Warwick yet in his way. Wherewith he took such displeasure and thought that the same night he said unto a secret page of his: "Ah! whom shall a man trust? Those that I have brought up myself, those that I had weened would most surely serve me, even those fail me and at my commandment will do nothing for me." "Sir" (quoth his page), "there lieth one on your pallet without that I dare well say, to do your Grace pleasure the thing were right hard that he would refuse." Meaning by this Sir James Tirrell. . . .

King Richard arose. . . . And calling up Sir James, brake to him secretly his mind in this mischievous matter. In which he found him nothing strange. Wherefore on the morrow he sent him to Brakenbury with a letter, by which he was commanded to deliver Sir James all the keys of the Tower for one night, to the end he might there accomplish the King's pleasure in such things as he had given him commandment. After which letter delivered, and the keys received, Sir James appointed the night next ensuing to destroy them, devising before and preparing the means. . . .

For Sir James Tirrell devised that they should be murdered in their beds. To the execution whereof he appointed Miles Forrest, one of the four that kept them, a fellow fleshed in murder beforetime. To him he joined one John Dighton, his own horsekeeper, a big, broad, square, and strong knave.

Then all the other being removed from them, this Miles Forrest and John Dighton about midnight (the seely children lying in their beds) came into the chamber and, suddenly lapping them up among the clothes, so to-bewrapped them and entangled them, keeping down by force the featherbed and pillows hard unto their mouths, that within a while, smothered and stifled, their breath failing, they gave up to God their innocent souls into the joys of heaven, leaving to the tormentors their bodies dead in the bed. Which after that the wretches perceived, first by the struggling with the pains of death, and after, long lying still, to be thoroughly dead, they laid their bodies naked out upon the bed and fetched Sir James to see them; which, upon the sight of them, caused those murderers to bury them at the stair foot, meetly deep in the ground, under a great heap of stones.

Then rode Sir James in great haste to King Richard and showed him all the manner of the murder; who gave him great thanks . . . they say that a priest of Sir Robert Brakenbury's took up the bodies again and secretly interred them. . . .

Some have I heard say that the Duke [of Buckingham], a little before his coronation, among other things required of the Protector the Duke of Hereford's lands, to the which he pretended himself just inheritor. And forsomuch as the title which he claimed by inheritance was somewhat interlaced with the title to the crown by the line of King Henry before deprived, the Protector conceived such indignation that he rejected the Duke's request with many spiteful and minatory words. Which so wounded his heart with hatred and mistrust that he never after could endure to look aright on King Richard, but ever feared his own life. . . .

The Duke . . . prepared open war against him . . . Sir Edward Courtney and Peter his brother, Bishop of Exeter, raised another army in Devonshire and Cornwall. In Kent Richard Gilford and other gentlemen collected a great company of soldiers and openly began war. . . .

The Duke of Buckingham, accompanied with a great power of wild Welshmen, . . . [was separated from them by a flood,] was of necessity compelled to fly . . . and he fell infortunately into the hands of the foaming boar, that tore him in pieces with his tusks. . . .

But when he had confessed the whole fact and conspiracy, upon All Souls' Day, without arraignment or judgment, he was at Salisbury, in the open market place, on a new scaffold beheaded and put to death. . . .

Henry Earl of Richmond prepared an army of five thousand manly Bretons and forty well-furnished ships . . . the Earl approached to the south part of the realm of England, even at the mouth of the haven of Poole in the county of Dorset, where he might plainly perceive all the sea banks and shores garnished and furnished with men of war and soldiers, appointed and deputed there to defend his arrival and landing. . . .

The Earl of Richmond, suspecting their flattering request to be but a fraud (as it was indeed) ... [returned to Brittany]. ...

King Richard [at Exeter] ... went about the city and viewed the seat of the same, and at length he came to the castle; and when he understood that it was called Rugemont, suddenly he fell into a dump and (as one astonied) said: "Well, I see my days be not long." He spake this of a prophecy told him, that when he came once to Richmond he should not long live after; which fell out in the end to be true, not in respect of this castle, but in respect of Henry Earl of Richmond. ...

[Richard] revolved in his wavering mind how great a fountain of mischief toward him should spring if the Earl of Richmond should be advanced to the marriage of his niece ... he himself would rather take to wife his cousin and niece the Lady Elizabeth. ... Wherefore he sent to the Queen (being in sanctuary) divers and often messengers, which first should excuse and purge him of all things before against her attempted or procured, and after should so largely promise promotions innumerable, and benefits, not only to her, but also to her son Lord Thomas, Marquis Dorset, that they should bring her (if it were possible) into some wanhope, or (as men say) into a fool's paradise.

The messengers, being men both of wit and gravity, so persuaded the Queen with great and pregnant reasons, and what with fair and large promises, that she began somewhat to relent, and to give to them no deaf ear; insomuch that she faithfully promised to submit and yield herself fully and frankly to the King's will and pleasure. ...

After this he procured a common rumor (but he would not have the author known) to be published and spread abroad among the common people, that the Queen [Anne] was dead; to the intent that she, taking some conceit of this strange fame, should fall into some sudden sickness or grievous malady; and to prove, if afterwards she should fortune by that or any other ways to lose her life, whether the people would impute her death to the thought or sickness, or thereof would lay the blame to him. ...

But howsoever that it fortuned, either by inward thought and pensiveness of heart, or by infection of poison (which is affirmed to be most likely), within few days after, the Queen departed out of this transitory life. . . .

Amongst the noble men whom he most mistrusted, these were the principal: . . . the Lord Stanley, because he was joined in matrimony with the Lady Margaret, mother to the Earl of Richmond. . . . For when the said Lord Stanley would have departed into his country to visit his family and to recreate and refresh his spirits (as he openly said, but the truth was, to the intent to be in a perfect readiness to receive the Earl of Richmond at his first arrival in England), the King in no wise would suffer him to depart before he had left as an hostage in the court George Stanley, Lord Strange, his first-begotten son and heir. . . .

[When Richmond invaded England,] the whole army came before the town of Tamworth; and . . . he privily departed again from his host to the town of Atherstone, where the Lord Stanley and Sir William his brother with their bands were abiding. There the Earl came first to his father-in-law, in a little close, where he saluted him and Sir William his brother; and after divers and friendly embracings, each rejoiced of the state of other and suddenly were surprised with great joy, comfort, and hope of fortunate success in all their affairs and doings. Afterward they consulted together how to give battle to King Richard, if he would abide, whom they knew not to be far off with an huge host. . . .

King Richard, which was appointed now to finish his last labor by the very divine justice and providence of God (which called him to condign punishment for his mischievous deserts), marched to a place meet for two battles to encounter, by a village called Bosworth, not far from Leicester; and there he pitched his field on a hill called Anne Beame, refreshed his soldiers, and took his rest.

The fame went that he had the same night a dreadful and terrible dream; for it seemed to him, being asleep, that he did see divers images like terrible devils, which pulled and haled him, not suffering him to take any quiet or rest. The which strange vision not so suddenly struck his heart with a sudden fear, but it stuffed his head and troubled his mind with many busy and dreadful imaginations. For incontinent after, his heart being almost damped, he prognosticated before the doubtful chance of the battle to come; not using the alacrity and mirth of mind and countenance as he was accustomed to do before he came toward the battle. And lest that it might be suspected that he was abashed for fear of his enemies, and for that cause looked so piteously, he recited and declared to his familiar friends in the morning his wonderful vision and fearful dream. . . .

[Richmond's army] exceeded not five thousand men, beside the power of the Stanleys, whereof three thousand were in the field under the standard of Sir William Stanley. The King's number was double so much and more. When both these armies were thus ordered, and all men ready to set forward, King Richard called his chieftains together and to them said as followeth.

The oration of King Richard the Third to the chieftains of his army. . . .

"Ye see . . . how a company of traitors, thieves, outlaws, and runagates of our own nation be aiders and partakers of his feat and enterprise, ready at hand to overcome and oppress us. You see also what a number of beggarly Bretons and fainthearted Frenchmen be with him arrived to destroy us, our wives and children. . . .

"And to begin with the Earl of Richmond, captain of this rebellion, he is a Welsh milksop, a man of small courage and of less experience in martial acts and feats of war, brought up by my mother's means and mine, like a captive in a close cage, in the court of Francis, Duke of Brittany. . . . Now, St. George to borrow, let us set forward. . . ."

The oration of King Henry the Seventh to his army:

"If ever God gave victory to men fighting in a just quarrel . . . I doubt not but God will rather aid us (yea, and fight for us) than see us vanquished and overthrown by such as neither fear him nor his laws, nor yet regard justice or honesty. . . . For what can be a more honest, goodly, or godly quarrel than to fight against a captain, being an homicide and murderer of his own blood or progeny, an extreme destroyer of his nobility? . . .

"Therefore labor for your gain and sweat for your right. . . . And this one thing I assure you, that in so just and good a cause, and so notable a quarrel, you shall find me this day rather a dead carrion upon the cold ground than a free prisoner on a carpet in a lady's chamber. . . . And therefore in the name of God and St. George, let every man courageously advance forth his standard." . . .

When King Richard saw the Earl's company was passed the marsh, he did command with all haste to set upon them. . . . Now being inflamed with ire and vexed with outrageous malice, he put his spurs to his horse and rode out of the side of the range of his battle, leaving the vanguard fighting, and like a hungry lion ran with spear in rest toward him. The Earl of Richmond . . . gladly proffered to encounter with him body to body and man to man. . . . King Richard's men were driven back and fled, and he himself, manfully fighting in the middle of his enemies, was slain, and (as he worthily had deserved) came to a bloody death, as he had led a bloody life. . . .

In this battle . . . of the nobility were slain John, Duke of Norfolk, which was warned by divers to refrain from the field, insomuch that the night before he should set forward toward the King, one wrote this rhyme upon his gate:

> Jack of Norfolk, be not too bold,
> For Dickon thy master is bought and sold. . . .

King Richard (as the fame went) might have escaped and gotten safeguard by fleeing. For . . . when the loss of the battle was imminent and apparent, they brought to him a swift and light horse, to convey him away. He, which was not ignorant of the grudge and ill will that the common people bare toward him, casting away all hope of fortunate success and happy chance to come, answered (as men say) that on that day he would make an end of all battles, or else there finish his life. . . .

When the Earl had thus obtained victory, and slain his mortal enemy, he kneeled down and rendered to almighty God his hearty thanks . . . he not only praised and lauded his valiant soldiers, but also gave unto them his hearty thanks. . . . Then the people rejoiced, and clapped their hands, crying up to heaven, "King Henry, King Henry!"

When the Lord Stanley saw the good will and gladness of the people, he took the crown of King Richard, which was found amongst the spoil in the field, and set it on the Earl's head. . . .

Anon after, he assembled together the sage councilors of the realm, in which council, like a prince of just faith and true of promise, to avoid all civil discord, he appointed a day to join in marriage with the Lady Elizabeth, heir of the house of York, with his noble person, heir to the line of Lancaster. . . . By reason of which marriage, peace was thought to descend out of heaven into England. . . .

Commentaries

CHARLES LAMB

Letter to Robert Lloyd

I am possessed with an admiration of the genuine Richard, his genius, and his mounting spirit, which no consideration of his cruelties can depress. Shakspeare has not made Richard so black a Monster as is supposed. Wherever he is monstrous, it was to conform to vulgar opinion. But he is generally a Man. Read his most exquisite address to the Widowed Queen to court her daughter for him—the topics of maternal feeling, of a deep knowledge of the heart, are such as no monster could have supplied. Richard must have *felt* before he could feign so well; tho' ambition choked the good seed. I think it the most finished piece of Eloquence in the world; of *persuasive* oratory far above Demosthenes, Burke, or any man, far exceeding the courtship of Lady Anne. Her relenting is barely natural, after all; the more perhaps S[hakespeare]'s merit to make *impossible* appear *probable,* but the *Queen's consent* (taking in all the circumstances and topics, *private and public* . . .) is probable. . . . This observation applies to many other parts. All the inconsistency is, that Shakespeare's better genius was forced to struggle against the prejudices which made a monster of Richard. He set out to paint a *monster,* but his human sympathies produced a *man.*   [1801]

From *Charles Lamb and the Lloyds*, ed. E. V. Lucas (London: Smith, Elder, & Company, 1898).

CHARLES LAMB

From Cooke's *Richard the Third*

We are ready to acknowledge that this actor presents us with a very original and very forcible portrait (if not of the *man Richard,* whom Shakspeare drew, yet) of the *monster Richard,* as he exists in the *popular idea,* in *his own exaggerated* and *witty self-abuse,* in the overstrained representations of the parties who were *sufferers* by his *ambition;* and, above all, in the impertinent and wretched *scenes,* so absurdly foisted in by some who have thought themselves capable of adding to what *Shakspeare wrote.*

But of Mr. Cooke's *Richard:*

1st, *His predominant and masterly simulation.*

He has a tongue can wheedle with the DEVIL.

It has been the policy of that ancient and gray simulator, in all ages, to hide his *horns* and *claws.* The *Richard* of Mr. Cooke perpetually obtrudes *his.* We see the effect of his deceit uniformly *successful,* but we do not comprehend *how* it *succeeds.* We can put ourselves, by a very common fiction, into the place of the individuals upon whom it acts, and say, that, in the like case, we should not have been alike credulous. The hypocrisy is too glaring and visible. It resembles more the shallow cunning of a mind which is its own dupe than the profound and practiced art of so powerful an intellect as *Richard's.* It is too obstreperous and loud, breaking out into *triumphs* and *plaudits* at its own success, like an unexercised *novitiate* to *tricks.* It has none of the silent confidence and steady self-command of the *experienced politician;* it possesses none of that *fine address* which was necessary to have betrayed the heart of

From *The Works of Charles Lamb,* ed. William MacDonald (London: J. M. Dent, 1903), Vol. III.

Lady Anne, or even to have imposed upon the duller wits of the Lord *Mayor* and *Citizens.*

2ndly, *His habitual jocularity,* the effect of buoyant spirits and an elastic mind, rejoicing in its own powers and in the success of its machinations. This quality of unstrained mirth accompanies *Richard* and is a prime feature in his character. It never leaves him; in plots, in stratagems, and in the midst of his bloody devices, it is perpetually driving him upon wit and jests and personal satire, fanciful allusions, and quaint felicities of phrase. It is one of the chief artifices by which the consummate master of dramatic effect has contrived to soften the horrors of the scene, and to make us contemplate a bloody and vicious character with delight. Nowhere, in any of his plays, is to be found so much of sprightly colloquial dialogue, and soliloquies of genuine humor, as in *Richard.* This character of unlabored mirth Mr. Cooke seems entirely to pass over, and substitutes in its stead the coarse, taunting humor and clumsy merriment of a low-minded assassin.

3dly, *His personal deformity.*— When the *Richard* of Mr. Cooke makes allusions to his own *form,* they seem accompanied with *unmixed distaste* and *pain,* like some obtrusive and *haunting* idea— But surely the *Richard* of Shakspeare mingles in these allusions a perpetual reference to his own powers and capacities, by which he is enabled to surmount these petty objections; and the joy of a defect *conquered,* or *turned* into an advantage, is one cause of these very allusions, and of the satisfaction with which his mind recurs to them. These allusions themselves are made in an ironical and good-humored spirit of exaggeration—the most bitter of them are to be found in his self-congratulating soliloquy spoken in the very moment and crisis of joyful exultation on the success of his unheard-of courtship.

[1802]

CHARLES LAMB

From On the Tragedies of Shakespeare, Considered with Reference to Their Fitness for Stage Representation

Not one of the spectators who have witnessed Mr. C[ooke]'s exertions in that part, but has come away with a proper conviction that Richard is a very wicked man and kills little children in their beds, with something like the pleasure which the giants and ogres in children's books are represented to have taken in that practice; moreover, that he is very close and shrewd and devilish cunning, for you could see that by his eye.

But is in fact this the impression we have in reading the Richard of Shakspeare? Do we feel anything like disgust, as we do at that butcherlike representation of him that passes for him on the stage? A horror at his crimes blends with the effect that we feel, but how is it qualified, how is it carried off, by the rich intellect which he displays, his resources, his wit, his buoyant spirits, his vast knowledge and insight into characters, the poetry of his part—not an atom of all which is made perceivable in Mr. C[ooke]'s way of acting it. Nothing but his crimes, his actions, is visible; they are prominent and staring. The murderer stands out, but where is the lofty genius, the man of vast capacity—the profound, the witty, accomplished Richard?   [1811]

From *The Works of Charles Lamb*, ed. William MacDonald (London: J. M. Dent, 1903), Vol. III.

A. P. ROSSITER

Angel with Horns: The Unity of *Richard III*

"Let's write 'good angel' on the devil's horn."
                              ——*Measure for Measure*, 2.4.16

In the Second Part of *Henry IV* (3.1) the King and Warwick are talking away the midnight, or the King's insomnia;
and the King remembers how Richard spoke like a prophet
of the future treachery of the Percies. Warwick replies that
those who look for rotations in history can indeed appear to
be prophets:

> There is a history in all men's lives,
> Figuring the nature of the times deceased;
> The which observed, a man may prophesy,
> With a near aim, of the main chance of things
> As yet not come to life, who in their seeds
> And weak beginning lie intreasurèd.
> Such things become the hatch and brood of time.

>   (80–86)

Richard, he explains, had observed "the necessary form" of
the events he had seen happen; and from that he could
"create a perfect guess" of some that were to ensue as "the
hatch and brood of time."

Men have always looked for such a predictability in history: it gives the illusion of a comfortably ordered world.
They have also often read—and written—historical records
to show that the course of events has been guided by a simple

From *Angel with Horns and Other Shakespeare Lectures* by A. P. Rossiter
(London: Longmans, Green & Co., Limited, 1961; New York: Theatre Arts
Books, 1961). © 1961 by Longmans, Green & Co., Limited. Reprinted by per-
mission of Longmans, Green & Co., Limited, and Theatre Arts Books.

process of divine justice, dispensing rewards and punishments here on earth and seeing to it that the wicked do *not* thrive like the green bay tree (as the Psalmist thought), and that virtue is not "triumphant only in theatrical performances" (as the humane Mikado put it: being a Gilbertian Japanese, not an Elizabethan Christian). The story matter of the Henry IV plays and of *Richard III* accepted both of these comforting and comfortable principles.

When I say "story matter" I mean what the Chronicles gave the author (or authors) of these four plays, and I wish to remain uncommitted as to whether their *plots* (and especially that of *Richard III*) work entirely within those reassuring limitations.

I am averse to source study, as material for lectures. Yet sad experience of human nature (and perhaps of historians) leads me to remind you how the Richard III myth ("story") came to reach Shakespeare. In the play, you remember, the Bishop of Ely, Morton, plots with Buckingham and runs away to join Richmond (Henry Tudor). He duly became one of Henry's ministers; and Thomas More grew up in his household—and later wrote the life of Richard III. It would only be human if Morton recounted all the worst that was ever said of the master he had betrayed: it is not surprising that Edward Halle should accept More's account, in writing his vast book on the "noble and illustre families of Lancastre and York"; and still more human that Raphael Holinshed (whom no one could call a historian) should copy extensively from Halle—and so leave room for all those since Horace Walpole who have had doubts about the historical character of this terrible monarch and the events of his times.

To think that we are seeing anything like sober history in this play is derisible naïvety. What we are offered is a formally patterned sequence presenting two things: on the one hand, a rigid Tudor *schema* of retributive justice (a sort of analogy to Newton's Third Law in the field of moral dynamics: "Action and reaction are equal and opposite"); and, on the other, a huge triumphant stage personality, an early old masterpiece of the art of rhetorical stage writing, a monstrous being incredible in any sober, historical scheme of things—Richard himself.

I will talk about the first, first. The basic pattern of retributive justice (or God's vengeance) is well enough illustrated in Holinshed, in the passage telling how Prince Edward (Henry VI's son and Margaret's) was murdered at the Battle of Tewkesbury. The prince was handed over to Edward IV on the proclamation of a promise that he would not be harmed; he was brought before the King, asked why he "durst so presumptuously enter into his realm" and replied courageously "To recover my father's kingdom and heritage" (and more to that purpose)—but let Holinshed say the rest:

> At which words king Edward said nothing, but with his hand thrust him from him, or (as some saie) stroke him with his gantlet; whom incontinentlie, George duke of Clarence, Richard duke of Glocester, Thomas Greie marquesse Dorcet, and William lord Hastings, that stood by, suddenlie murthered; for the which cruell act, the more part of the dooers in their latter daies dranke of the like cup, by the righteous justice and due punishment of God.

There you have the notional pattern, in little, of the whole framework of *Richard III*: Clarence—"false, fleeting, perjured Clarence" (who took the sacrament to remain true to Henry VI of Lancaster and deserted him); Gray—one of the group of Queen Elizabeth Woodeville's relations, who fall to Richard and Buckingham next after Clarence; Hastings, who says he will see "this crown of mine hewn from its shoulders / Before I see the crown so foul misplaced" (on Richard's head) (3.2.43–44)—and *does* (if a man can be said to see his own decapitation). Holinshed really understates the matter in writing "the more part of the dooers . . . dranke of the like cup"; for of those he names, everyone did. On the one hand, that is what *Richard III* is about: what it is composed of. A heavy-handed justice commends the ingredients of a poisoned [cup].

This notional pattern of historic events rigidly determined by a mechanical necessity is partly paralleled by, partly modified by, the formal patterns of the episodes (or scenes) and the language. By "formal patterns" I mean the unmistakably iterated goings-on in scenes so exactly parallel that if the first *is* passable on a modern stage as quasi-realistic costume-play stuff, the second (repeating it always *more* unrealistically) cannot be. The two wooing scenes (Richard with Anne and Elizabeth) are the simplest case; but in the lamentation scenes—where a collection of bereft females comes together and goes through a dismal catalogue of *Who was Who* and *Who has lost Whom* (like a gathering of historical Mrs. Gummidges, each "thinking of the old 'un" with shattering simultaneity)—there, even editors have found the proceedings absurd; and readers difficult. When Queen Margaret, for example, says:

> I had an Edward, till a Richard killed him;
> I had a husband, till a Richard killed him.
> Thou hadst an Edward, till a Richard killed him;
> Thou hadst a Richard, till a Richard killed him.
>
> (4.4.40–43)

a reader may *just* keep up (and realize that the last two are the Princes in the Tower, so that Queen Elizabeth is being addressed); but when the Duchess of York takes up with

> I had a Richard too, and thou didst kill him;
> I had a Rutland too, thou holp'st to kill him,   (44–45)

it is likely that you are lost, unless your recollection of a *Henry VI* and the ends of Richard, Duke of York, and his young son (Edmund) is unusually clear.

It is not only the iteration of scene that is stylized: the stiffly formal manipulation of echoing phrase and sequence of words within the scenes is even more unrealistic. A closely related parallelism exists in the repeated occurrence of a sort of "single-line traffic" in sentences: the classicist's *stichomythia.* One speaker takes from the other exactly the same ration of syllables, and rejoins as if under contract to repeat the form of the given sentence as exactly as possible, using the maximum number of the same words or their logical opposites, or (failing that) words closely associated with them. I describe the game pedantically, because it *is* an exact and scientific game with language, and one of the graces and beauties of the play Shakespeare wrote. If we cannot accept the "patterned speech" of *Richard III,* its quality must remain unknown to us. "Early work" is an evasive, criticism-dodging term. Early it may be; but the play is a triumphant contrivance in a manner which cannot properly be compared with that of any other tragedy—nor of any history, except *3 Henry VI* (where the manner takes shape, and particularly in 3.2) and *King John* (which is not half so well built or integrated as this).

I have emphasized the stylization of verbal patterning (with its neatly overexact adjustments of stroke to stroke, as in royal tennis), because the sequence of most of the important events offers very much the same pattern. I might remark, in passing, that these verbal devices were offering to the Elizabethans an accomplished English equivalent to the neat dexterities they admired in Seneca (a point made by T. S. Eliot years ago; though he did not examine how the dramatic ironies of the action run in parallel with these counterstroke reversals of verbal meaning, and form a kind of harmony). But we miss something more than Shakespeare's rhetorical game of tennis if merely irritated by, e.g.:

> *Anne.* I would I knew thy heart.
>
> *Richard.* 'Tis figured in my tongue.
>
> *Anne.* I fear me both are false.
>
> *Richard.* Then never man was true.   (1.2.192–95)

Those reversals of intention (*heart-tongue*; *false-true*) are on precisely the pattern of the repeated reversals of human expectation, the reversals of events, the anticipated reversals (foreseen only by the audience), which make "dramatic irony." The patterned speech of the dialogue—the wit that demonstrates that a sentence is but a cheveril glove, quickly turned the other way—is fundamentally one with the ironic patterns of the plot. "Dramatic irony" here is verbal *peripeteia.*

You will see that simply exemplified if you read Buckingham's speech at the beginning of Act 2, where he calls a curse on himself if ever he goes back on his reconciliation

with the Queen (and is quite specific about it); then turn
straight to his last lines in 5.1, when he is on the way to execution: "That high All-seer, which I dallied with." He has
got exactly what he asked for. He did not mean the words he
used, but they have been reversed into actuality, in exactly
the same way as verbal terms are reversed in the tennis-court
game of rhetoric.

The same irony plays all over *Richard III*. It lurks like a
shadow behind the naïvely self-confident Hastings; it hovers
a moment over Buckingham when Margaret warns him
against "yonder dog" (Richard) and, on Richard's asking
what she said, he replies, "Nothing that I respect, my gracious lord" (1.3.295)—and this at a time when Buckingham
is under no threat whatsoever.

Its cumulative effect is to present the personages as
existing in a state of total and terrible uncertainty. This is
enhanced if we know the details of what comes into the play
from *3 Henry VI*, but is there even if we know only a few
bare essentials of what has gone before. We need to know
who Margaret is; how Lancaster has been utterly defeated,
and King Henry and his son murdered; how Clarence
betrayed his King and returned to the Yorkists; and how
Richard, his younger brother, has already marked him as his
immediate obstruction on his intended way to the crown. We
need to know too that the Duchess of York is mother to that
unrewarding trio, Edward IV, Clarence, Gloucester; that
Edward IV has married an aspiring commoner, Elizabeth
Grey (*née* Woodeville); and that she has jacked up her relations into nobility. Beyond those half-dozen facts we do not
need back-reference to *3 Henry VI* for any but the finer
points—so far as the essential ironies of the plot go.

Far more important than these details is the simple over-
riding principle derived from the Tudor historians: that England rests under a chronic curse—the curse of faction, civil
dissension, and fundamental anarchy, resulting from the de-
position and murder of the Lord's Anointed (Richard II) and
the usurpation of the house of Lancaster. The savageries of
the Wars of the Roses follow logically (almost theologi-
cally) from that; and Elizabeth's "All-seeing heaven, what a
world is this!" says but half. It is a world of absolute and

hereditary moral ill, in which *everyone* (till the appearance of Richmond-Tudor in Act 5) is tainted with the treacheries, the blood and the barbarities of civil strife, and internally blasted with the curse of a moral anarchy which leaves but three human *genera*: the strong in evil, the feebly wicked, and the helplessly guilt-tainted (such as the Princes, Anne— all those despairing, lamenting women, whose choric wailings are a penitential psalm of guilt and sorrow: England's guilt, the individual's sorrow). The "poor painted Queen's" "What a world" needs supplementing with the words of the pessimistically clear-sighted Third Citizen:

> All may be well; but, if God sort it so,
> 'Tis more than we deserve or I expect.   (2.2.36–37)

I have in effect described the meaning of the framework of the play: presented it as "moral history," to be interpreted in abstract terms. But the play itself is also a symphonic structure which I can only describe in terms of music: a rhetorical symphony of five movements, with first and second subjects and some Wagnerian leitmotifs. The playmaking framework is Senecan revenge, the characterization largely Marlovian; but the orchestration is not only original, but unique. It can be sketched like this.

The first movement employs five "subjects": Richard himself, his own overture; the wooing theme (to be repeated in the fourth movement); Richard among his enemies (repeating the duplicity with which he has fooled Clarence); Margaret's curse; and the long dying fall of Clarence. It occupies the whole of Act 1.

The second movement includes Act 2 and scenes 1–4 of Act 3. It begins with the King's feeble peacemaking— in which Buckingham invites his curse—and its other subjects are: a lamentation after the King's death (repeated in the fourth movement); the fall of the curse on Rivers, Grey, and Vaughan (when the curse is remembered), and on Hastings (the curse briefly recalled again). The future subject of Richard's moves against the Princes is introduced between-whiles.

The third movement cuts across the act divisions and

runs from 3.5 to 4.3. Its main subject is the Gloucester-Buckingham plot for the crown, with the magnificently sardonic fooling of the London *bourgeoisie* with a crisis-scare, a brace of bishops, and the headline story that here is a highly respectable unlibidinous monarch for decent England. On its success, Anne is called to be Queen, and thus to meet the curse she herself called on Richard's wife before he wooed her in that humor and won her (the first movement is here caught up). Buckingham now makes himself one of Richard's future victims by showing reluctance for the plot against the Princes, and Richard throws him off with a snub. The Princes are dealt with (the account of Forrest and Deighton echoing that of the murderers of Clarence, one of whom had a temporary conscience); and Richard concludes with a brisk summary and prospectus:

> The sons of Edward sleep in Abraham's bosom,
> And Anne my wife hath bid this world good night;
>
> (4.3.38–39)

and so, since Richmond plans to marry "young Elizabeth, my brother's daughter," "To her go I, a jolly thriving wooer" (Richard's last jocularity). The movement ends with the first murmurs of Richmond. Previously there has been slipped in the trivial-sounding prophecy about "Rugemont," besides Henry VI's prophecy (4.2.94 ff.). The flight of the Bishop of Ely (Morton) really troubles Richard.

The fourth movement brings down the curse on Buckingham (5.1 is obviously misplaced, so the movement runs from 4.4 to 5.1 inclusive). Mainly it repeats themes heard before: with a long lamentation scene (the Blake-like weeping Queens); a repetition of Margaret's curse with the curse of Richard's mother added; the second wooing scene; the subject of Nemesis repeated by Buckingham. In it the sound of Richmond's advance has become clearer; and Richard's self-command and certainty begin to waver.

The fifth movement is all at Bosworth: the fall of the curse on Richard himself. There is the dream-prologue of the procession of contrapuntal Ghosts (including all those so qualified from the four previous movements) and, like all ghosts, they are reminiscent and repetitive. The play ends with the epilogue to the Wars of the Roses—spoken by Queen Elizabeth's grandfather—calling a blessing on the English future, and inverting the opening lines of Richard's prologue:

> Now is the winter of our discontent
> Made glorious summer.   (1.1.1–2)

The deliberateness of this highly controlled workmanship needs but little comment. I shall take up a single musical phrase: one that intertwines its plangent undertones throughout the whole symphony, a true leitmotif.

At first sight, Clarence's dream (1.4.9 ff.) appears to contribute little to the play, nothing to the plot; and it may seem a rhetorical indulgence, even if we accept Mr. Eliot's judgment that it shows "a real approximation in English to the magnificence of Senecan Latin at its best. . . . The best of Seneca has here been absorbed into English."[1] But first recollect the setting. Clarence has been sent to the Tower, by the machinations of the Queen's party (so he thinks), and he is confident that his brother Richard will stand good friend to him. He believes Richard's worried "We are not safe, Clarence, we are not safe" (1.1.70); cannot possibly see the ironical joke Richard is cracking with himself; has no idea that he has been first on Richard's list since that moment in *3 Henry VI* (5.6) when his brother muttered, "Clarence, beware; thou keep'st me from the light."[2] (A line that follows a passage predetermining the gulling of both Clarence and Anne to follow:

> I have no brother, I am like no brother;
> And this word "love," which graybeards call divine,
> Be resident in men like one another,
> And not in me! I am myself alone.)   (80–83)

---

[1] *Selected Essays*, 1932, p. 90; reprinted from Introduction to *Seneca His Tenne Tragedies*, 1927.

[2] This contradicts R. G. Moulton, *Shakespeare as a Dramatic Artist*, 1885 (p. 92), who says Richard is *not* "ambitious" (as Macbeth is): "never found dwelling upon the prize in view." This presumes a complete disconnection between *3 Henry VI* and *Richard III*. No such assumption is acceptable nowadays—nor was it sensible even then.

Clarence had not been there to hear that: knows nothing of
the typically sharp reversal of Richard's solemnly hypocritical fooling now with:

> Go tread the path that thou shalt ne'er return.
> Simple plain Clarence, I do love thee so
> That I will shortly send thy soul to heaven,
> If heaven will take the present at our hands.
>
> (1.1.117–20)

Clarence has his nightmare in the Tower: a vision prophetic of
doom, and thick with curdled guilt. He dreams that Richard
blunderingly knocks him overboard from a vessel; he drowns;
goes to hell; and his guilt-sick mind spews up its own evil:

> *Keeper.* Awaked you not in this sore agony?
>
> *Clarence.* No, no, my dream was lengthened after life.
> O, then began the tempest to my soul!
> I passed, methought, the melancholy flood,
> With that sour ferryman which poets write of,
> Unto the kingdom of perpetual night.
> The first that there did greet my stranger soul
> Was my great father-in-law, renownèd Warwick,
> Who spake aloud, "What scourge for perjury
> Can this dark monarchy afford false Clarence?"
> And so he vanished. Then came wand'ring by
> A shadow like an angel, with bright hair
> Dabbled in blood, and he shrieked out aloud,
> "Clarence is come, false, fleeting, perjured Clarence,
> That stabbed me in the field by Tewkesbury.
> Seize on him, Furies, take him unto torment!"   (1.4.42–57)

It is as fine a passage in that style as English can offer: calculated to leave its solemn music in even half-attentive ears.
In the second movement of the play (2.2.43 ff.), Queen Elizabeth announces the King's death:

> If you will live, lament; if die, be brief,
> That our swift-wingèd souls may catch the King's,

> Or like obedient subjects follow him
> To his new kingdom of ne'er-changing night.

It is scarcely a proper-wifely expectation of the fate of her husband's spirit: but the echo of "Unto the kingdom of perpetual night" is the effect intended, not Elizabeth's notions. The actors who put together the Q. text of 1597 showed that they appreciated, if clumsily, the author's intention. They made it "To his new kingdom of perpetuall rest": catching the echo rightly, while missing the point.

The same "dark monarchy" awaits all these people: they are the living damned. That is the translation of this echo-technique of leitmotifs; and why I call the play's anatomy "musical." Nor is that all: the phrase returns again. But before I come to that, remark how Hastings philosophizes on his fall at the end of the second movement:

> O momentary grace of mortal men,
> Which we more hunt for than the grace of God!
> Who builds his hope in air of your good[3] looks
> Lives like a drunken sailor on a mast,
> Ready with every nod to tumble down
> Into the fatal bowels of the deep.   (3.4.95–100)

We have heard that surging rhythm before. And with it the feeling of being aloft, in air, unbalanced: the rhythm of Clarence dreaming:

> As we paced along
> Upon the giddy footing of the hatches,
> Methought that Gloucester stumbled, and in falling
> Struck me (that thought to stay him) overboard
> Into the tumbling billows of the main.   (1.4.16–20)

Pattern repeats pattern with remarkable exactitude. "Into the fatal bowels of the deep" is where the giddy Hastings also goes. "O Lord, methought what pain it was to drown" might be extended to all these desperate swimmers in the tide of pomp and history. The elaboration of the dream is no mere

---

[3] Q2. faire.

exercise in fine phrase on Latin models: it offers a symbol of choking suspense above black depths (the ocean, and perpetual night) which epitomizes the "momentary grace" of all these "mortal men" and women. And the sea as figure of "the destructive element" appears again in Elizabeth's lines in the second wooing scene:

> But that still use of grief makes wild grief tame,
> My tongue should to thy ears not name my boys
> Till that my nails were anchored in thine eyes;
> And I, in such a desp'rate bay of death,
> Like a poor bark of sails and tackling reft,
> Rush all to pieces on thy rocky bosom.   (4.4.230–35)

"Bay" of death suggests also an animal at bay; just plausibly relevant, since Richard (the boar) would be at bay when she *could* scratch his eyes out. But the repetition of the rather too emphatic anchors and the eyes from Clarence's dream is much more striking.

You will find a further echo of the "night motif" in the last movement. Richard suspects Stanley (confusingly also called Derby), and reasonably so: for he was husband to the Countess of Richmond, Henry Tudor's mother, the famous Lady Margaret Beaufort; and therefore keeps his son, George Stanley, as hostage. Before Bosworth, he sends a brisk message to warn the father of the black depths beneath the son; and again Shakespeare sounds his doom music from the Clarence sequence:

> bid him bring his power
> Before sunrising, lest his son George fall
> Into the blind cave of eternal night.   (5.3.60–62)

Need I remark that Clarence was "George" too, and lightly called that by Richard when he was afraid that King Edward might die before he signed his brother's death warrant?

> He cannot live, I hope, and must not die
> Till George be packed with post horse up to heaven.
>   (1.1.145–46)

I could further exemplify the play's tight-woven artistry by taking up that very remarkable prose-speech on "conscience" by Clarence's Second Murderer (1.4.136 ff.), and following the word into Richard's troubled mind in Act 5 before Margaret's curse attains its last fulfillment. But to reduce attention to Richard himself in his own play, beyond what I am already committed to by my insistence on taking the play as a *whole* (as a dramatic pattern, not an exposition of "character"), would be to do it—and Shakespeare—an injustice.

Richard Plantagenet is alone with Macbeth as the Shakespearean version of the thoroughly bad man in the role of monarch and hero; he is unique in combining with that role that of the diabolic humorist. It is this quality which makes it an inadequate account to say that the play is "moral history," or that the protagonists are the personality of Richard and the curse of Margaret (or what it stood for in orthodox Tudor thinking about retributive justice in history)—for all that these opposed "forces" *are* central throughout. The first movement establishes both, and emphatically. First, Richard, stumping down the stage on his unequal legs, forcing his hitched-up left shoulder and his withered arm on us, till we realize that *this* is what the "winter of our discontent" in *3 Henry VI* has produced, *this* the proper "hatch and brood of time"; and then, Richard established, his cruel and sardonic effectiveness demonstrated on Clarence and Anne, there arises against his brazen Carl Orff-like music the one voice he quails before (if but slightly): the subdominant notes of Margaret and her prophecy of doom, to which the ghosts will walk in the visionary night before Bosworth. It is a conflict between a spirit and a ghost: between Richard, the spirit of ruthless will, of daemonic pride, energy and self-sufficiency, of devilish gusto and *Schadenfreude* (he *enjoys* wickedness even when it is of no practical advantage to his ambitions or to securing himself by murder: it may be only wickedness in *words*, but the spirit revealed is no less evilly exultant for that); and the ghost, as I call her—for what else is Margaret, Reignier's daughter picked up on a battlefield by Suffolk and married to that most etiolated of Shakespeare's husbands, Henry VI, but the living ghost of Lancaster, the walking dead, memorializing the long, cruel,

treacherous, bloody conflict of the years of civil strife and
pitiless butchery?

You can, of course, see more there if you will. Make
her the last stage or age of woman-in-politics: she who has
been beautiful, fiercely passionate, queenly, dominating,
master of armies, *generalissima*; now old, defeated, empty
of everything but fierce bitterness, the illimitable bitterness
and rancor of political zeal. What did Yeats write of *his*
equivalent symbol? It is in "A Prayer for my Daughter." For
her he prays:

> An intellectual hatred is the worst,
> So let her think opinions are accursed.
> Have I not seen the loveliest woman born
> Out of the mouth of Plenty's horn,
> Because of her opinionated mind
> Barter that horn and every good
> By quiet natures understood
> For an old bellows full of angry wind?

Margaret is that, if you like; but, not to go beyond Shakespeare, I cannot but think that when the old Duchess of York
sits down upon the ground for the second lamentation scene
(to tell "sad stories of the death of kings"), the *author's* mind
ran more upon Margaret as he wrote:

> Dead life, blind sight, poor mortal living ghost, . . .
> Brief abstract and record of tedious days,
> Rest thy unrest on England's lawful earth,
> Unlawfully made drunk with innocent blood!
>
> (4.4.26, 28–30)

Here Shakespeare devises a new variation on the Senecan
visitant from another world howling for revenge, by making
the specter nominal flesh and blood; the tune of the Dance of
Death to which all dance to damnation is played by Margaret; and one aspect of the play is our watching the rats go
into the Weser, compelled by that fatal tune.

But Richard himself is not simply the last and most important (and worst) of the victims—if those justly destroyed
can be called "victims." That is just where the label "moral

history" is inadequate. For Richard has grown a new dimension since his abrupt and remarkable development in *3 Henry VI*: he has become a wit, a mocking comedian, a "vice of kings"—but with a clear inheritance from the old Vice of the Moralities: part symbol of evil, part comic devil, and chiefly, on the stage, the generator of roars of laughter at wickednesses (whether of deed or word) which the audience would immediately condemn in real life. On the one hand, his literary relations with the Senecan "Tyrant" (author of *"In regna mea Mors impetratur,"* etc.) are clear enough; as they are with the Elizabethan myth of "the murderous Machiavel" ("feared am I more than loved / Let me be feared," etc.): enough has been written on them. But only the medieval heritage—from the comic devils with their *Schadenfreude*, and the Vice as comic inverter of order and decency—can fully explain the new Richard of this apparent sequel to the *Henry VI* series.

I have said that the Christian pattern imposed on history gives the simple plot of a cast accursed, where all are evil beings, all deserve punishment. Look, then, with a believing Tudor eye, and ought you not to *approve* Richard's doings? *Per se,* they are the judgment of God on the wicked; and he

> *Ein Teil von jener Kraft*
> *Die stets das Böse will, und stets das Gute schafft.*[4]

But that is not all. Richard's sense of humor, his function as clown, his comic irreverences and sarcastic or sardonic appropriations of things to (at any rate) *his* occasions: all those act as underminers of our assumed naïve and proper Tudor principles; and we are on his side much rather because he makes us (as the Second Murderer put it) "take the devil in [our] mind," than for any "historical-philosophical-Christian-retributional" sort of motive. In this respect a good third of the play is a kind of grisly *comedy*; in which we meet the fools to be taken in on Richard's terms, see them with his mind, and rejoice with him in their stultification (in which execution is the ultimate and unanswerable practical

---

[4] "A part of that Power which always wills evil and yet always brings about good." (Goethe's *Faust*)

joke, the absolutely final laugh this side of the Day of Judgment). Here, Richard is a middle-term between Barabas, the Jew of Malta (*c.* 1590) and Volpone (1606). He inhabits a world where everyone deserves everything he can do to them; and in his murderous practical joking he is *inclusively* the comic exposer of the mental shortcomings (the intellectual and moral deformities) of this world of beings depraved and besotted. If we forget to pity them awhile (and he does his best to help us), then his impish spirit urges us towards a positive reversal of "Christian charity" until the play's fourth movement (which is when the Elizabethan spectator began to back out, I take it)—or even beyond that point.

An aspect of Richard's appeal, which has, I fancy, passed relatively unexamined,[5] is one that we can be confident that William Shakespeare felt and reflected on. I mean the appeal of the actor: the talented being who can assume every mood and passion at will, at all events to the extent of making others believe in it. Beyond question, all our great actors have regarded the part as a fine opportunity. The extent to which the histrionic art (as Shakespeare thought and felt about it) contributed to the making of this great stage figure is to me more interesting.

The specific interest here is the *power* that would be in the hands of an actor consummate enough to make (quite literally) "all the world a stage" and to work on humanity by the perfect simulation of every feeling: the appropriate delivery of every word and phrase that will serve his immediate purpose; together with the complete dissimulation of everything that might betray him (whether it be his intentions, or such obstructive feelings as compunction, pity or uncertainty of mind). This appears at once when Gloucester first takes shape as the man self-made to be King, in the long soliloquy in *3 Henry VI* (3.2). The closing lines are specifically on histrionic genius:

> Why, I can smile, and murder whiles I smile,
> And cry "Content!" to that which grieves my heart,

[5] [J. Middleton Murry, *Shakespeare*, 1936, pp. 125–26, quotes the theatrical metaphors and remarks briefly on the conception of Richard as an actor.]

> And wet my cheeks with artificial tears,
> And frame my face to all occasions.   (182–85)

And then, after a little bragging prospectus on his intended deadlines, he ends:

> I can add colors to the chameleon,
> Change shapes with Proteus for advantages,
> And set the murderous Machiavel to school.
> Can I do this, and cannot get a crown?
> Tut, were it farther off, I'll pluck it down.   (191–95)

M. R. Ridley notes here that "Machiavelli . . . seems to have been to the Elizabethans a type of one who advocated murder as a method of cold-blooded policy."[6] It is true that that marks off one point of difference between the "Senecan" tyrant-villainy (which is primarily for revenge) and the "Machiavellian" (which is for power, or self-aggrandizement: "We that are great, our own self-good still moves us"): though I do not think that the distinction can be maintained, if you read Seneca. But surely Ridley's note misses the point, in its context? What the "Machiavel" allusion represents is, I believe, Shakespeare's recognition that the program set before the Prince in *Il Principe* is one that demands exactly those histrionic qualities I have just described: a lifelong, unremitting vigilance in relentless simulation and impenetrable deception. There, precisely, lies the super-humanity of the Superman. The will-to-power is shorn of its effective power without it. He is an *artist* in evil.

Now Richard in his own play shows this power—these powers—to perfection. Except to the audience, he is invisible; but the audience he keeps reminded not only of his real intentions, but equally of his actor's artistries. The bluff plain Englishman, shocked at ambitious go-getters and grievingly misunderstood, is perfectly "done" before the Queen's relations:

> Because I cannot flatter and look fair,
> Smile in men's faces, smooth, deceive, and cog,

[6] *New Temple* ed., p. 140.

> Duck with French nods and apish courtesy,
> I must be held a rancorous enemy.
> Cannot a plain man live and think no harm
> But thus his simple truth must be abused
> With silken, sly, insinuating Jacks?   (1.3.47–53)

A little later, it is: "I am too childish-foolish for this world," (*ibid.*, 141); and even: "I thank my God for my humility" (2.1.74).

Then, left to himself and the audience, after egging on all their quarrels:

> But then I sigh, and with a piece of Scripture
> Tell them that God bids us do good for evil;
> And thus I clothe my naked villainy
> With odd old ends stol'n forth of holy writ,
> And seem a saint when most I play the devil.
>
> (1.3.333–37)

The stage direction, *"Enter two Murderers,"* caps this nicely. It is not simply that Richard is a hypocrite and (like other stage villains) tells us so. The actor's technique of "asides" is the essence of his chuckling private jokes—made to "myself alone." (You might say that Shakespeare is giving not merely "the acting of drama," but also "the drama of consummate *acting*.")

The same reminders, nudging the audience's attention, appear in his swift-switched actual asides: e.g., his thoroughly unholy reception of his mother's blessing, spoken as he gets up off his dutiful knees:

> Amen! And make me die a good old man!
> That is the butt end of a mother's blessing;
> I marvel that her Grace did leave it out.   (2.2.109–11)

Or, again, we have Richard's insinuating equivocations in talking to the prattling little Princes; in one of which he acknowledges his theatrical-historical legacy from the Moralities: "Thus, like the formal Vice, Iniquity, / I moralize two meanings in one word" (3.1.82–83). Over and above this there is that striking passage (3.5.1–11) where he and

Buckingham are working up a crisis (appearing ill dressed in old rusty armor, as if they had armed in desperate haste), when Richard specifically inquires whether Buckingham can "do the stage tragedian":

> *Richard.* Come, cousin, canst thou quake and change thy color,
>   Murder thy breath in middle of a word,
>   And then again begin, and stop again,
>   As if thou wert distraught and mad with terror?

> *Buckingham.* Tut, I can counterfeit the deep tragedian,
>   Speak and look back, and pry on every side,
>   Tremble and start at wagging of a straw,
>   Intending deep suspicion. Ghastly looks
>   Are at my service, like enforcèd smiles;
>   And both are ready in their offices
>   At any time to grace my stratagems.

It is all sardonically jocular; but nothing shows more clearly the artist's delight in his craft: call it illusion or deception, it makes no odds. It is this dexterity that his other rapid reversals of tone keep us aware of; whether he is half-amazedly rejoicing in his conquest of Anne, or poking unfilial fun at his mother (a performance more shocking to Elizabethans than to our more child-foolish days).

Yet again, there is that admirable moment when the Londoners are being fooled into believing that he must be persuaded to be king; when Buckingham pretends to lose patience, with "Zounds, I'll entreat no more." And Richard, bracketed aloft with two Bishops, is distressed: "O, do not swear, my lord of Buckingham" (3.7.219). (It is like the moment in *Eric or Little by Little* (ch. 8) when Eric refers to the usher as a "surly devil"; and the virtuous Russell exclaims: "O Eric, that is the first time that I have heard you swear.") It is this unholy jocularity, the readiness of sarcastic, sardonic, profane, and sometimes blasphemous wit, the demonic gusto of it all, which not only wins the audience over to accepting the Devil as hero, but also points us towards the central paradox of the play. And, through that, to a full critical awareness of its unity: with a few remarks on which I shall conclude.

To begin with Richard. On the face of it, he is the demon-Prince, the cacodemon born of hell, the misshapen toad, etc. (all things ugly and ill). But through his prowess as actor and his embodiment of the comic Vice and impish-to-fiendish humor, he offers the false as more attractive than the true (the actor's function), and the ugly and evil as admirable and amusing (the clown's game of value reversals). You can say, "We don't take him seriously." I reply, "That is exactly what gets most of his acquaintances into Hell: just what the devil-clown relies on." But he is not only this demon incarnate, he is in effect God's agent in a predetermined plan of divine retribution: the "scourge of God." Now by Tudor-Christian historical principles, this plan is *right*. Thus, in a real sense, Richard is a king who "can do no wrong"; for in the pattern of the justice of divine retribution on the wicked, he functions as an avenging angel. Hence my paradoxical title, "Angel with Horns."

The paradox is sharpened by what I have mainly passed by: the repulsiveness, humanely speaking, of the "justice." God's will it may be, but it sickens us: it is as pitiless as the Devil's (who is called in to execute it). The contrast with Marlowe's painless, dehumanized slaughterings in *Tamburlaine* is patent.

This overall system of *paradox* is the play's unity. It is revealed as a constant displaying of inversions, or reversals of meaning: whether we consider the verbal patterns (the *peripeteias* or reversals of act and intention or expectation); the antithesis of false and true in the histrionic character; or the constant inversions of irony. Those verbal capsizings I began by talking about, with their deliberate reversals to the opposite meaning in equivocal terms, are the exact correlatives of both the nature of man (or man in power: Richard) and of the nature of events (history); and of language too, in which all is conveyed.

But, start where you will, you come back to history; or to the pattern made out of the conflict of two "historical myths." The orthodox Tudor myth made history God-controlled, divinely prescribed and dispensed, to move things towards a God-ordained perfection: Tudor England. Such was the *frame* that Shakespeare took. But the total effect from Halle: a very different meaning. Dr. Duthie may write, "But there is no doubt that Shakespeare saw history in the same light as Halle saw it."[7] I say there *is* doubt. Dover Wilson has nothing to offer but what he summarizes from Moulton, but his last sentence points my doubting way: "it appears, to me at least, unlikely that Shakespeare's 'main end' in *Richard III* was 'to show the working out of God's will in English history.' "[8] (The quotation he is discussing is from Tillyard's *Shakespeare's History Plays* [1944], p. 208.) He can go no further because his own limitations on *Henry IV* inhibit his ever observing that the comic Richard has no more place in Halle's scheme than Falstaff has.

The other myth is that of Richard the Devil-King: the Crookback *monstrum deforme, ingens* whom Shakespeare *found* as a ready-made Senecan tyrant and converted into a quite different inverter of moral order: a ruthless, demonic comedian with a most un-Senecan sense of humor and the seductive appeal of an irresistible gusto, besides his volcanic Renaissance energies. They are themselves demoralizing: *Tapfer sein ist gut*[9] is the antithesis of a Christian sentiment.

The outcome of this conflict of myths was Shakespeare's display of constant inversions of meaning; in all of which, two systems of meaning impinge and go over to their opposites, like the two "ways" of the cheveril glove. This applies equally to words and word-patterns; to the actor-nature; to dramatic ironies; and to events, as the hatch and brood of time, contrasted with opposite expectations.

As a result of the paradoxical ironic structure built from these inversions of meaning—built above all by Richard's demonic appeal—the naïve, optimistic, "Christian" principle of history, consoling and comfortable, modulates into its opposite. The "Christian" system of retribution is undermined, counterbalanced, by historic irony. (Do I need to insist that the coupling of "Christian" and "retribution" itself is a paradox? That the God of vengeance is *not* a Christian God; that his opposite is a God of mercy who has no representation in this play. If I do, I had better add that the so-called "Christian" frame is indistinguishable from a pagan one of

[7] G. I. Duthie, *Shakespeare*, 1951, p. 118.
[8] *Richard III* (*New Cambridge* ed., 1954), p. xiv.
[9] "To be bold is good."

Nemesis in which the "High all-seer" is a Fate with a cruel sense of humor.)

But do not suppose I am saying that the play is a "debunking of Tudor myth," or that Shakespeare is disproving it. He is not "proving" anything: not even that "Blind belief is sure to err / And scan his works in vain" (though I think that is *shown*, nevertheless). Contemporary "order"-thought spoke as if naïve faith saw true: God was above God's Englishmen and ruled with justice—which meant summary vengeance. This historic myth offered absolutes, certainties. Shakespeare in the Histories always leaves us with relatives, ambiguities, irony, a process thoroughly dialectical. Had he entirely accepted the Tudor myth, the frame and pattern of order, his way would have led, I suppose, towards writing *moral history* (which is what Dr. Tillyard and Dr. Dover Wilson and Professor Duthie have made *out* of him). Instead, his way led him towards writing *comic history*. The former would never have taken him to tragedy: the latter (paradoxically) did. Look the right way through the cruel-comic side of Richard and you glimpse Iago. Look back at him through his energy presented as evil, and you see Macbeth. And if you look at the irony of men's struggles in the nets of historic circumstances, the ironies of their pride and self-assurance, you will see Coriolanus; and you are past the great tragic phase and back in history again.

ROBERT ORNSTEIN

Richard III

A stunning success in Shakespeare's time, *Richard III* has
been a favorite of succeeding generations of actors and audiences. Like *Hamlet*, it has never failed to hold the stage
because it is superbly theatrical—inspired by the stage and
by an actor's awareness of the power which a virtuoso performer has over his audiences. It is also daringly conceived
to mingle contrarieties: gothic shapes and Renaissance energies; tragic pathos and ironic comedy; high-spirited farce
and Senecan gloom. Not content simply to allow Crookback
to display his melodramatic genius before he falls into his
destined role of scapegoat, Shakespeare endows Richard's
tragic career with monumental artistic form. He imagines
the darkness befôre the dawn of Tudor deliverance as the
setting for a vast revenge tragedy which unfolds with proph-
esies of doom and choric lamentations, a full freight of
medieval moralizing, a chilling figure of Nemesis, and a
pageant of accusing ghosts. For the first time in *Richard III*
Shakespeare's plotting in the History Plays has vertical as
well as horizontal form, because each step of Richard's rise
and fall offers a fresh discovery of political and moral
reality. Seemingly surefooted in his ascent to the throne,
Richard suffers an astonishing vertigo at the pinnacle of his
career and regains his equilibrium again only when he
touches ground—when he fights on foot against overwhelming odds at Bosworth.

In Richard III Shakespeare had a historical subject worthy

From *A Kingdom for a Stage: The Achievement of Shakespeare's History
Plays* by Robert Ornstein (Cambridge, Massachusetts: Harvard University
Press, 1972). Copyright © 1972 by the President and Fellows of Harvard Col-
lege. Reprinted by permission. Several footnotes have been omitted.

of his rapidly maturing powers. He found in More's *History*[1] a brilliant characterization and a biography that had already been given an artistic shape and interpretation. Having made use of More's conception of Richard in developing his portrait of Gloucester in *Henry VI Part 3*, he could now fashion his plot directly out of More's terse, coherent, absorbing historical narrative and directly appropriate More's ironic humor and penetrating insights. Fascinating as is More's account of the sinister, misshapen Richard, Shakespeare's portrait is more dazzling and memorable still. For, though More is willing to grant Richard his cleverness, sardonic humor, and theatrical instinct, he describes him as an explorer might describe a rare and horrifying species of poisonous snake. Never allowing his reader to savor Richard's histrionic performances, More makes each of Richard's successes an occasion for moral outrage, disgust, and scorn. It is Shakespeare who endows Richard with his exuberance and extraordinary vitality. It is Shakespeare who makes him an engaging, heroic, and honest villain, one who opens his heart to the audience in soliloquies and asides and who plays the moral teacher for quite a long time before he becomes the moral lesson of the play.

In speaking of Shakespeare's transformation of the "accepted view" of Richard, we should keep in mind that More's was not the only portrait current. Almost certainly Shakespeare read *The True Tragedy of Richard III* (printed in a debased version in 1594), in which Richard is portrayed more like a conscience-ridden Macbeth than the vicious monster whom More describes.[2] Shakespeare does not go half as far in humanizing More's villain; what he does is make Richard's perversity credible and, more than that, enjoyable, for the heartless murderer More depicts becomes in Shakespeare's play a humorist and a comedian so cheeky, frank, and enthusiastic in his wickedness that most of his

[1]*The History of Richard III,* first printed with Hardyng's *Chronicle* in 1543, was incorporated in Hall's *Chronicle* and again in Holinshed.
[2]*The True Tragedy* probably gave Shakespeare the inspiration for the pageant of ghosts which visits Richard during his nightmare on the eve of Bosworth. Other verbal echoes are identified by Geoffrey Bullough in the footnotes to his excerpts from *The True Tragedy* in Volume III of *Narrative and Dramatic Sources of Shakespeare,* pp. 317–45.

betters seem unpardonably dishonest and dreary. A gloating dissimulator in *Henry VI Part 3*, he is in *Richard III* a thoroughly accomplished *farceur*, an urbane masquerader who literally plots the course of the dramatic action, which he dominates from beginning to end. He is the supreme individualist; the other characters, with the exception of the harridan Margaret, are variations on a theme. They cannot fathom him, but he can play them at sight; and none of them can stand against him until they have been schooled by his treachery. Even after Richmond enters the play, Richard is the only antagonist worthy of Richard and destined to be his own nemesis.

Although more the superman than before, Richard leaves behind the Marlovian hyperboles of his soliloquies in *Henry VI Part 3*. When he walks out on stage to open the play, his speech is measured, his figures neatly contained within the caesuras of his blank verse lines. He can wield words like a rapier, but he has no passion for the grandiose. His bent of mind, like that of the other characters, is rhetorical rather than poetic, and when, late in the play, he grows dull, his rhetoric grows as artificial and as tedious as theirs. Since Richard at his best is incomparable, one wonders why more of the play is not cut to the measure of his brilliance. Often his speeches are the only flashes of life and energy in the tedious bickering of the Court, and that bickering seems highly dramatic compared to the turgid formality of the choric and ritual scenes. Even if we grant that Elizabethans had more taste than we do for sententiousness and rhetorical flourish, we must still wonder why calamity in *Richard III* must be so full of words, why every moral account in the play must be explicitly summed and every irony pointed out and underlined. It is almost as if Shakespeare, unwilling to trust his audiences' perception of the subtle ironies of his plot, provides a more obvious key to the moral drama in Margaret's prophecies and the ostentatious hypocrisies of the courtiers, who damn themselves in swearing falsely. Although the sense of the past evoked in the rhetoric of the choric and ritual scenes is necessary to the play, it is a burden on modern audiences, who must sort-out current intrigues and factious alignments even as they try to make sense of the references made to earlier events—the atrocities committed at Wakefield, Towton, and Tewkesbury. We need not assume, however, that Shakespeare's audiences were so familiar with *Henry VI Part 3* or with the Chronicles that they could interpret each of the allusions to the past. Nor need we attempt to provide extensive historical notes for modern audiences, because the play provides what information they need. It does not matter precisely what crimes Clarence, Hastings, Rivers, or Grey committed (or allowed) in the past; what matters is that all were involved to some degree in the atrocities of the civil war. Some participated in the murder of children, others watched; few hands are clean in Edward's court, and few pious protestations can be taken at face value.

Of course, the days of vendetta are long since over, and even the memory of atrocity is blurred and fragmentary, because except for Margaret, who nurtures her ghastly memories, the characters of *Richard III* would turn their backs on the past and forget the ways in which they rose to eminence and power. Opportunists for the working day and Christians enough for their world, they do not rage against their enemies and plot their destruction as York did. Moderate in their factionalism, they would be part-time accomplices of the Protector and settle for minor portions of the spoils. Hastings, loyal to Edward and his sons, would be content with a high position and the power to punish his enemies. Buckingham, less scrupulous and less loyal, would be satisfied with the earldom of Hereford—if he did not have to murder the Princes. Although such men bicker, backbite, and scheme against each other, they leave the commission of murder, judicial or otherwise, to Richard, and they know the pangs of belated conscience, because they would die well even though they live ill. The survivors of catastrophe, they have all learned how to bend with the wind; they have all mastered the art of accommodation which enables a man successfully to turn his coat. They know when to be obtuse and when to equivocate or turn casuist. The noble Buckingham can argue with conviction that innocent children do not deserve the sanctuary which is the right of criminals, and the dying Edward can lament that none of his courtiers prevented him from condemning his brother Clarence. All know the importance of seeming earnest, and all have the gift of fine words. Clarence is an accomplished and unctuous orator, Buckingham a master of the political platform, and Richard a very genius at sanctimony.

John Danby makes the penetrating comment that "in Richard . . . the corruption of his time is made aware of itself. This is the ambiguity of his role: to be the logical outcome of his society, and yet a pariah rejected by that society; a hypocrite, yet more sincere in his self-awareness than those he ruins and deceives."[3] If it were true, however, that Richard takes "the average practice of his world" and erects it "into a conscious principle of action," then England would be like him irredeemable. Although seemingly a very man o' the time, he is not its archetype; on the contrary, his plots are an attempt to call back the yesterday which the other characters shudder to remember. Men like Hastings and Buckingham can enjoy the pleasures of rank and influence, but Richard, bored and restless in "this weak piping time of peace," wants to relive again the thrilling danger of the battlefield. Like Margaret, he is an anachronism, a creature for whom time has stopped; and when he must fully reveal himself by his deeds and words, he resembles no one else in the play—he is very obviously an aberration, uniquely deformed in spirit as in body. Richard falls, among other reasons, because he is not enough like other men and women to know how they think and feel. Although he can manipulate those who are credulous and corruptible, he does not know the difference between his absolute unscrupulousness and the lesser equivocations of his accomplices and victims. Utterly cynical, he cannot gauge the force of their half-hearted principles or predict their hesitations, and he makes a catastrophic error in thinking that the people can be mollified by pious shows when they know that he has committed unpardonable crimes.

In *Richard III*, as in *Henry VI Part 3*, Richard is still the outsider. If he seems now to belong, it is not because his society is made up of men like him but because time has rubbed smooth the sharp edges of his malcontent. Able to get along with men as well as to get rid of them, Richard is

[3]*Shakespeare's Doctrine of Nature*, p. 60.

completely at ease with himself as well as with others. No longer envious of those of better person, no longer itching to hack his way through his own flesh and blood, he takes a detached, ironic, almost kindly, view of such victims as "simple plain Clarence." One does not feel that Richard has become so skillful at duplicity that he completely masks the hatreds he voices in *Henry VI Part 3*; one simply cannot imagine the suave plotter of *Richard III* raging at the world. An entrepreneur and impresario of villainy, he is always removed from the murderous acts he perpetrates. His wit flashes rather than his knife; he kills with words rather than swords, and though we have no doubt that he could stab anyone, he is too fastidious to bloody his hands needlessly. He enjoys entrapping Hastings and allows others the pleasure of beheading him. Instead of eating a bloody supper in the Tower, he is content to beg some good strawberries from Ely's garden and look at Hastings's severed head before he dines.

Acting as prologue as well as puppetmaster, Richard introduces the action he contrives and dominates; and when he lets the audience in on stratagems he dares not reveal to any one else, they enjoy the confidence because his ambition is devoid of personal malice or envy:

> But I, that am not shaped for sportive tricks
> Nor made to court an amorous looking glass;
> I, that am rudely stamped, and want love's majesty
> To strut before a wanton ambling nymph;
> I, that am curtailed of this fair proportion,
> Cheated of feature by dissembling Nature,
> Deformed, unfinished, sent before my time
> Into this breathing world, scarce half made up,
> And that so lamely and unfashionable
> That dogs bark at me as I halt by them;
> Why, I, in this weak piping time of peace,
> Have no delight to pass away the time,
> Unless to see my shadow in the sun
> And descant on mine own deformity.
> And therefore, since I cannot prove a lover
> To entertain these fair well-spoken days,
> I am determined to prove a villain
> And hate the idle pleasures of these days. (1.1.14–31)

Is this a man tormented by the deformity which he describes with such humor and sweet reasonableness? Or one driven to seek power by a gnawing sense of his own inferiority? If there is any burden of anguish in this frank declaration, it is very deeply submerged, for Richard sounds bored, not embittered. He wants work, an opportunity to bustle, a goal worthy of his extraordinary energies and talents. His calculated changes of mood are unpredictable; his melodramatic gestures are lightninglike, but he is never impulsive. His style is elegant and even studied. He savors, and stamps with his fastidious personality, the alliterations, antitheses, and rhetorical flourishes which are conventional in the speeches of others.[4] An instigator of disorder, he seems, until his failure of nerve, immensely rational and self-controlled, so much so that his aplomb is more frightening than his sudden squalls of passion, which are as calculated as his sudden fits of piety. Unlike the gormandizing Falstaff, who affects a Puritanical preciseness, Richard is genuinely ascetic in his appetites. He does disapprove of lechery, whether Edward's or Hastings's—or rather he despises men who waste their time chasing women.

A born teacher, Richard delights even as he instructs. His mimicking of pious cant is so perfect that, though we are not seduced, we are amused by revelations that should horrify us. The snarling Richard of *Henry VI Part 3* was less threatening, because his pathology conformed to and confirmed traditional moral assumptions. A creature warped from birth, he could be explained by Freudian theory as well as Elizabethan ethical psychology as a slave to monstrous passions. But the Richard who makes a cheerful vocation of the evil to which he is drawn by natural instincts and gifts is not so comfortably explained away. To be sure, his posturing is absurdly theatrical; he is a melodramatist who can be enjoyed because he is so patently "fictitious." Yet even as we cheer ourselves with the thought that Richard is unreal, we know he is a more credible and convincing representation of human nature than is Richmond. No stereotype of villainy,

[4]Olivier caught very well the fastidiousness of Richard's manner in his film version of *Richard III*. As Richard, he spoke in a somewhat high-pitched voice and phrased his lines precisely and elegantly.

Richard has his individual bent of speech, a sinister command of homely phrases and a sardonic humor. More "observed" than conceived, he speaks of our own world, and we laugh at his ingenious stratagems partly because they lay bare eternal truths of political and moral behavior. Some critics believe his cheerful dedication to a life of evil is a fiction invented to soothe his lacerated ego. Others suggest that he is tormented secretly by his deformity, which he treats as a badge of his uniqueness and a convenient excuse for his inhumanity. But it is hard to imagine that Richard hungers to be normal or that he seeks power as a compensation for his sexual inadequacies, when his conquest of Lady Anne suggests that, had he applied himself to seduction, he might have rivaled Casanova.

Perhaps, like Iago, Richard needs to believe in his reasonableness and cannot admit the sense of inferiority that sparks his malice. But whom does Richard envy? There is no beauty in Hastings's or Buckingham's life that makes his seem ugly, and it is impossible to equate the elegant aristocratic Richard with the vulgar, lying, cheating Ancient. If Richard's self-acceptance is only a mask, it is a mask that does not, like Iago's pose of robust cynicism, slip to disclose a perverted and lacerated ego. What is revealed on the eve of Bosworth is not Richard's long concealed bitterness and spite but his despairing sense of isolation. Unlike Iago, Richard in conversation and in soliloquy is very much the same creature; because he lacks Iago's insistent need for self-justification, he does not lie to himself about his motives or about how he feels or acts. And because he lacks Iago's sadistic cravings, his pleasure in using people is almost wholly impersonal and professional. He does not need to degrade them; he has no knack for gratuitous cruelty. To enter, as Freudian critics will, the subterranean corridors of Richard's psyche is to lose contact with the Richard of the play or to mistake him for the more conventionally conceived malcontent who briefly appears in the last acts of *Henry VI Part 3*. Like Elizabethans, we may wish to believe that heartless criminals lead lives of quiet desperation, for if we must have unconscionable villains, we would prefer them warped and tormented, just as if we must have extermination camps, we would have them run by sadists and perverts, not by fussy bureaucrats who take pride in their fanatical efficiency, in an unpleasant job well done. We do not want to believe that men may commit horrible acts just because they are lacking in emotional sympathies or moral sensitivity, because, like Richard, they regard other human beings as objects to be manipulated, acquired, or disposed of.

The cool, ironical Richard of the first acts is not the whole of Shakespeare's portrait. The more he reveals himself during the play, the less attractive he appears. Even before the lines of strain mar his splendid composure, his brilliance loses its fascination; even before he reaches the crown, the "moral holiday" of the opening scenes, created by his witty, conscienceless audacity and preposterous poses, draws to an end. Or rather there is never in *Richard III* a moral holiday comparable to the escape from moral judgments which Lamb finds in Restoration comedy. If we check our morals with our coats when we see a performance of *The Country Wife*, it is because moral judgments are irrelevant to Wycherley's characters. His wives and sweethearts may prove unfaithful, but they cannot be seduced from scruples of chastity because they do not have any; they cannot be corrupted because they are never innocent. Similarly, the victimized husbands and lovers do not arouse our pity because they are too gross to be cheated and too insensitive to be pained. Because Wycherley's point of view is insistently arch and his situations artificial, he threatens nothing by his farcing of adultery. He amuses and titillates; he allows us to enjoy a very bourgeois dirty joke even while we think ourselves very sophisticated and worldly.

Richard III evokes a more complex response because its perspective is moral and because an audience's pleasure in Richard's brilliant plotting is countered by some measures of sympathy for his victims. Even Clarence, the first of Richard's dupes, is a dignified and poignant figure. Little more than a shallow opportunist in *Henry VI Part 3*, he has on the night of his murder some touch of poetry and even some unconscious intuition of Richard's treachery. Stirred by remorseful memories and fearful of his life, he prays that his innocent children will not suffer for his misdeeds. One does not feel too sorry, however, for Clarence, who confesses himself false and perjured, because his murderers are so entertaining and so much more brutally honest with themselves about the nuisance of conscience. The balancing of tones in the scene is daring; one moment we sigh for Clarence, the next laugh at the joke of the butt of Malmsey, in which he will have wine enough. At first Clarence would play the orator with his assassins and dissuade them with finespun casuistry, theological arguments, and moral exhortations. But when he appeals to God, they remind him of his crimes and declare themselves instruments of divine justice. The slickness of Clarence's pious sentences and the hypocrisy of the assassins' replies are a sardonically amusing exposure of the moral way of the world. At the very last, however, the joke of scruple and remorse turns out to be no joke at all, for the more reluctant of the murderers is appalled by his deed and will have none of the reward that earlier stilled the whisper of his conscience.

The comedy of Richard's initial successes is enjoyable because there is an ironic justice in the fates of men like Hastings and Buckingham, who think themselves Richard's accomplices, not his puppets, and who betray themselves by their vanity and ambition. The confidence game Richard plays could not succeed if men like Hastings and Buckingham were as moral as they claimed to be or less eager for illicit gains. Delighted to have a seat in the inner circle, and savoring their power to destroy other men, they are fatuously confident that they can outwit Richard or use him to their own ends. Poor Hastings thinks Catesby is *his* spy, and, pleased by the executions of Rivers and Grey, he plans, amidst some pious exclamations, to send a few more packing. Buckingham, a tragic figure in More's *History*, is more comic in *Richard III*, where he preens himself on his political genius when he is only running Richard's errands and parroting his ideas. Ironies multiply as Hastings and Buckingham play their studied roles at the council that is to choose a date for the coronation of Edward's son. Taking a page from Richard's book, Hastings chooses to appear as childish-foolish and naive as the Protector; he remarks to the others about the openness of Richard's feelings. Also playing the innocent, Buckingham declares (more truly than he knows) that he and Richard know each other's faces but not each other's hearts.

Clinging to their shabby ends of morality, Hastings and Buckingham must lose their heads to find themselves—or at least to recognize the vanity of their politic careers. Completely honest with himself, Richard is fully conscious of his hypocrisies and pretenses. Where Hastings shudders at the crimes he contemplates, Richard openly enjoys the company of murderers; and his frank sanctimony is a refreshing breeze in the stifling cant of the Court. He does not release an audience from the burden of morality; he frees it from the burden of the simpering hypocrisy that often passes for moral conviction, from the clichés of brotherhood and charity that substitute for generous thought and Christian deeds.

Iago's plans succeed because Othello and others believe he is honest; Edmund's plots prosper in *King Lear* because he appears a loyal and natural son. Richard's successes are more ironic still because everyone except his gullible brothers knows pretty much what he is and fears him. His counterfeit professions pass current, nevertheless, because in a world of surfaces, of facile words and meaningless oaths, no man can afford to question another man's gestures. We know what Richard believes because he speaks his mind. What the others actually believe is difficult to say. Does Anne really believe when she surrenders to Richard that she does not know his heart? Is the Archbishop of Canterbury convinced that innocent children do not deserve sanctuary? Does Hastings think that Richard lacks guile or the Mayor believe that Hastings is guilty? The will to self-deception is strong when there are advantages to being obtuse, and when accommodation and pliancy are the wisdom of the times.

Cleverer than all the rest, free from sham, and flawless in his Machiavellian virtuosity, Richard surmounts incredible obstacles to the throne. Like Marlowe's Tamburlaine, he seems a transcendent and irresistible force, so resourceful that every challenge or rebuff affords an opportunity for another dazzling performance. Other Elizabethan villains—Marlowe's and Jonson's, for example—overreach in obvious ways; infatuated with their successes, they underestimate their opponents or hoist themselves with their own petards. Richard is too witty, however, and too skeptical to grow infatuate with success. He knows, even as he relishes the seduction of Anne, that he is no thing of beauty, and he takes the accurate measure of almost all of his opponents. He does not gloat like a Barabas or a Guise over his power to destroy: Nothing too much is his political philosophy. Yet he falters at the very moment of his ultimate triumph, and his fall is as precipitous as his ascent was meteoric.

The geometry of Richard's career has a superb logic as well as an artful symmetry. His fall is the mirror image of his rise because the very techniques which carry him to the throne ensure that he will not keep it long. His is the politics of faction and corruption. His plots feed on the intrigues and rivalries of the Court, which provide him with both accomplices and scapegoats. At first he can easily enlist the support of Hastings and Buckingham, who hate the Queen's relatives, and he can win the reluctant assent of Rivers and Grey to his apparently reasonable proposals about the Princes. With each step Richard takes toward the crown, however, his ambition grows more transparent, his accomplices fewer, and his enemies more numerous. He uses his brother Edward to eliminate Clarence; then he uses Hastings to get rid of Rivers and Grey. Buckingham helps him to murder Hastings, and finally he rids himself of Buckingham. Thus, each of Richard's triumphs is purchased with a diminishing Machiavellian capital, and though his political debts are self-liquidating, so too are his political assets. When he gains the pinnacle of power, he stands alone, isolated from other men by his criminality, and hated by those whose allegiance he nominally commands. Not once could he gain the support of ordinary men like the Scrivener, who immediately sees the fraud of Hastings's indictment. At the Guildhall, the citizens failed to respond to Buckingham's exhortations; and their silence was so ominous that the Mayor, we are told, began to back away from Richard's campaign. Another man might have hesitated at this point, but Richard plunged on because he was too self-confident to value the aid of others. Convinced that shows of piety and popular support were enough, he finds at Bosworth that he has on his side only such shows of loyalty as Stanley offers.

Richard's fall is not political in any conventional sense. He is not toppled from power by the superior forces of Richmond or deposed by his subjects. His defeat at Bosworth puts the seal on a catastrophe that begins the moment he takes his place on the throne. In More's *History* as in Shakespeare's play, the murder of the Princes is the turning point of Richard's career. More relates that after the murder of his nephews, Richard had no rest or quiet of mind, only the torment of conscience and cowardly fears. Shakespeare alters this conception by placing Richard's crisis of confidence before the murder of the Princes, not after it. When Buckingham does not immediately consent to their death in the coronation scene, Richard, who did not blanch at the report of the citizens' silence in the Guildhall, grows angry, gnaws his lip, and speaks for the first time of fear and uncertainty, even though he wears the crown. His response is strikingly out of proportion to its cause. He does not need Buckingham to commit the murders when there are willing cutthroats in the Court, nor does he need his consent or compliance. Yet when Buckingham hesitates, Richard grows furious enough to commit a disastrously unpolitic act. Unwilling to wait for Buckingham's reply (which will soon enough be volunteered), he treats his old ally with brutal insolence. Indeed, he goes out of his way to humiliate Buckingham by denying him the earldom of Hereford, which Richard had specified as his henchman's reward. How extraordinary that, even while he declares that his kingdom stands on brittle glass, Richard insults and casts off the accomplice whose army might have tipped the scales at Bosworth. After this peevishness, Richard grows even more irritable and indecisive. Lethargic, and unable to concentrate, he responds in a confused and uncertain fashion to reports of impending invasion and disaffection among his people. What a fall is there from the masterly Richard of the first act to the cringing despondent general of the last act, who seeks reassurance from the men he should lead and who stoops to spying on his own troops.

John Palmer sees Richard as unnerved by his own success. Having achieved the impossible in gaining the throne, Richard, he suggests, finds himself with no new worlds to

conquer, and no goal worthy of his extraordinary energies.[5]
I would put this a slightly different way, because it seems to
me that Richard is unnerved, not because he has nothing left
to win, but because having won, he has now everything to
lose. An instinctive gambler, he delights in winning Anne
"all the world to nothing"; and having won her, he will
wager his "dukedom to a beggarly denier" on his good
looks. In the same vein, he declares that he "will stand the
hazard of the die" at Bosworth because he has bet his life on
victory. He is at his best, as in the seduction of the Lady
Anne, when the impossibility of a venture challenges his
daring. Needing the odds against him, he recovers his old
vitality at Bosworth, when with the battle nearly lost, he can
again stake everything, including his life, in an impossible
venture. What shakes Richard's confidence as he ascends
the throne in the coronation scene is an awareness that he is
now on the defensive: he must stop all growths that threaten
him. Better equipped to seize the crown than wear it, he
lacks, as he ironically predicted in a moment of mock self-
deprecation, the ability to rule.

Although Richard's failure of nerve betrays itself in his
psychological responses, the crux of the coronation scene is
unmistakably moral. In More's *History*, Richard falls out
with Buckingham over political issues that have no connection to the murder of the Princes. Richard fears and mistrusts
his chief ally, More relates, because the ambitious Buckingham was a potential rival, and the earldom of Hereford,
which he claimed was "interlaced with the title to the
crowne." In *Richard III* Buckingham, too docile to inspire
suspicion, aims no higher than the reward which Richard
had earlier promised. But he does enrage Richard in the
coronation scene when he refuses to consent immediately to
the King's request for the murder of his nephews. Earlier
Richard had wooed the Lady Anne and had sent Catesby to
court Hastings. Now as King he finds it necessary to woo
Buckingham to commit a horrid deed, and he discovers to
his chagrin that Buckingham knows how to play the bashful

[5]John Palmer, *Political Characters of Shakespeare* (London: Macmillan,
1952), pp. 103–104. Although sometimes patronized as an "amateur" effort
in Shakespearean criticism, this book is a treasure of acute insight and penetrating interpretation.

maiden as well as he. Given the nature of the request, Buckingham's coyness and obtuseness are understandable: at this point any man might pretend dullness. More puzzling is Richard's oblique manner of wooing, because suddenness once was his supreme tactic. Now he moves sideways like a crab towards his goal and stoops to playing guessing games with his puppet. He wants Buckingham not only to consent to the murder of Edward's sons but also to volunteer to perform the deed which Richard is unwilling to call by its name. And, though Buckingham is not shocked by the idea of killing the boys, Richard is enraged by his hesitation, which forces him to state his purpose openly.

This revelation of Richard's nature is extraordinary. He has no scruples in the ordinary sense of the word; only once does he speak of sin and shudder at the thought of wading through blood. But he has the need—the "moral" need—for Buckingham's company in hell. To ascend the heights of power Richard has had to ascend the heights of villainy. Each step upward demanded a crime worse than the last, and at each step another accomplice faltered or held back. First one of the murderers of Clarence fled, then Hastings refused to see Richard crowned. When Buckingham draws away from the murder of the boys, as do Tyrrel and the hired assassins, Richard finds himself without another damned soul. The other crimes Richard willed. The murder of the Princes is one which he must commit whether he wills it or not, because he *needs* the Bastards dead. For the first time he is not in control of his destiny; he is commanded by the necessities which his ambition created. Now he speaks of what he must do:

> I must be married to my brother's daughter,
> Or else my kingdom stands on brittle glass.
> Murder her brothers, and then marry her!
> Uncertain way of gain! But I am in
> So far in blood that sin will pluck on sin.   (4.2.59–63)

In *Richard III* as in *Henry VI Part 3*, the murder of children is a crowning villainy which only a Richard could cold-bloodedly plan and only a Margaret rejoice in. Despite his qualms, Richard keeps to his dreadful course and, though he has no stomach for this crime, invites Tyrrel to come to him after dinner to describe how the boys were murdered. Contemptuous of Tyrrel's show of remorse, Richard greets him sardonically as "kind Tyrrel" and "gentle Tyrrel," but the mockery will not stick because Tyrrel's remorse is genuine. Before, the very frankness of Richard's dedication to evil had a certain charm. Now the pitilessness of his response to Tyrrel is horrifying. Wanting the natural touch, Richard is unable to feel anything for another human being.

The portrayal of Richard's loss of control in the coronation scene is masterful. Thereafter, his uncertainties grow repetitious and his hesitations undramatic. I do not think that Shakespeare becomes bored with his plot at this point. Rather he becomes too interested in working out the symmetries of Richard's pyramidal career. Wanting to fashion a literal peripeteia, to make Richard's decline a precise inversion of his ascent, he devotes too much space to his wooing of the widowed Elizabeth in Act 4, hoping perhaps that his audience will grasp the subtle ways that Richard's failure parodies his triumphant seduction of the Lady Anne. Measured against ordinary reality both wooing scenes are preposterous because no man in his right mind would attempt to seduce women even as they mourned for those whom he has murdered. But the attempt on Anne is something of a lark, a *jeu d'esprit*, in which Richard flatters himself with impossibilities, whereas his encounter with Elizabeth is a political necessity; he must win her daughter to shore his tottering state.

Richard's success with Anne can be made more credible if she is thought of as the "everlasting trollop."[6] But we cannot look at her in this way when every character except Richard treats her with respect and sympathy even after she has married him. Shallow in her grieving over Henry VI, whose corpse she abandons to Richard at the close of the scene, she is not so foolish that she believes Richard's outrageous lies, nor so pliant that she yields to his arguments loathing his nature. His triumph is more of a rape than a seduction, for though he seems to cringe and fawn, he bul-

---

[6]Palmer remarks of this scene: "The eternal bully speaks to the everlasting trollop—and knows that he will prevail" (*Political Characters*, p. 83). But surely Anne is nobler than this.

lies and intimidates and mocks her high moral tone by appeals to Christian charity. Instead of attempting to persuade her of his sincerity, he shakes her belief in her own scruples by answering her hyperboles of outrage with hyperboles that are outrageous. In *Henry VI Part 3* he played the chorus to Edward's courtly wooing of Elizabeth. Now he assumes the ludicrously incongruous pose of a sighing Petrarchan lover and casts Anne as his Laura, his saint, his cruel fair who pretends disdain where she means love. And how can she remain cruel when he confesses that he has performed the ultimate service of love—murdered her husband and father-in-law to win her? She cannot believe the fantastic lie that he did all for her beauty, but she must prefer to accept its flattery than to admit the brutality of Richard's contempt for her.

Richard's knack of improvisation is dazzling: Anne's talk of killing him prompts his Petrarchan posturing, and it is only a step from the cliché of her killing eyes to the cliché of his helpless tears. She is vulnerable because she cannot match his brutal will except with words; and even as his exaggerated passion is a mere tissue of words, so too her hatred seems at last nothing more than words, for she cannot bring herself to kill him even when he offers her his sword and volunteers to kill himself if she commands him to:

> Nay, do not pause, for I did kill King Henry,
> But 'twas thy beauty that provoked me.
> Nay, now dispatch, 'twas I that stabb'd young Edward,
> But 'twas thy heavenly face that set me on.
> > *She falls the sword.*
> Take up the sword again, or take up me.　　(1.2.179–83)

The frankness of his confession shatters her last defense. Flattered, humiliated, and terrified, she can escape from knowing herself only by pretending not to understand Richard: "I would I knew your heart."

It is a far less confident and resourceful Richard who claims in Act 4 to be a jolly, thriving wooer. Now he faces a worthy antagonist in Elizabeth, who knows Richard's heart and has been schooled in vindictiveness by the railing Margaret. This time the match is even, because it pits realist against realist. Or rather, from the beginning, it is uneven, because Elizabeth has Richard's former strength while he has Anne's vulnerability. He comes armed only with conventional sentiments, platitudes, and hypocritical rationalizations, while Elizabeth speaks with shrewd and bitter cynicism of her willingness to degrade her daughter and to slander herself. Before Richard was the Petrarchan wooer; now Elizabeth, who would teach him how to woo her daughter, suggests that he use the Petrarchan emblem of a pair of bleeding hearts, an appropriate conceit for the murderer of her sons. As the rhetorical patterning of the lines reveals, Richard is on the defensive. It is Elizabeth who interrupts him, who has the brilliant unanswerable ripostes and the last stichomythic words, while he pleads with her not to mock him or confound his meanings. When the arguments and poses that dazzled Anne do not succeed—when casualness and candor are impossible—Richard must stoop to outright falsehood, lying oaths, and disgusting bribes. Accustomed to dealing with human beings as objects, he tries to bargain with Elizabeth like a peddler: so much recompense for so much loss, so many grandchildren to come for children murdered. Because he is unable to love, he cannot judge the horror of his commerce of flesh and blood or the futility of his cynical promises of profit:

> If I did take the kingdom from your sons,
> To make amends I'll give it to your daughter.
> If I have killed the issue of your womb,
> To quicken your increase I will beget
> Mine issue of your blood upon your daughter.
> A grandam's name is little less in love
> Than is the doting title of a mother;
> They are as children but one step below,
> Even of your metal, of your very blood. . . .
> Again shall you be mother to a king,
> And all the ruins of distressful times
> Repaired with double riches of content.
> What! We have many goodly days to see.
> The liquid drops of tears that you have shed
> Shall come again, transformed to orient pearl,

> Advantaging their loan with interest
> Of ten times double gain of happiness.   (4.4.294–324)

Although Richard speaks of womb, fruit, and harvest, he is the enemy of increase. His state is threatened by the growth of hopes, and his nature is as kind "as snow in harvest." Once careful to avoid the hypocrisies that damned Hastings and Buckingham, now, desperate and bankrupt, he writes out a canting promissory note that falls due at Bosworth field:

> As I intend to prosper and repent,
> So thrive I in my dangerous affairs
> Of hostile arms! Myself myself confound!
> Heaven and fortune bar me happy hours!
> Day, yield me not thy light, nor, night, thy rest!
> Be opposite all planets of good luck
> To my proceedings if, with dear heart's love,
> Immaculate devotion, holy thoughts,
> I tender not thy beauteous princely daughter![7]
>
> (397–405)

Knowing that Elizabeth mocks him, Richard has to believe nevertheless that he has won her over, though she promises only to send her answer. There is no pleasure, however, in this "triumph," none of the exuberant self-congratulation that followed the winning of Anne, only a sneering contempt for this "relenting fool, and shallow changing woman." But the joke is on Richard, and so certain was Shakespeare that his audience would understand it that he makes only a casual reference later in the play to Richmond's betrothal of Elizabeth's daughter.

It is appropriate that Richard, who deceived so many others, should at last deceive and confound himself. And it is fittingly ironic that, having cast off all human ties, he is cursed and disowned by the woman who bore him. Once he put on the role of childish-foolishness, but now he finds himself like a child afraid of the dark, and he is unable to trust

---

[7]The wording of Richard's oath is a precise echo of the false protestations which earlier damned Hastings and Buckingham. See 2.1.11, and 32–40.

anyone including himself. Indeed, he is more frightened by the shadows of his own thought at Bosworth than by Richmond's army. Prompted perhaps by *The True Tragedy of Richard III*, Shakespeare stages Richard's "dreadful and terrible dreame" on the eve of Bosworth as a ghostly pageant in which Richard's victims, each in his proper turn, bless Richmond's enterprise and curse Richard. Thus, the past returns to bear witness against Richard, and the nightmare becomes a ritual of excommunication, in which he is anathematized and cast out by the dead as he has been by the living.

The pageant of ghosts seems an appropriately archaic device with which to recapitulate the past; the attempt to make Richard bear witness against himself as he awakens is less successful:

> What do I fear? Myself? There's none else by.
> Richard loves Richard: that is, I am I.
> Is there a murderer here? No. Yes, I am.
> Then fly. What, from myself? Great reason why!
> Lest I revenge. What, myself upon myself?
> Alack, I love myself. Wherefore? For any good
> That I myself have done unto myself?
> O no! Alas, I rather hate myself
> For hateful deeds committed by myself.
> I am a villain. Yet I lie, I am not.   (5.3.183–192)

These broken, disjointed phrases and abrupt contradictions express too crudely and rhetorically a very sophisticated and "modern" psychological conception. Like one of Dostoevski's heroes, Richard sneers at the slave morality in his waking thoughts but cannot escape the reckoning of his unconscious nature that takes the form of terrible dreams. That Richard would suffer from nightmares at the crisis of Bosworth seems reasonable enough. It is harder to accept Anne's assertion (4.1.83–85) that he was often afflicted with "timorous dreams," because this revelation does not square with Richard's personality; we cannot imagine the nerveless villain of the first three acts taking more than ten minutes to fall soundly asleep. Only later will the bankruptcy of Richard's credo of ego become evident. Only in the last scenes will it become clear that the supreme egotist does not know how to love himself.

Richard's spiritual failure is England's salvation, because even as he falls apart, others unite against him. Repaying perjury with perjury, treachery with treachery, murder with murder, he has settled all the criminal accounts of the past except his own; and then with perfect justice he becomes his own nemesis. At Bosworth he stands alone for sacrifice, the only one left with bloody hands, a scapegoat laden with all the sins of his time. At Towton and Wakefield both sides committed vile acts. At Bosworth field, however, the moral oppositions are as clearly drawn again as they were in *Henry VI Part 1*, where chivalry opposed witchcraft and was betrayed by policy. When Richmond and Richard share the stage, good stands against evil, love opposes hate, and the communal impulse is set against the predatory instincts of the lone wolf.

Those who want proof that virtue is stronger than vice must find it somewhere else, however, because *Richard III* dramatizes Richard's failure rather than Richmond's success. Hardly a mention is made in the play of the preparations for Richmond's campaign which have so important a place in More's *History*, and Richmond does not even appear until the fifth act. I do not mean that Shakespeare risked angering Elizabeth by slighting Richmond's part in bringing peace and unity to England, only that he keeps his focus on Richard and does not conceive of Richmond as another Talbot or as England's champion in a Morality combat between the forces of darkness and light. So little emphasis, in fact, is placed on Richmond's military prowess that, were it not for the stage direction of the last scene of the play, we would not know that he kills Richard in combat. Under the banner of the Red Cross Knight, Richmond sallies forth against a dragon who is already doomed—deserted by his followers, sapped of vitality, and sick at heart. Even before Richmond enters the play, moreover, York and Lancaster make peace with one another as Margaret, Elizabeth, and the Duchess of York join together to grieve their losses. No less symbolic of the reunification of England is the pageant of ghosts, Yorkist and Lancastrian, who make common cause against Richard and for Richmond. The

future belongs to Richmond, not because he is the greater
soldier but because he answers the longing of the nation that
there be an end to violence and rage. Richmond's mission is
to deliver England not only from Richard's tyranny but also
from the hatreds of the past that live on in Margaret's thirst
for vengeance.

In a sense Margaret is the presiding genius of the revenge
plot in *Richard III*, who makes explicit its pattern of crime
and punishment, sin and retribution. But that pattern of
vengeance is sickening, because it includes in Margaret's
mind the murder of innocents, and because the instrument of
this vengeance is Richard, who "punishes" the guilty by
making them the steppingstones to his bloody tyranny.
Loathsome physically and morally, Margaret is a Senecan
Fury, let shrieking out of hell, whose cry for revenge is the
direct antithesis of Richmond's appeal for reconciliation.
Even when she joins the widowed Elizabeth and Duchess of
York in lamentation, she is isolated by her warped emotions.
Wanting an eye for an eye, and capable of relishing the suffering of others, she prays to a pitiless deity whose "justice"
is an unmitigated horror:

> O upright, just, and true-disposing God,
> How do I thank thee that this carnal cur [Richard]
> Preys on the issue of his mother's body
> And makes her pewfellow with others' moan!
>
> (4.4.55–58)

Where Richard can speak of Elizabeth's children as so much
merchandise, Margaret can balance out the murder of children as if she were counting sacks of grain. When the
Duchess of York protests that she has wept for Margaret's
losses, Margaret continues her sickening arithmetic:

> Bear with me; I am hungry for revenge,
> And now I cloy me with beholding it.
> Thy Edward he is dead, that killed my Edward;
> The other Edward dead, to quit my Edward;
> Young York he is but boot, because both they
> Matched not the high perfection of my loss.   (61–66)

From Margaret, Elizabeth can learn to curse and forego sleep. The greater lesson of mercy, so necessary to England's future, requires a nobler teacher, Richmond.

By portraying Richmond as a spiritual leader who brings a new dispensation of mercy to England, Shakespeare avoids the ticklish question of the Tudor claim to the succession and Richmond's role as "rebel." In his oration to his army Richmond does not offer a theoretical justification for rebellion; he portrays the battle against Richard as an act of self-defense by which Englishmen protect their homes and families against a ravening predator. And Richmond need not expound his claim to the throne because his "legitimacy" is moral, not genealogical. The time of rival claimants is past; the new age demands a new royal house, one untouched by dynastic feuds. Thus, while contempt is heaped on Englishmen who support the French invaders in *King John*, England's salvation in *Richard III* can come from France and with French aid, because England needs an "outsider" as king, a monarch who has not bloodied his hands in the civil wars.

In themselves, Richmond's speeches sound conventionally pious. In dramatic context, juxtaposed against the collapse of Richard's cynical schemes, they have a genuine power. To bring *Richard III* to a close, Shakespeare does not retreat from political realism to moral clichés. The chorus of weeping women and the pageant of ghosts recall the toll of violence, so even as we rejoice in the rescue of the young George Stanley, whom Richard would have executed, we remember Rutland, Margaret's son, Richard's nephews, and all the innocents who were not spared. The mood at the end is one of somber reflection, not of joyous celebration. Instead of proclaiming the Tudor millennium, Richmond prays that England will escape a past when

> The brother blindly shed the brother's blood,
> The father rashly slaughtered his own son,
> The son, compelled, been butcher to the sire.
>
> (5.5.24–26)

Although there is no doubt that the heavens to which Richmond prays have had their part in England's deliverance, the moral drama of the last scenes is acted out by men on earth. The victory at Bosworth is won, not by armies of angels, but by a people determined to be rid of their oppressor; and if Richard is damned, it is to a spiritual hell on earth from which he can find no exit except the excitement of battle. Despite his nightmare, he is unregenerate on the morrow; having recovered his old zest in combat, he finds at Bosworth the heroic death that was his only possible fulfillment.

In the *Henry VI* plays the well-being of England seemed to depend upon the valor of its legendary champions. But when chivalry died in *Part 1,* and the battlefield became a setting for atrocity in *Part 3,* heroism ceased to be an ultimate value. Chivalric deeds will not in themselves rescue a country inured to violence; there must be an end to the appetite for war which is Richard's and England's sickness. Thus, while the tetralogy begins with eulogies of the mighty Henry V, whose "brandish'd sword did blind men with his beams," it concludes with Henry VII's invocation of a peaceful agrarian world in which men may enjoy "fair prosperous days" and taste "this land's increase." Once again at Bosworth, as at Wakefield and Towton, men band together to hunt down their foe, only now the hunt is the communal act of peace-loving men who join forces to kill a savage boar. After Bosworth men pray, not for an England once again united and invincible, but for an England in which concord and brotherhood will at last prevail.

COPPÉLIA KAHN

"Myself Alone": *Richard III* and the Dissolution of Masculine Identity

In the patriarchal world of Shakespeare's history plays, a man's identity is determined by his relationship to his father; it is the father from whom men strive to separate themselves or with whom they merge. What Roland Barthes says of the father in Racine is also true of the father in these plays:

> his being is his anteriority; what comes after him is descended from him, ineluctably committed to a problematics of loyalty. The Father is the past. . . . The only movement permitted to the son is to break, not to detach himself.[1]

The first tetralogy, the three parts of *Henry VI* and *Richard III*, traces the decline of the father-son bond, from the son's emulation of his father in a feudal context, then to the son as his father's avenger, and finally to the breakdown of all filial bonds in *Richard III*, from which emerges Richard's distinctively isolated, asocial, self-consciously theatrical form of masculine selfhood.[2]

From Coppélia Kahn, *Man's Estate: Masculine Identity in Shakespeare* (University of California Press, 1981). Revised for the Signet Classic edition of *Richard III*. Used by permission of the publisher and author.
[1] Roland Barthes, *On Racine*, tr. Richard Howard (New York: Hill and Wang, 1964), pp. 37–8.

[2] Jean E. Howard and Phyllis Rackin characterize Richard as hero of a tragedy rather than of a history play, in that he exemplifies "the emergent conception of an autonomous masculine identity defined in performance," instead of "an older conception of masculine identity rooted in patrilineal inheritance." Richard, they argue, represents a demonized form of this more modern masculinity which is replaced by that of Richmond, "a figure who embodies successful compromise between modernity and tradition, between performance and genealogy as warrants for his rule" (pp. 113–14). See their *Engendering a Nation: A Feminist Account of Shakespeare's English Histories* (London: Routledge, 1997).

The wailing and cursing queens, mothers, and wives of *Richard III*, whose primary purpose was to bear sons, are survivors of dynasties that have virtually eliminated each other in the name of lineal succession through the male line. What is pursued in the name of the filially defined masculine self—loyalty to the father, family honor, and personal honor—destroys both the collective self of the family line and the individual men who are part of it. This self-reflexive and self-destructive quality is the essence of masculine identity conceived as the son's emulation of the father. The men of the first tetralogy gaze backward into their families' pasts, seeking to repeat their fathers either in virtue or in vengeance, enmeshed in rivalries with other men, fearful of and easily entrapped by women, incapable of making new alliances that break with the past and transform the future.

Critics have often interpreted *Richard III* as the lump of chaos born of England's chaos, the incarnation of its untrammeled slaughter of sons, brothers, fathers. Wolfgang Clemen argues that, though Richard is never at a loss for an explanation, none of his explanations suffices for the monstrosities he commits; he is more a symbolic than a realistic character.[3] Free of guilt or inner conflict, the aloof though appreciative spectator of his own performances, he thus accomplishes what few men would be capable of. But finally he destroys himself. The dominant pattern of Richard's character is the pattern of the play and of the tetralogy, a ricochet pattern of self-reflexiveness and self-destruction. England and Richard swallow themselves. The curses that only turn back on those who hurl them, the several small and the one large nemesis action running through the play, and Richard himself who "preys on the issue of his mother's body" (4.4.57)—all are analogous to the backward-looking, self-swallowing process by which men have defined themselves in the tetralogy.

There is a realistic psychological dimension to Richard's

[3] Wolfgang Clemen, *A Commentary on Shakespeare's Richard III*, tr. Jean Bonheim (London: Methuen, 1968), pp. 6–7. For the argument that Richard is plausibly motivated by "a perversion . . . of his frustrated will to sexual power," see Murray Krieger, "The Dark Generations of Richard III," in *The Design Within: Psychoanalytic Approaches to Shakespeare*, ed. Melvin Faber (New York: Science House, 1970), pp. 347–66.

character as well as the symbolic one, however. *Richard III* of all the history plays most strongly suggests the importance of the mother, rather than the father, in the formation of masculine identity—but negatively, by showing how alienation from the mother helps turn a physical monster into a moral one. Taking into account the extent to which theatrical convention inspires Richard's confessions of his villainy, we must also heed his insights into his condition, which are borne out by other characters as well. In the first of his two great soliloquies in *3 Henry VI*, he cries, "Why, love foreswore me in my mother's womb" (3.2.153), and goes on to describe the hideous deformity that makes him

> Like to a chaos, or an unlick'd bear whelp
> That carries no impression like the dam.   (161–62)

As Michael Neill argues, these lines suggest the mirroring process discerned by Winnicott, in which the mother, by responding actively and lovingly to her child, gives him back an image of himself and the basis for an identity. Richard, Neill says, "cannot know himself because he cannot love himself, and he cannot love himself because he has never been loved."[4] Confronted with the lumpish whelp her womb had formed, Richard's mother failed to lick it into shape, to imprint on it the "impression" of being loved and accepted. The circumstances of Richard's entrance into the world are mentioned frequently enough to demand our consideration: a difficult labor, a breech birth, his limbs deformed but his teeth already in his head, as even the young Duke of York has heard somewhere.[5] His mother's remembrance tends to confirm his contention that he was never loved:

[4]Michael Neill, "Shakespeare's Halle of Mirrors: Play, Politics, and Psychology in *Richard III*," *Shakespeare Studies* 8 (1976): 99–129. In a brilliant analysis, Neill goes on to argue that Richard's well-known theatricalism emanates from his lack of a self. As "dramatist, producer, prologue, and star performer of his own rich comedy," he narcissistically creates his own roles and through them, the roles of others, in effect making up "a false self to be the object of his consuming need for love."

[5]See *3 Henry VI*, 3.2.153–62; 5.6.69–79; *Richard III*, 1.3.227–31; 2.4.27–28; 4.1.53–55; 4.4.47–55, 167–75.

> Thou cam'st on earth to make the earth my hell.
> A grievous burden was thy birth to me,
> Tetchy and wayward was thy infancy.
>
> (*Richard III*, 4.4.167–169)

Lacking that crucial two-way exchange with the mother as the primary representative of the human community, he never feels he is part of it.[6] Thus, as he says,

> I have no brother, I am like no brother;
> And this word "love," which greybeards call divine,
> Be resident in men like one another,
> And not in me: I am myself alone.
>
> (*3 Henry VI*, 5.6.80–83)

Deprived of love, he is filled with rage, and puts his untimely teeth to use: he bites, as we are often reminded by the stream of canine images figuring his murderous aggression.[7] Henry VI interprets Richard's teeth as the sign of what he was fated to be:

> Teeth hadst thou in thy head when thou wast born,
> To signify thou camst to bite the world.
>
> (*3 Henry VI*, 5.6.53–54)

But the play also supports the psychological reading suggested by another "dog," Shylock:

> Thou call'dst me dog before thou hadst a cause.
> But since I am a dog, beware my fangs.
>
> (*The Merchant of Venice*, 3.3.6–7)

---

[6]See Janet Adelman, *Suffocating Mothers: Fantasies of Maternal Origin in Shakespeare's Plays, "Hamlet" to "The Tempest"* (London: Routledge, 1992), for a fascinating interpretation of the soliloquy in *3 Henry VI* in which Richard vows "to catch the English crown." She argues that in his image of the "thorny wood" from which he vows to free himself by hewing his way out "with a bloody axe," he fantasizes his scramble for the throne as counterviolence against an originary maternal malevolence—a fantasy that "predicts the peculiar turn of Richard's violence away from common familial enemies and toward the matrix of his own family" (p. 3).

[7]See *3 Henry VI*, 5.6.53–54; *Richard III*, 1.3.288–90; 2.4.27–34; 4.4.47–58, 78.

and by Richard himself:

> Then since the heavens have shap'd my body so,
> Let hell make crook'd my mind to answer it.
>
> (*3 Henry VI*, 5.6.78–79)

Thus Richard stands out from the men of the Henry VI plays, who even when they murdered did so in the name of their fathers. Though Richard resembles his father in ruthless ambition, he cannot be said to emulate him, in either the sense of following his example or of competing with him. He travesties the examples of family loyalty preceding him. Having no brother in the sense of having no kinship with people who are lovable and who love, being himself alone emotionally, in his utter lack of pity, as well as physically, he pursues the crown for himself alone. He sets his brothers against each other, by mimicking a brotherly love he has never felt so as to deceive and entrap them and by killing off or otherwise disposing of their children as obstacles to his succession. Perhaps his most shameless parody of the principle of succession that dominated the previous three plays is to sow the rumor that his brother Edward is illegitimate and thus not the true heir to the throne, so that *he* can claim, in Buckingham's words, to restore to its proper purity "the lineal glory of your royal house," "successively, from blood to blood," even as he murders its children (3.7.117–40). What began in the first play as dedication to the continuity of the family through the succession from father to son ends in the destruction of the family, and in the dissolution of masculine identity paternally defined.[8]

---

[8] "The Family and the Yorkist Cycle," a talk given by Norman Rabkin at the Special Session on Marriage and the Family in Shakespeare at the Modern Language Association's annual meeting in Chicago, December 27, 1977, first suggested the idea of Richard's destruction of the family to me and provided the stimulus for this essay.

Richard III on Stage and Screen

Richard Burbage (1573–1619), a friend of Shakespeare and the leading actor in his plays, was especially famous for playing Richard III, Hamlet, Othello, and Lear. In a student play at Cambridge, *The Second Part of The Return from Parnassus* in 1602, Burbage pays a student the doubtful compliment, "I like your face and the proportion of your body for Richard the Third," and asks him to try out by speaking the opening lines. John Manningham, a law student at the Middle Temple, in the same year wrote in his diary a story that once, when Burbage played Richard, a woman was so taken with him that she invited him to come to her that night by the name of Richard III; Shakespeare, overhearing, came first and sent his friend the message that "William the Conqueror was before Richard the Third." One writer called Burbage "the Atlas of your sphere" (the Globe playhouse); another wrote that "he was a delightful Proteus," wholly transforming himself into his part, and "an excellent orator, animating his words with speaking, and speech with action," as Hamlet advises the players to do. But exactly what Burbage made out of Richard we do not know. Later actors, we know, have tended to see Richard chiefly as devilish, sometimes as soldierly, and (recently) as psychotic, but of Burbage's Richard we know only that it was greatly esteemed by the public.

We do, however, know something about the way in which the play was staged. In Burbage's and Shakespeare's day, at the Theatre or the Globe a play moved swiftly and continuously, with no curtain to raise or lower, no pause to change scenery, and no intermission to break the mood. Most of the scenes in *Richard III* take place on the open-air platform stage, which can be imagined as a street in London, as a room in the palace, as a place in or near the Tower of London, or as Bosworth Field. The upper stage is used in 3.5 to represent the walls of the Tower, from which Richard speaks to the Mayor. In 3.7 it is the roof of Baynard's Castle, Richard's London mansion, from which he addresses the Mayor and citizens. In 4.2 a curtain at the back of the main stage probably opened to disclose a throne. This is the only fixed property needed in the play, but it is essential: Richard's ascent to sit upon the throne is the visual symbol that he has risen to absolute power. In 5.3 Richard orders his soldiers to pitch his tent in a field near the town of Bosworth. Richmond has his tent pitched at the opposite end of the stage. and both tents are open so that the audience can see the two generals as they speak, sleep, and dream. When they go out, the soldiers carry off the tents in order to clear the field for battle.

There is very little evidence of revivals of *Richard III* in the later seventeenth century, but in 1700 Colley Cibber adapted and streamlined the play into a version that was to hold the stage well into the nineteenth century, and indeed it has even been done in the twentieth. Because Shakespeare's play is immensely long (with 3600 lines, it is exceeded only by *Hamlet*), and it cannot possibly be acted within three hours, Cibber reduced it to 2050 lines, partly by eliminating the roles of Margaret, Clarence, Edward IV, and Hastings. He also rewrote many passages, simplifying the language. But the changes were not always in the direction of cutting. He added some passages from other plays, notably *3 Henry VI*, including the soliloquy in 3.2, "Ay, Edward will use women honorably." Curiously, some of Cibber's own lines have become almost inseparable from the play. Few persons know that such famous lines as "Off with his head, so much for Buckingham," and "Richard's himself again" are by Cibber, not Shakespeare. Cibber's version was acted more times on the London stage in the eighteenth century than any other Shakespeare play except *Hamlet* and *Macbeth*. When in 1821 William Charles Macready restored much of Shakespeare and deleted some of Cibber, the public indicated its disapproval with Macready's tampering, and not until 1845, when Samuel Phelps at Sadler's Wells cut all of Cibber, did a post-Shakespeare audience hear only Shakespeare's lines.

David Garrick, the most brilliant actor of his time, made himself famous by appearing as Richard, in Cibber's text, in 1741, when he was only twenty-four, and he acted the role at Drury Lane until 1776. Arthur Murphy wrote of Garrick as Richard that "the power of his imagination was such that he transformed himself into the very man. . . . His look, his voice, his attitude, changed with every sentiment. . . . His soliloquy in the tent scene discovered the inward man." William Hogarth painted a striking picture of Garrick in this scene of Richard struggling with his conscience on the last night of his life.

Garrick's Richard changed and developed in each act of the play. In Act 1 he murdered Henry VI in the Tower and boasted that he had neither pity, love, nor fear: "I am—myself alone." In Act 2 he played his role as lover so persuasively that Anne in the end believed him. Thomas Newton wrote to Garrick that "Our Ladies are almost in love with Richard as much as Lady Anne." Garrick staged the last scene of Act 3 in a new way: after he was hailed as king and told the bishops, "I must unto my holy work again," as soon as they left he flung away his prayer book, "a simple and most natural gesture, yet marked with originality." "Dissimulation," a critic wrote in Bell's acting edition of 1774, "was never displayed in a more conspicuous light. . . . Each act rises above the other. . . . The whole piece is alive, with increasing spirit, to the end." Richard's full revelation of his character in Act 4, the same critic wrote, "places an audience on the topmost bent of expectation." In the last act Garrick clutched his sword instinctively when he woke from his dream. An eloquent silence followed before he said, "Have mercy, heaven! ha! Soft, 'twas but a dream; But then so terrible, it shakes my soul." Finally he dismissed the dream: "Conscience avaunt! Richard's himself again." During the battle "his courage mounted to a blaze," and he died as a great warrior. Garrick's voice was powerful and his action vigorous. Shakespeare was right, the critic in the acting edition wrote, to make Richard "a confirmed, uniform villain: nothing in the medium way would have been half so striking on the stage." The play, he summed up, "must always read well, but act better."

John Philip Kemble, who played the role from 1783, was stately and eloquent, but more like an orator than an actor. More exciting was George Frederick Cooke, whose diabolical Richard was admired (though not by Charles Lamb) for his "intense, enduring energy of passion," both at Covent Garden and in New York, where he died in 1812.

Edmund Kean, one of the greatest English actors, took London by storm in 1814 as Shylock and as Richard III. Byron wrote in his diary: "Just returned from seeing Kean in Richard. By Jove! he is a soul! Life, nature, truth, without exaggeration or diminution. . . . Richard is a man, and Kean is Richard." Coleridge said that seeing Kean act was like "reading Shakespeare by flashes of lightning," and Keats praised his "intense power of anatomizing the passions." Hazlitt wrote of him: "He is more refined than Cooke; more bold, varied, and original than Kemble in the same character. . . . He gives to the last two acts of the play the greatest animation and effect." Kean acted mainly at Drury Lane, but Richard was his most popular role when he toured the United States in 1820 and in 1825.

Kean spoke his opening lines in natural tones, and rendered the line "But I, that am not shaped for sportive tricks" with a mixture of ironical contempt and self-approval. His wooing of Anne was a wonderful exhibition. Hazlitt wrote: "An enchanting smile played upon his lips, while a courteous humility bowed his head. . . . He seemed, like the first tempter, to approach his prey, certain of the event and as if success had smoothed his way before him." He was so convincing that Anne, like a fluttered bird, could not escape his fascination. When Buckingham asked him what to do if Hastings would not join them, the offhandedness of his answer, "Chop off his head," showed how little he cared for anyone who opposed him. The play gave Kean chances to display the whole range of his virtuosity: his violent passions, his pantherlike gaiety, his energy and power. In the last act he held his audience spellbound. His awakening from his nightmare sent a shudder of terror through the spectators. He staggered forward, sank on one knee, then started back as if he were trying to rise. His free hand, held high in the air, shook violently. With an effort of will he thrust his fears behind him, brandished his sword over his head, and shouted triumphantly, "Richard's himself again." One reviewer called this scene "one of the finest pieces of acting we have ever beheld, or perhaps that the stage has ever known." Hazlitt described Kean in battle: "he fought like one drunk with wounds, and the attitude in which he stands with his hands stretched out, after his sword is taken from him, had a preternatural and terrific grandeur."

The first black theater troupe in America, the African Company, opened in 1821 in New York with Richard III acted by James Hewlett, a handsome and impressive figure. The most famous black actor, Ira Aldridge, began with the African Company but went abroad and played Richard, Othello, and other roles throughout Europe, from London to Serbia and Moscow, between 1824 and 1867. Charles Winter Wood, who became director of the Tuskegee Players, began playing Richard in Chicago in 1886, with his own company.

Junius Brutus Booth, who made himself up to resemble Kean, acted Richard at Covent Garden and then for many years throughout America, from New York to San Francisco. He acted, William Winter wrote, with "a prodigious force and an impetuous, fiery, terrible passion." Once in New York he entered into his part so completely that he thought he was Richard and tried to kill Richmond in battle. William Charles Macready played Richard in 1819 at Covent Garden and later at Drury Lane. Charles Kean, son of Edmund, staged the most magnificent productions of the play ever seen, in New York in 1846 and in London in 1854. More than one hundred actors, with rich costumes and heraldic banners, marched in the funeral procession for Henry VI, the coronation procession of Richard, and the final battle. Costumes and scenery, however, nearly smothered the play. Richard Mansfield in 1889 was still producing the play as a splendid pageant.

Plays in Performance: Richard III (1981) reproduces portraits or photographs of eleven actors of Richard: Garrick, Cooke, Kean, J. B. Booth, Barry Sullivan, Henry Irving, Balliol Holloway, Donald Wolfit, Laurence Olivier, Ian Holm, and Ramaz Chkivadze. Charles H. Shattuck in *Shake-*

speare on the American Stage (1976) pictures Cooke, Edmund and Charles Kean, J. B. Booth, and his son Edwin Booth, Edwin Forrest, and John McCullough. The finest American actor, Edwin Booth, William Winter wrote in his biography, showed "Richard's subtle wit and devilish irony, his duplicity and his tremendous intensity of purpose and courage, with overwhelming force."

Laurence Olivier is the twentieth-century successor to Kean as Richard. His first acting of Richard in 1944, J. C. Trewin wrote, was "one of the exciting Shakespeare nights of the century." Olivier was "thinker and doer, mind and mask," "a figure truly diabolical," and Sybil Thorndike as Margaret had "one scene of shivering venom." John Gielgud was so impressed by his friend's triumph that he gave Olivier the very sword that Kean and Irving had used as Richard. Olivier played Richard in Paris and Hamburg, Antwerp and Ghent, and with Vivien Leigh as Anne in Australia, New Zealand, and again in London. In 1955, he made his great film, which will be discussed later.

Olivier writes in his book *On Acting* (1986): "I wanted to look the most evil thing there was"; but he also had to win Anne and to make the audience like Richard, so "They must be won over by his wit, his brilliantly wry sense of humor," and his "veneer of smiling sophistication." As Olivier limped, very slowly, out of the shadows to speak his first lines, W. A. Darlington wrote, "He seemed malignity incarnate. All the complications of Richard's character—its cruelty, its ambition, its sardonic humor—seemed implicit in his expression and his walk." Olivier describes the voice he used for the part as "thin and rapier-like, but all-powerful—venom coated with sugar." The scene in which he mesmerizes Anne with his voice and eyes, he writes, is pure magic: "I can't wait to get on the stage to play it." The way he played it won Anne and the audience as well. Trewin called Olivier's Richard "the marriage of intellect and dramatic force."

Many modern directors, trying to be different from Olivier, have presented a Richard who was anti-heroic, less theatrical, and less dramatic. Tyrone Guthrie directed Alec Guinness as Richard in Canada in 1953 and Hume Cronyn at Minneapolis in 1965, both fine actors but better as humorists than as devils. Christopher Plummer at Stratford-on-Avon in 1961 acted the play as "a threateningly contemporary account of political ambition," but he "missed no opportunity for sardonic comedy" in "a highly intelligent, and richly satisfying performance." Alan Bates in Canada in 1967 played Richard, and Zoe Caldwell Anne, as "alienated souls struggling in a predetermined, mechanical universe," with "a stark atmosphere reflecting the influence of Brecht and Kott" (*Shakespeare Around the Globe*, pp. 612–13). I remember the performance, however, as much more exciting than this sounds; Bates, except at the end, was a strong Richard. Ian Holm as Richard at Stratford in 1963 and Alan Howard in 1980 suffered from extreme paranoia. Holm's Richard, Trewin wrote, "was no longer a daemonic theatrical personage" but a man who "played the power game and was trapped in a situation we still know well." Kevin Kline in 1983, in the fifth production of the play at the New York Shakespeare Festival, was more effective because "instead of malevolence, he opted for a more subtle, crafty evil, and brought considerable humor and credibility to the role."

Shakespeare Around the Globe: A Guide to Notable Postwar Revivals, edited by Samuel L. Leiter in 1986, describes a wide variety of modern productions of *Richard III* in Britain, Canada, the United States, Sweden, Poland, West Germany, France, Belgium, Italy, Norway, and the Soviet Union. The annual bibliographies in *Shakespeare Quarterly* add further productions since 1977 in Czechoslovakia, Yugoslavia, Rumania, Spain, Australia, New Zealand, and Japan. Four of these productions put special emphasis on the relevance of *Richard III* to the world today.

In the Royal Theater at Stockholm in 1947 Alf Sjöberg directed a Richard who, he wrote, "was not at all hard to identify while Europe was still living in the rubble of the world war, and we continually watched great ideological con-men rise up and try to seize power." This Richard mesmerized others by his mastery of words, but he died in desperate anguish, knowing that he had never been loved, only feared. Tora Teje as Margaret, "still every inch a queen," brought a sense of tragic intensity to her bitter speeches and prophecies. The expressionistic setting for the play was "a dark, nightmarish image of a world in ruins."

Jan Kott based many of his ideas in *Shakespeare Our Contemporary* (1964) on a production of *Richard III* that he saw in Warsaw in 1960. Here Richard was not an individual but a man who moved the cogs of the universal mechanism of history, a catalyst who probed the dark side of human nature. When he dies, nothing will change. History will repeat itself, and the struggle for power will go on as before.

Kott's thesis inspired an "epic" staging of the play at the Avignon Festival in 1966, where the set and properties resembled threatening machines that suggested the cyclical process of history. Everyone in the play was corrupt, Richard no more than the rest. Roger Planchon, the director, made him young and handsome, "a Richard as he is seldom seen, a charming, cunning, incredibly calculating Richard, at once savage and attractive, a pathologically warped personality, but a man almost ingenuous in his villainy," wrote Gaylord Todd in *Drama Survey* (1967). He could win over Anne and Elizabeth as easily as he could convince and betray his brother Clarence and his friends Hastings and Buckingham. This production has been called one of the best ever seen in France.

An even more Brechtian production was brought to London in 1980 by a company from Tbilisi, Georgia, with Ramaz Chkivadze as Richard (photograph in *Plays in Performance*). The director, Robert Sturua, changed Shakespeare's drama into a morality play of power politics and the corruption of the human soul. Margaret stage managed the play, reading from a promptbook to introduce the characters and locales. Richmond, dressed in white, an angel to Richard's devil, was onstage from the start and shadowed every move Richard made. Sturua added a jester like the Fool in *Lear* who pointed out all the contrasts between aspiration and reality. The set of the play was suggested by Bosch's painting of the Last Judgment, a fitting backdrop to a drama of murder and retribution.

The play has had a remarkable career also on film and television. In early silent films Richard III was usually an actor who had toured in the part for years: William V. Ranous in 1908 (one reel only), Frank R. Benson in 1911 (key scenes in three reels), and Frederick B. Warde in 1913 (five reels with 1500 persons and 200 horses). They acted before the camera as they had acted on the stage. Benson's was filmed in one week on the stage at Stratford. André Calmettes directed a French film in 1912 and Max Reinhardt a German film in 1919, with Conrad Veidt as Richard.

Olivier in 1955 directed the first film of the play to have color and sound. It was beautifully acted by Olivier as Richard, Claire Bloom as Anne, John Gielgud as Clarence, Cedric Hardwicke as Edward IV, and Ralph Richardson as Buckingham. The early part showed the dominating symbol, the crown of England, suspended over the throne as Edward IV is crowned, in a splendid pageant without words. Then Richard spoke "the most dramatic opening speech of any Shakespeare play," as Olivier writes in *On Acting*. He talked directly to the camera, as though to every viewer personally. "I wanted to convince the audience of the mind behind the mask," he says, "a demonic mind, a witty mind." When he came to "Cheated of feature by dissembling Nature," he turned away from the camera to suggest his bitterness. He made clear his plans with lines from *3 Henry VI*, such as "I'll make my heaven to dream upon the crown" and "Can I do this, and cannot get a crown?" Olivier changed Shakespeare's play freely, and he omitted all the scenes with Queen Margaret.

A tracking camera followed Olivier wherever he went and showed his eyes piercing Clarence or Anne or Hastings and his body running like a spider down a long hall to greet with joy the men who were to murder Clarence. He broke the scene with Anne into two scenes: in the first she resisted, but at last his magnetism roused her to passion. The wonderful voice of Gielgud as Clarence expressed the terror of his dream and made a moving plea for mercy, in vain. At the Tower Olivier put on a splendid comic show as he buried his nose in a prayer-book and pretended to refuse the crown before he finally accepted it. Once the citizens left, he seized a bell-rope and slid down it to the ground in triumph. His eyes showed how much he was to be feared: when the young York taunted him, he glared at the child, and when he turned on Buckingham his malignity was overwhelming. The night before the battle was a dark night for Richard. Olivier showed his struggle with despair, his fears and doubts. Then he overcame them and said quietly to himself, "Richard's himself again." In the battle he fought desperately, on horseback and on foot with his sword, killing everyone who came near. When his enemies surrounded him and stabbed him, he raised his sword in a last defiance. The crown rolled from his head along the ground under the horses' hooves until it came to rest in a thorn bush. Richmond held it up for all to see in the final image. Olivier's *Richard III* ranks with his *Henry V* as one of the finest film interpretations ever made from Shakespeare's plays.

A severely cut film version (1995) starring Ian McKellen was indebted to McKellen's stage version of 1990. Set in England in the 1930s, Richard and his followers evoke Sir Oswald Mosley's fascist blackshirts; in the earlier scenes, the uniforms are British, but as the film progresses, uniforms, armbands, and banners increasingly call Hitler's Nazis to mind. It's a bit hard to understand what is gained by this suggestion that Britain's history in the 1930s was something other than what it was, but most of the acting is excellent and the visual elements are striking, so the film consistently holds a viewer's interest. A single detail: When Richard utters the most famous line in the play, "A horse! A horse! My kingdom for a horse!" (5.4.13) he is in a stalled vehicle.

Before turning to versions made for television, we should glance at one other film, *Looking for Richard* (1996), written and directed by Al Pacino, and starring Pacino. He had played Richard on the stage and had hoped to make a film version of the play; *Looking for Richard*, something of a documentary of his efforts, opens and closes with shots of The Cloisters, a museum of medieval art in New York City, and it is here that we get shots of scenes of a production, in period costumes, with Kevin Spacey as Buckingham and Alec Baldwin as Clarence. Although some reviewers were deeply distressed by Pacino's diction, these scenes are not at all bad. In between shots of the play we get Pacino and friends talking about it, and interviews with the famous (e.g. Kenneth Branagh, John Gielgud, and Vanessa Redgrave), the distinguished but not-so-famous (e.g. Professor Emrys Jones), and the unknown (various unidentified average guys and girls in the street), who give their opinions about what Shakespeare means, or doesn't mean, to the general public. An interesting novelty.

Three productions have been made specifically for the television screen, but they have not come close to equaling the powerful dramatic effect of Olivier's *Richard III*. The first of these was the British Broadcasting Corporation's brave attempt (1960) to condense eight of Shakespeare's history plays, from *Richard II* to *Richard III*, into fifteen episodes, shown one a week. The series was called *An Age of Kings*; the last two episodes were "The Dangerous Brother" and "The Boar Hunt." Paul Daneman of the Stratford company was a competent Richard, but he was no threat to Olivier. The actors spoke too fast, perhaps because the director, Peter Dews, tried to cram too much into each episode of only ninety minutes. The camera work was not very enterprising. Television can use close-ups effectively to show an actor soliloquizing, but it should not use them continuously, as *An Age of Kings* did. The camera needs to shift to middle-distance shots and long shots for variety, even though they do not work so well on a small screen as they do on a larger screen or on a more spacious stage. Viewers find it hard to follow all that is going on in a scene with many characters or one of swift action. They may see only part of the pageantry of a coronation or of a battle between armies. Olivier believed that his film lost most of its effect when it was reduced for television. A television director has to find ways of appealing to the imagination in order to overcome the limitations of the medium. *An Age of Kings* did not discover such ways. For the most part it merely recorded certain parts of the staged action.

The Wars of the Roses in 1964 was more successful in terms of television in dramatizing *Richard III*. Peter Hall and John Barton had directed the Royal Shakespeare Company at Stratford-on-Avon in a sequence of three plays abridged from the plays on Henry VI and Richard III. The leading actors in the third play were Ian Holm as Richard, Janet Suzman as Anne, Peggy Ashcroft as Margaret, and Eric Porter as Richmond, all experienced in playing Shakespeare. While they were still acting the play on the stage, they took time to rehearse for a second and different production for television. They used the same shortened text, except that they left out the talk of the citizens in 2.3, and the whole play took only about two and a half hours. Two directors from BBC Television, with a staff of fifty, worked with Hall and Barton of the Royal Shakespeare Company to make the action more vivid for television audiences. Richard and the other characters talked directly to the viewers. Instead of filming the whole stage, cameras focused on faces in different groups, and these close shots contrasted with the full stage picture shown in processions and battle sequences. One camera shot scenes from above the stage and another from a pit in front of the stage, while other cameras on a platform before the stage were free to move to different angles, and a hand-held camera took the viewer into the thick of battle. The directors aimed at a more thorough realism, but they overshot the mark, since the stage production was already full of blood and violence. The play in the theater opened with a series of heads spiked upon the walls; Clarence was drowned onstage instead of off, and the bodies of his murderers were later shown broken on wheels, an unnecessary addition to Shakespeare. Peter Hall interpreted the plays on Henry VI and Richard III as "a horrific analysis of power politics and violence." *The Wars of the Roses* was exciting television drama, but it was very different from Shakespeare's plays. It emphasized stage pictures and action rather than revealing the characters and emotions of men and women. Ian Holm as Richard seemed more mad than bad. The reviewer for *The Times* wrote that he "fails totally to develop into Satanic magnitude," and the reviewer for the *Sunday Telegraph* that "when every prop and every confrontation is designed to dwarf him, his midget monarch develops an insect insanity which scarifies us like the sight of an ant with its feet on the button of the H bomb" (*Plays in Performance,* p. 72). They were writing about the stage production, but on television Richard came across as even more insignificant. He was not left out, as traveling actors once left out the part of Hamlet from *Hamlet*. Richard was merely diminished.

The BBC recorded *Richard III* in 1982 as one of its series of all Shakespeare's plays for television. Jane Howell, the director, saw the play as a picture of the breakdown of

England from the unity shown in *Henry V*. It is about all the people, she emphasized, not only about Richard: "It's not a play about a single man. It's a play about a society." She felt that it was frightening because it was like a nightmare; except for Richard "you see nobody killed; just people going away, being taken away—so much like today; they're just removed. There's a knock on the door and people are almost willing to go. There's no way out of it." Shadows are a continuing theme. As the film opens you see Richard's shadow before you see him; he talks about seeing his shadow in the sun; at the end of the play the sun does not shine on Richard, but it shines on Richmond. The actors in this version spoke nearly all the lines that Shakespeare wrote: only sixty-eight were cut, including twenty-seven in 1.3 and twenty-five in 4.4. The director gave an effective interpretation of some of the great scenes, especially in the last act. On the night before the battle Ron Cook as Richard sees the ghosts of his victims come to haunt him and to prophesy his death. Then each turns to Richmond to prophesy his victory. Whereas Olivier shows only a few shadows summoned up by Richard's conscience, Howell shows all eleven speaking both to Richard and to Richmond. Unlike the despairing Richard in *The Wars of the Roses*, this Richard does not give up easily; he is a hard man to kill. Fighting to the last, he holds at bay a whole band of spearmen, until they finally encircle him and Richmond kills him. The last shot is of Margaret on top of a pile of bodies, holding the dead Richard and laughing in triumph. This television version makes an interesting contrast with the stage production that Jane Howell directed in New York in 1983. Here she created a morality-play atmosphere in which those who hold power do so briefly and Richmond becomes just another crafty politician, as in the Warsaw production of 1960 described by Kott. The king's portrait at the back of the stage changes from Edward IV to Edward V, to Richard III, then to Henry VII, but nothing else will be very different.

Bibliographic Note: For further reading see Julie Hankey's edition of *Richard III* in the Plays in Performance Series (2nd ed., 1988), which has an eighty-page introductory essay on the stage history, and the text of the play with annotations on the facing pages indicating how speeches and scenes were performed over the centuries. For a stage history that comes up to the Royal Shakespeare Company's 1990 production with Ian McKellen, see Scott Colley, *Richard's Himself Again: A Stage History of "Richard III"* (1992). On Olivier's film, see Constance A. Brown, in *Focus on Shakespearean Films*, ed. C. W. Eckert (1972); Dale Silviria, *Laurence Olivier and the Art of Film Making* (1985); R. Chris Hassel, Jr., *Song of Death: Performance, Interpretation, and the Text of "Richard III"* (1987). On the BBC television version with Ron Cook as Richard, see Hassel's book, and see also Hugh Richmond, *Richard III* (1989), a volume in the Shakespeare in Performance Series. (Richmond compares several productions of the later twentieth century.)

Suggested References

The number of possible references is vast and grows alarmingly. (The *Shakespeare Quarterly* devotes one issue each year to a list of the previous year's work, and *Shakespeare Survey*—an annual publication—includes a substantial review of biographical, critical, and textual studies, as well as a survey of performances.) The vast bibliography is best approached through James Harner, *The World Shakespeare Bibliography on CD-Rom: 1900–Present.* The first release, in 1996, included more than 12,000 annotated items from 1990–93, plus references to several thousand book reviews, productions, films, and audio recordings. The plan is to update the publication annually, moving forward one year and backward three years. Thus, the second issue (1997), with 24,700 entries, and another 35,000 or so references to reviews, newspaper pieces, and so on, covered 1987–94.

Though no works are indispensable, those listed below have been found especially helpful. The arrangement is as follows:

1. Shakespeare's Times
2. Shakespeare's Life
3. Shakespeare's Theater
4. Shakespeare on Stage and Screen
5. Miscellaneous Reference Works
6. Shakespeare's Plays: General Studies
7. The Comedies
8. The Romances
9. The Tragedies
10. The Histories
11. *The Tragedy of Richard III*

The titles in the first five sections are accompanied by brief explanatory annotations.

1. Shakespeare's Times

Andrews, John F., ed. *William Shakespeare: His World, His Work, His Influence,* 3 vols. (1985). Sixty articles, dealing not only with such subjects as "The State," "The Church," "Law," "Science, Magic, and Folklore," but also with the plays and poems themselves and Shakespeare's influence (e.g., translations, films, reputation)

Byrne, Muriel St. Clare. *Elizabethan Life in Town and Country* (8th ed., 1970). Chapters on manners, beliefs, education, etc., with illustrations.

Dollimore, John, and Alan Sinfield, eds. *Political Shakespeare: New Essays in Cultural Materialism* (1985). Essays on such topics as the subordination of women and colonialism, presented in connection with some of Shakespeare's plays.

Greenblatt, Stephen. *Representing the English Renaissance* (1988). New Historicist essays, especially on connections between political and aesthetic matters, statecraft and stagecraft.

Joseph, B. L. *Shakespeare's Eden: the Commonwealth of England 1558–1629* (1971). An account of the social, political, economic, and cultural life of England.

Kernan, Alvin. *Shakespeare, the King's Playwright: Theater in the Stuart Court 1603–1613* (1995). The social setting and the politics of the court of James I, in relation to *Hamlet, Measure for Measure, Macbeth, King Lear, Antony and Cleopatra, Coriolanus,* and *The Tempest.*

Montrose, Louis. *The Purpose of Playing: Shakespeare and the Cultural Politics of the Elizabethan Theatre* (1996). A poststructuralist view, discussing the professional theater "within the ideological and material frameworks of Elizabethan culture and society," with an extended analysis of *A Midsummer Night's Dream.*

Mullaney, Steven. *The Place of the Stage: License, Play, and Power in Renaissance England* (1988). New Historicist analysis, arguing that popular drama became a cultural institution "only by . . . taking up a place on the margins of society."

Schoenbaum, S. *Shakespeare: The Globe and the World*

(1979). A readable, abundantly illustrated introductory book on the world of the Elizabethans.

Shakespeare's England, 2 vols. (1916). A large collection of scholarly essays on a wide variety of topics, e.g., astrology, costume, gardening, horsemanship, with special attention to Shakespeare's references to these topics.

2. Shakespeare's Life

Andrews, John F., ed. *William Shakespeare: His World, His Work, His Influence,* 3 vols. (1985). See the description above.

Bentley, Gerald E. *Shakespeare: A Biographical Handbook* (1961). The facts about Shakespeare, with virtually no conjecture intermingled.

Chambers, E. K. *William Shakespeare: A Study of Facts and Problems,* 2 vols. (1930). The fullest collection of data.

Fraser, Russell. *Young Shakespeare* (1988). A highly readable account that simultaneously considers Shakespeare's life and Shakespeare's art.

———. *Shakespeare: The Later Years* (1992).

Schoenbaum, S. *Shakespeare's Lives* (1970). A review of the evidence and an examination of many biographies, including those of Baconians and other heretics.

———. *William Shakespeare: A Compact Documentary Life* (1977). An abbreviated version, in a smaller format, of the next title. The compact version reproduces some fifty documents in reduced form. A readable presentation of all that the documents tell us about Shakespeare.

———. *William Shakespeare: A Documentary Life* (1975). A large-format book setting forth the biography with facsimiles of more than two hundred documents, and with transcriptions and commentaries.

3. Shakespeare's Theater

Astington, John H., ed. *The Development of Shakespeare's Theater* (1992). Eight specialized essays on theatrical companies, playing spaces, and performance.

Beckerman, Bernard. *Shakespeare at the Globe, 1599–1609* (1962). On the playhouse and on Elizabethan dramaturgy, acting, and staging.

Bentley, Gerald E. *The Profession of Dramatist in Shakespeare's Time* (1971). An account of the dramatist's status in the Elizabethan period.

———. *The Profession of Player in Shakespeare's Time, 1590–1642* (1984). An account of the status of members of London companies (sharers, hired men, apprentices, managers) and a discussion of conditions when they toured.

Berry, Herbert. *Shakespeare's Playhouses* (1987). Usefully emphasizes how little we know about the construction of Elizabethan theaters.

Brown, John Russell. *Shakespeare's Plays in Performance* (1966). A speculative and practical analysis relevant to all of the plays, but with emphasis on *The Merchant of Venice, Richard II, Hamlet, Romeo and Juliet,* and *Twelfth Night.*

———. *William Shakespeare: Writing for Performance* (1996). A discussion aimed at helping readers to develop theatrically conscious habits of reading.

Chambers, E. K. *The Elizabethan Stage,* 4 vols. (1945). A major reference work on theaters, theatrical companies, and staging at court.

Cook, Ann Jennalie. *The Privileged Playgoers of Shakespeare's London, 1576–1642* (1981). Sees Shakespeare's audience as wealthier, more middle-class, and more intellectual than Harbage (below) does.

Dessen, Alan C. *Elizabethan Drama and the Viewer's Eye* (1977). On how certain scenes may have looked to spectators in an Elizabethan theater.

Gurr, Andrew. *Playgoing in Shakespeare's London* (1987). Something of a middle ground between Cook (above) and Harbage (below).

———. *The Shakespearean Stage, 1579–1642* (2nd ed., 1980). On the acting companies, the actors, the playhouses, the stages, and the audiences.

Harbage, Alfred. *Shakespeare's Audience* (1941). A study of the size and nature of the theatrical public, emphasizing the representativeness of its working class and middle-class audience.

Hodges, C. Walter. *The Globe Restored* (1968). A conjectural restoration, with lucid drawings.

Hosley, Richard. "The Playhouses," in *The Revels History of Drama in English*, vol. 3, general editors Clifford Leech and T. W. Craik (1975). An essay of a hundred pages on the physical aspects of the playhouses.

Howard, Jane E. "Crossdressing, the Theatre, and Gender Struggle in Early Modern England," *Shakespeare Quarterly* 39 (1988): 418–40. Judicious comments on the effects of boys playing female roles.

Orrell, John. *The Human Stage: English Theatre Design, 1567–1640* (1988). Argues that the public, private, and court playhouses are less indebted to popular structures (e.g., innyards and bear-baiting pits) than to banqueting halls and to Renaissance conceptions of Roman amphitheaters.

Slater, Ann Pasternak. *Shakespeare the Director* (1982). An analysis of theatrical effects (e.g., kissing, kneeling) in stage directions and dialogue.

Styan, J. L. *Shakespeare's Stagecraft* (1967). An introduction to Shakespeare's visual and aural stagecraft, with chapters on such topics as acting conventions, stage groupings, and speech.

Thompson, Peter. *Shakespeare's Professional Career* (1992). An examination of patronage and related theatrical conditions.

———. *Shakespeare's Theatre* (1983). A discussion of how plays were staged in Shakespeare's time.

4. Shakespeare on Stage and Screen

Bate, Jonathan, and Russell Jackson, eds. *Shakespeare: An Illustrated Stage History* (1996). Highly readable essays on stage productions from the Renaissance to the present.

Berry, Ralph. *Changing Styles in Shakespeare* (1981). Discusses productions of six plays (*Coriolanus*, *Hamlet*, *Henry V*, *Measure for Measure*, *The Tempest*, and *Twelfth Night*) on the English stage, chiefly 1950–1980.

————. *On Directing Shakespeare: Interviews with Contemporary Directors* (1989). An enlarged edition of a book first published in 1977, this version includes the seven interviews from the early 1970s and adds five interviews conducted in 1988.

Brockbank, Philip, ed. *Players of Shakespeare: Essays in Shakespearean Performance* (1985). Comments by twelve actors, reporting their experiences with roles. See also the entry for Russell Jackson (below).

Bulman, J. C., and H. R. Coursen, eds. *Shakespeare on Television* (1988). An anthology of general and theoretical essays, essays on individual productions, and shorter reviews, with a bibliography and a videography listing cassettes that may be rented.

Coursen, H. P. *Watching Shakespeare on Television* (1993). Analyses not only of TV versions but also of films and videotapes of stage presentations that are shown on television.

Davies, Anthony, and Stanley Wells, eds. *Shakespeare and the Moving Image: The Plays on Film and Television* (1994). General essays (e.g., on the comedies) as well as essays devoted entirely to *Hamlet, King Lear*, and *Macbeth*.

Dawson, Anthony B. *Watching Shakespeare: A Playgoer's Guide* (1988). About half of the plays are discussed, chiefly in terms of decisions that actors and directors make in putting the works onto the stage.

Dessen, Alan. *Elizabethan Stage Conventions and Modern Interpretations* (1984). On interpreting conventions such as the representation of light and darkness and stage violence (duels, battles).

Donaldson, Peter. *Shakespearean Films/Shakespearean Directors* (1990). Postmodernist analyses, drawing on Freudianism, Feminism, Deconstruction, and Queer Theory.

Jackson, Russell, and Robert Smallwood, eds. *Players of Shakespeare 2: Further Essays in Shakespearean Performance by Players with the Royal Shakespeare Company* (1988). Fourteen actors discuss their roles in productions between 1982 and 1987.

————. *Players of Shakespeare 3: Further Essays in Shake-*

spearean Performance by Players with the Royal Shakespeare Company (1993). Comments by thirteen performers.

Jorgens, Jack. *Shakespeare on Film* (1977). Fairly detailed studies of eighteen films, preceded by an introductory chapter addressing such issues as music, and whether to "open" the play by including scenes of landscape.

Kennedy, Dennis. *Looking at Shakespeare: A Visual History of Twentieth-Century Performance* (1993). Lucid descriptions (with 170 photographs) of European, British, and American performances.

Leiter, Samuel L. *Shakespeare Around the Globe: A Guide to Notable Postwar Revivals* (1986). For each play there are about two pages of introductory comments, then discussions (about five hundred words per production) of ten or so productions, and finally bibliographic references.

McMurty, Jo. *Shakespeare Films in the Classroom* (1994). Useful evaluations of the chief films most likely to be shown in undergraduate courses.

Rothwell, Kenneth, and Annabelle Henkin Melzer. *Shakespeare on Screen: An International Filmography and Videography* (1990). A reference guide to several hundred films and videos produced between 1899 and 1989, including spinoffs such as musicals and dance versions.

Sprague, Arthur Colby. *Shakespeare and the Actors* (1944). Detailed discussions of stage business (gestures, etc.) over the years.

Willis, Susan. *The BBC Shakespeare Plays: Making the Televised Canon* (1991). A history of the series, with interviews and production diaries for some plays.

5. Miscellaneous Reference Works

Abbott, E. A. *A Shakespearean Grammar* (new edition, 1877). An examination of differences between Elizabethan and modern grammar.

Allen, Michael J. B., and Kenneth Muir, eds. *Shakespeare's Plays in Quarto* (1981). One volume containing facsimiles of the plays issued in small format before they were collected in the First Folio of 1623.

Bevington, David. *Shakespeare* (1978). A short guide to hundreds of important writings on the subject.

Blake, Norman. *Shakespeare's Language: An Introduction* (1983). On vocabulary, parts of speech, and word order.

Bullough, Geoffrey. *Narrative and Dramatic Sources of Shakespeare*, 8 vols. (1957–75). A collection of many of the books Shakespeare drew on, with judicious comments.

Campbell, Oscar James, and Edward G. Quinn, eds. *The Reader's Encyclopedia of Shakespeare* (1966). Old, but still the most useful single reference work on Shakespeare.

Cercignani, Fausto. *Shakespeare's Works and Elizabethan Pronunciation* (1981). Considered the best work on the topic, but remains controversial.

Dent, R. W. *Shakespeare's Proverbial Language: An Index* (1981). An index of proverbs, with an introduction concerning a form Shakespeare frequently drew on.

Greg, W. W. *The Shakespeare First Folio* (1955). A detailed yet readable history of the first collection (1623) of Shakespeare's plays.

Harner, James. *The World Shakespeare Bibliography*. See headnote to Suggested References.

Hosley, Richard. *Shakespeare's Holinshed* (1968). Valuable presentation of one of Shakespeare's major sources.

Kökeritz, Helge. *Shakespeare's Names* (1959). A guide to pronouncing some 1,800 names appearing in Shakespeare.

———. *Shakespeare's Pronunciation* (1953). Contains much information about puns and rhymes, but see Cercignani (above).

Muir, Kenneth. *The Sources of Shakespeare's Plays* (1978). An account of Shakespeare's use of his reading. It covers all the plays, in chronological order.

Miriam Joseph, Sister. *Shakespeare's Use of the Arts of Language* (1947). A study of Shakespeare's use of rhetorical devices, reprinted in part as *Rhetoric in Shakespeare's Time* (1962).

The Norton Facsimile: The First Folio of Shakespeare's Plays (1968). A handsome and accurate facsimile of the first collection (1623) of Shakespeare's plays, with a valuable introduction by Charlton Hinman.

Onions, C. T. *A Shakespeare Glossary*, rev. and enlarged by

R. D. Eagleson (1986). Definitions of words (or senses of words) now obsolete.

Partridge, Eric. *Shakespeare's Bawdy*, rev. ed. (1955). Relatively brief dictionary of bawdy words; useful, but see Williams, below.

Shakespeare Quarterly. See headnote to Suggested References.

Shakespeare Survey. See headnote to Suggested References.

Spevack, Marvin. *The Harvard Concordance to Shakespeare* (1973). An index to Shakespeare's words.

Vickers, Brian. *Appropriating Shakespeare: Contemporary Critical Quarrels* (1993). A survey—chiefly hostile—of recent schools of criticism.

Wells, Stanley, ed. *Shakespeare: A Bibliographical Guide* (new edition, 1990). Nineteen chapters (some devoted to single plays, others devoted to groups of related plays) on recent scholarship on the life and all of the works.

Williams, Gordon. *A Dictionary of Sexual Language and Imagery in Shakespearean and Stuart Literature*, 3 vols. (1994). Extended discussions of words and passages; much fuller than Partridge, cited above.

6. Shakespeare's Plays: General Studies

Bamber, Linda. *Comic Women, Tragic Men: A Study of Gender and Genre in Shakespeare* (1982).

Barnet, Sylvan. *A Short Guide to Shakespeare* (1974).

Callaghan, Dympna, Lorraine Helms, and Jyotsna Singh. *The Weyward Sisters: Shakespeare and Feminist Politics* (1994).

Clemen, Wolfgang H. *The Development of Shakespeare's Imagery* (1951).

Cook, Ann Jennalie. *Making a Match: Courtship in Shakespeare and His Society* (1991).

Dollimore, Jonathan, and Alan Sinfield. *Political Shakespeare: New Essays in Cultural Materialism* (1985).

Dusinberre, Juliet. *Shakespeare and the Nature of Women* (1975).

Granville-Barker, Harley. *Prefaces to Shakespeare*, 2 vols. (1946–47; volume 1 contains essays on *Hamlet, King*

Lear, Merchant of Venice, Antony and Cleopatra, and *Cymbeline*; volume 2 contains essays on *Othello, Coriolanus, Julius Caesar, Romeo and Juliet, Love's Labor's Lost*).

——. *More Prefaces to Shakespeare* (1974; essays on *Twelfth Night, A Midsummer Night's Dream, The Winter's Tale, Macbeth*).

Harbage, Alfred. *William Shakespeare: A Reader's Guide* (1963).

Howard, Jean E. *Shakespeare's Art of Orchestration: Stage Technique and Audience Response* (1984).

Jones, Emrys. *Scenic Form in Shakespeare* (1971).

Lenz, Carolyn Ruth Swift, Gayle Greene, and Carol Thomas Neely, eds. *The Woman's Part: Feminist Criticism of Shakespeare* (1980).

Novy, Marianne. *Love's Argument: Gender Relations in Shakespeare* (1984).

Rose, Mark. *Shakespearean Design* (1972).

Scragg, Leah. *Discovering Shakespeare's Meaning* (1994).

——. *Shakespeare's "Mouldy Tales": Recurrent Plot Motifs in Shakespearean Drama* (1992).

Traub, Valerie. *Desire and Anxiety: Circulations of Sexuality in Shakespearean Drama* (1992).

Traversi, D. A. *An Approach to Shakespeare,* 2 vols. (3rd rev. ed, 1968–69).

Vickers, Brian. *The Artistry of Shakespeare's Prose* (1968).

Wells, Stanley. *Shakespeare: A Dramatic Life* (1994).

Wright, George T. *Shakespeare's Metrical Art* (1988).

7. The Comedies

Barber, C. L. *Shakespeare's Festive Comedy* (1959; discusses *Love's Labor's Lost, A Midsummer Night's Dream, The Merchant of Venice, As You Like It, Twelfth Night*).

Barton, Anne. *The Names of Comedy* (1990).

Berry, Ralph. *Shakespeare's Comedy: Explorations in Form* (1972).

Bradbury, Malcolm, and David Palmer, eds. *Shakespearean Comedy* (1972).

Bryant, J. A., Jr. *Shakespeare and the Uses of Comedy* (1986).

Carroll, William. *The Metamorphoses of Shakespearean Comedy* (1985).

Champion, Larry S. *The Evolution of Shakespeare's Comedy* (1970).

Evans, Bertrand. *Shakespeare's Comedies* (1960).

Frye, Northrop. *Shakespearean Comedy and Romance* (1965).

Leggatt, Alexander. *Shakespeare's Comedy of Love* (1974).

Miola, Robert S. *Shakespeare and Classical Comedy: The Influence of Plautus and Terence* (1994).

Nevo, Ruth. *Comic Transformations in Shakespeare* (1980).

Ornstein, Robert. *Shakespeare's Comedies: From Roman Farce to Romantic Mystery* (1986).

Richman, David. *Laughter, Pain, and Wonder: Shakespeare's Comedies and the Audience in the Theater* (1990).

Salingar, Leo. *Shakespeare and the Traditions of Comedy* (1974).

Slights, Camille Wells. *Shakespeare's Comic Commonwealths* (1993).

Waller, Gary, ed. *Shakespeare's Comedies* (1991).

Westlund, Joseph. *Shakespeare's Reparative Comedies: A Psychoanalytic View of the Middle Plays* (1984).

Williamson, Marilyn. *The Patriarchy of Shakespeare's Comedies* (1986).

8. The Romances (*Pericles, Cymbeline, The Winter's Tale, The Tempest, The Two Noble Kinsmen*)

Adams, Robert M. *Shakespeare: The Four Romances* (1989).

Felperin, Howard. *Shakespearean Romance* (1972).

Frye, Northrop. *A Natural Perspective: The Development of Shakespearean Comedy and Romance* (1965).

Mowat, Barbara. *The Dramaturgy of Shakespeare's Romances* (1976).

Warren, Roger. *Staging Shakespeare's Late Plays* (1990).

Young, David. *The Heart's Forest: A Study of Shakespeare's Pastoral Plays* (1972).

9. The Tragedies

Bradley, A. C. *Shakespearean Tragedy* (1904).

Brooke, Nicholas. *Shakespeare's Early Tragedies* (1968).

Champion, Larry. *Shakespeare's Tragic Perspective* (1976).

Drakakis, John, ed. *Shakespearean Tragedy* (1992).

Evans, Bertrand. *Shakespeare's Tragic Practice* (1979).

Everett, Barbara. *Young Hamlet: Essays on Shakespeare's Tragedies* (1989).

Foakes, R. A. *Hamlet versus Lear: Cultural Politics and Shakespeare's Art* (1993).

Frye, Northrop. *Fools of Time: Studies in Shakespearean Tragedy* (1967).

Harbage, Alfred, ed. *Shakespeare: The Tragedies* (1964).

Mack, Maynard. *Everybody's Shakespeare: Reflections Chiefly on the Tragedies* (1993).

McAlindon, T. *Shakespeare's Tragic Cosmos* (1991).

Miola, Robert S. *Shakespeare and Classical Tragedy: The Influence of Seneca* (1992).

———. *Shakespeare's Rome* (1983).

Nevo, Ruth. *Tragic Form in Shakespeare* (1972).

Rackin, Phyllis. *Shakespeare's Tragedies* (1978).

Rose, Mark, ed. *Shakespeare's Early Tragedies: A Collection of Critical Essays* (1995).

Rosen, William. *Shakespeare and the Craft of Tragedy* (1960).

Snyder, Susan. *The Comic Matrix of Shakespeare's Tragedies* (1979).

Wofford, Susanne. *Shakespeare's Late Tragedies: A Collection of Critical Essays* (1996).

Young, David. *The Action to the Word: Structure and Style in Shakespearean Tragedy* (1990).

———. *Shakespeare's Middle Tragedies: A Collection of Critical Essays* (1993).

10. The Histories

Blanpied, John W. *Time and the Artist in Shakespeare's English Histories* (1983).

Campbell, Lily B. *Shakespeare's "Histories": Mirrors of Elizabethan Policy* (1947).

Champion, Larry S. *Perspective in Shakespeare's English Histories* (1980).

Hodgdon, Barbara. *The End Crowns All: Closure and Contradiction in Shakespeare's History* (1991).

Holderness, Graham. *Shakespeare Recycled: The Making of Historical Drama* (1992).

——, ed. *Shakespeare's History Plays: "Richard II" to "Henry V"* (1992).

Leggatt, Alexander. *Shakespeare's Political Drama: The History Plays and the Roman Plays* (1988).

Ornstein, Robert. *A Kingdom for a Stage: The Achievement of Shakespeare's History Plays* (1972).

Rackin, Phyllis. *Stages of History: Shakespeare's English Chronicles* (1990).

Saccio, Peter. *Shakespeare's English Kings: History, Chronicle, and Drama* (1977).

Tillyard, E. M. W. *Shakespeare's History Plays* (1944).

Velz, John W., ed. *Shakespeare's English Histories: A Quest for Form and Genre* (1996).

11. *Richard III*

For references concerning the play on the stage, see pages 244–45. For reviews of recent productions, consult *Shakespeare Quarterly* and an annual publication, *Shakespeare Survey*. For studies of *Richard III* in the context of Shakespeare's history plays, see the works cited in Section 10 of this list of Suggested References.

Carroll, William. " 'The Form of Law': Ritual and Succession in *Richard III*," in *True Rites and Maimed Rites*, ed. Linda Woodbridge and Edward Berry (1992), pp. 203–19.

Clemen, Wolfgang. *A Commentary on Shakespeare's "Richard III"* (1968).

Hodgdon, Barbara. *The End Crowns All* (1991).

Jones, Emrys. *The Origins of Shakespeare* (1977).

Moore, James A. *"Richard III": An Annotated Bibliography* (1986).

Moulton, Richard G. *Shakespeare as a Dramatic Artist* (1901).

Skura, Meredith Anne. *Shakespeare the Actor and the Purposes of Playing* (1993).

Watkins, Donald C. *Shakespeare's Early History Plays: Politics at Play on the Elizabethan Stage* (1990).